Complete Guide to OneNote

W. FREDERICK ZIMMERMAN

Complete Guide to OneNote
Copyright ©2004 by W. Frederick Zimmerman

ISBN (pbk): 1-59059-216-6

Printed and bound in the United States of America 12345678910

Trademarked names may appear in this book. Rather than use a trademark symbol with every occurrence of a trademarked name, we use the names only in an editorial fashion and to the benefit of the trademark owner, with no intention of infringement of the trademark.

Technical Reviewer: Andrew Watt

Editorial Board: Dan Appleman, Craig Berry, Gary Cornell, Tony Davis, Steven Rycroft, Julian Skinner, Martin Streicher, Jim Sumser, Karen Watterson, Gavin Wray, John Zukowski

Assistant Publisher: Grace Wong

Project Manager: Tracy Brown Collins

Copy Editors: Kim Wimpsett, Ami Knox

Production Manager: Kari Brooks

Production Editor: Laura Cheu

Proofreader: Linda Seifert

Compositor: Susan Glinert Stevens

Indexer: Valerie Perry

Artist: Kinetic Publishing Services, LLC

Cover Designer: Kurt Krames

Manufacturing Manager: Tom Debolski

Distributed to the book trade in the United States by Springer-Verlag New York, Inc., 175 Fifth Avenue, New York, NY, 10010 and outside the United States by Springer-Verlag GmbH & Co. KG, Tiergartenstr. 17, 69112 Heidelberg, Germany.

In the United States: phone 1-800-SPRINGER, email orders@springer-ny.com, or visit http://www.springer-ny.com. Outside the United States: fax +49 6221 345229, email orders@springer.de, or visit http://www.springer.de.

For information on translations, please contact Apress directly at 2560 Ninth Street, Suite 219, Berkeley, CA 94710. Phone 510-549-5930, fax 510-549-5939, email info@apress.com, or visit http://www.apress.com.

For my lovely and much-loved wife, Cheryl,
first, last, and always.

Contents at a Glance

Contents

Foreword

THE MICROSOFT ONENOTE TEAM is excited about making people more productive. Fred Zimmerman shares that enthusiasm. He's been tracking Microsoft OneNote since the first news reports about the program began to emerge, more than a year ago, because he shared our vision that developing a new note-taking program was a crucial opportunity to improve professional productivity. Fred's a J.D. with many years experience developing online information services for students, lawyers, businesspeople, and scientists, so he, like the OneNote team, has spent a lot of time thinking about how to make people more productive.

While we at Microsoft were beginning to explore ways to enrich Microsoft Office 2003, Fred was working for LexisNexis, the online information company, where he led the development of prototype products intended to help law students prepare for class and exams. Improved methods for taking, managing, and reviewing notes were, of course, essential to those prototypes. As a result of those projects, Fred knew that note taking was a crucial task in professional workflow and that existing productivity software wasn't truly adequate for note-taking. So when Fred heard about OneNote, he was one of the first to become involved with the fledgling OneNote community.

Fred wrote the chapter on Microsoft OneNote for *First Look Microsoft Office 2003,* the Microsoft Press "beta book" about Office 2003, and established OneNoteInfoCenter.com, the first independent Web site devoted to OneNote (now folded into Fred's multitopic Zimmerblog at http://www.wfzimmerman.com.) In recognition of Fred's contributions to peer-to-peer support for OneNote, Fred was named as one of the first two Microsoft MVPs for OneNote. Throughout the beta cycle, as the OneNote team has been working to refine OneNote and prepare it for launch, Fred has been writing this book, whose fundamental purpose is to help you get the most out of your work.

We're very pleased to see this book come out—at the most basic level, its very existence is a validation that authors and publishers believe that OneNote is going to be significant and will draw enthusiastic audiences. It's also a good feeling to see that an accomplished professional, completely independent of our team, is willing to make the very substantial commitment of time and effort necessary to bring out a book devoted solely to our work. Thanks, Fred!

We encourage you to try OneNote, explore it, live with it, and let it become a central element of your daily work life. We strongly believe that OneNote will make you more productive, and Fred's book is an important tool that can help you achieve that goal.

Chris Pratley
Group Program Manager, Office Authoring Services (Word, OneNote, Publisher)
Microsoft Corporation
Redmond, Washington

About the Author

W. Frederick Zimmerman is a technology author, consultant, trainer, and speaker. Fred is a Microsoft OneNote MVP and is the editor of the independent Web site OneNoteInfoCenter.com. He wrote the OneNote chapter for *First Look: Microsoft Office 2003* (Microsoft Press, 2003) and is the author of the forth-coming book *End-to-End Product Development for Tablet PC* (Apress, 2004).

Fred is a research scientist for ISCIENCES, *L.L.C.,* a provider of scientific infor-mation services and technologies. Previously, he directed emerging technology strategy for LexisNexis, a division of Reed Elsevier. He has a J.D. and has been a member of the State Bar of Michigan as well as a certified project management professional. Fred lives in Ann Arbor, Michigan, with wife, Cheryl, and their children, Kelsey and Parker.

About the
Technical Reviewer

Andrew Watt is an independent consultant and experienced author who wrote his first computer programs almost 20 years ago. His focus currently is on XML and its application-to-business effectiveness. OneNote 2003 doesn't yet have XML, but its ease of use and its effectiveness in idea capture mean that OneNote has a good chance of replacing his all-time favorite program, Lotus Notes, in his affections.

Acknowledgments

THANKS TO ALL those who helped me learn about OneNote, write this book, and share it with readers.

At Microsoft, Bill Thacker, John Voorhies, Alex Blanton, Roan Kang, Robert Scoble, Mike Sampson, Tom Oliver, and Chris Pratley. Thanks to the OneNote team for a great product!

At ActiveWords, Burt Bruggeman. At MindManager, Hobie Swan. At InfoSelect, Tom Wolf.

At LexisNexis, Joe Kornowski, Rich Miller, and Harry Silver.

At Elsevier, Andrea Kravetz and David Marques, who encouraged my interest in electronic lab notebooks.

At Evolved Media Networks, Dan Woods.

At the Ann Arbor IT Zone, Lauren Bigelow.

At Toshiba, Craig Marking, and at the Benjamin Group, Angelo Griffo.

At Cambridge University, Markus Kuhn.

At Louis Rosenfeld, LLC, himself.

At Stockholm University, Jacob Palme.

In the OneNote community, Andrew Watt (my technical reviewer), Ben Schorr, Diane Poremsky, Charles Hawkins, Christopher L. Thompson, Dallas Snell, David Salahi, Don Lipper, Brian Collins, Ed Garay, Ed Kress, Ken Brown, Kye Lewis, Harry Leung, Marc Orchant, David Terron, Donna Currie, Ken Brown, and David Parody.

At Studio B, Neil Salkind and Jackie Coder.

At Apress, Dan Appleman, John Zukowski, Tracy Brown Collins, Kim Wimpsett, Ami Knox, Beth Christmas, Jessica Dolcourt, Hollie Fischer, and Laura Cheu.

At home, Barbara and Terry and Cheryl, Kelsey, and Parker.

Introduction

WELCOME! You're going to take a deep dive into Microsoft OneNote. This book is intended to make *everyone* who reads it, from novice to maestro, a powerful user of this new and exciting program. Like any prudent diver, you're going to look before you leap. You'll begin with the basics and work your way up to advanced topics. Like true aficionados of any sport, you'll take some time to learn about the background of the subject and learn from masters of the practice. Like champions in any sport, you're going to be very skillful by the time you're done. And, like participants in any sport, you're going to have fun while you're at it!

What Is Microsoft OneNote?

Microsoft OneNote is a new addition to the Microsoft Office 2003 family. Like the other programs in the Office suite, it's an *application* program, which means it's intended to help you *apply* the computer to carry out a particular task. In the case of OneNote, it's specifically intended to help you capture, manage, and use the notes you take. In a moment, you'll take a "guided tour" of Microsoft OneNote.

First, let's get a few key technical facts on the table:

- OneNote complements, but doesn't require, Microsoft Office 2003.

- OneNote complements, but doesn't require, Microsoft's Tablet PC platform.

- OneNote needs you to run Microsoft Windows 2000 Service Pack 3 (or higher) or Windows XP on a fairly modern personal computer (Pentium 133MHz or faster).

What this means is that if you have a reasonably modern computer, originally purchased in 2000 or later, you can probably run OneNote.

Why a Book About OneNote?

Like its siblings Word, Excel, PowerPoint, and so on, OneNote is a powerful, complex application that you can use to do a lot of useful things. Unlike its siblings, OneNote is exploring "new territory." OneNote brings the Windows-powered personal computer into an important part of the workday that has traditionally been dominated either by hasty, primitive scribblings or by tools, such as Microsoft

Word, that are too powerful for the task at hand: sledgehammers swinging at gnats. Unlike Word, which is full of features intended to help the user create a complex final work product, everything in OneNote is focused exclusively on helping you take notes and get the most out of them going forward.

This is a new goal and an important one. How often do you take notes? Every day? Every meeting? Every phone call? According to research conducted by Microsoft as part of the development of OneNote, most people aren't satisfied with the way they take and manage their notes. Most of us would agree that there's certainly room for improvement!

OneNote provides new tools to help you accomplish this goal:

- "Write-anywhere" page surface

- "Containers" for typed, ink, or image notes

- Notebook pages organized into sections and folders

- Meeting audio synchronized with your written notes

- Side Notes that are always available, like a Post-It

- Auto-outlining…sortable, customizable "note flags"

- Integration with Office 2003 and SharePoint

- And more

It's a new type of user interface and a new type of program in the Office family. It's a new approach to an important part of your daily activities.

In short, Microsoft OneNote is new enough, innovative enough, and important enough that there will probably be a lot of people, like you, who want to learn more about it.

Why *This* Book About Microsoft OneNote?

I got excited enough to write *this* book about Microsoft OneNote when I realized I could structure this book so that users of every skill level, and every personality type, can benefit from it.

Users of Every Skill Level Will Benefit

If you know nothing about OneNote except that you have a glimmer of interest in it, I'll provide a concise, friendly introduction.

If you already know a bit about OneNote, perhaps have even installed it and begun to experiment, I'll help you learn *everything* that the program can do to help you.

If you're already an active user of OneNote and think you understand most of its features, I'll help you go beyond that.

If you want to become the office "guru," I'll provide tricks and tips to help you overcome subtle problems such as how to paste Hypertext Markup Language (HTML) pages into a OneNote page.

If you're a system administrator who needs to integrate OneNote into your enterprise's Office 2003 environment, I'll provide you with the guidance you need.

No matter what your skill level, you'll benefit from a series of insightful Q&As and sidebars with leading usability experts, productivity gurus, tech visionaries, and industry-specific experts.

There's Something Here for Every Learning Style

Let's face it, we all have different learning styles. Some of us learn best by doing, some by observing, and some by teaching. (And those who can't teach, write!) This fact is important for readers of this book because learning styles and personality type play a huge role in how people react to version 1.0 software. No matter what your personality type:

- A naturally inquisitive, nasty, skeptical-minded person like me (trained first in academia, then law school)

- An energetic pragmatist such as Scarlett O'Hara ("As God is my witness, I'll never be unproductive again…")

- An enthusiastic optimist such as Little Orphan Annie ("The sun will come up tomorrow/bet your bottom dollar that/tomorrow, there'll be sun…)

there's something here for you. For the skeptical-minded, I'll offer substantive research and information to back up the proposition that OneNote will, in fact, make you more productive. For the pragmatic, I'll help you ramp up fast. For the optimistic, I'll show you how to wrap your whole life into OneNote!

How This Book Is Organized

This book is organized in a structure that roughly parallels the process of becoming a power user of Microsoft OneNote. This introduction will give you an overview of OneNote, as if you're about to sit down next to a knowledgeable friend who will show you the program for the first time and will tell you why he thinks you may find it useful. Then I'll place OneNote in its immediate context as part of Microsoft Office 2003 and then in a broader context as one of many Microsoft applications that run on many flavors of Microsoft Windows.

Chapter 1 will provide interesting background about OneNote—where it came from, its place in the overall history of personal computing, and how it fits into what I know about how information workers use software to become more productive. If you want to get right down to installing and using the software, you can skip Chapter 1 and go straight to Chapter 2, "Installing OneNote." In subsequent chapters, I'll take you through the process of learning the core functionality of the program. I'll do this in a task-by-task manner, as opposed to feature by feature. In other words, I'll show you how to tackle typical tasks that you might try to master early in your experience with the program, such as taking notes at your first meeting, as opposed to marching you through the menu structure command by command.

A Friendly Overview of OneNote

Scene: A standard 8×10 cubicle in an anonymous CUBICLE FARM. The cubicle is neither crowded nor overly large, but there are some small touches (a LARGE FLAT-SCREEN MONITOR, a new PC, a SOOTHING WATER FOUNTAIN, a collection of USELESS CRYSTAL STATUES honoring corporate achievements, a very small STAR TREK ICON), which show the presence of an enlightened and well-respected spirit. Seated in the cubicle and greeting you with a friendly expression is FRED, a knowledge worker who looks like he has been kept inside too long except that he has now become so productive and well-organized that he has time for weekend windsurfing trips.

FRED: Welcome to my humble abode! I'm looking forward to showing you OneNote. I know it's a busy day, so I'll just "hit the high points" and show you a few figures and some key features.

Here's how you start the program: You start it the first time just like any other Microsoft program (see Figure I-1).

Figure I-1. Start ➤ All Programs ➤ Microsoft OneNote 2003

 NOTE There are several other ways to launch OneNote. My favorite is pressing Windows-N on the keyboard.

Once you've started OneNote the first time, the OneNote program icon will show up in the Start menu just like any other recently used program (see Figure I-2).

Microsoft Office OneNote 2003

Figure I-2. Microsoft OneNote program icon

Figure I-3 shows the main program screen.

Let me draw your attention to a few major features of the layout. This is a typical Windows application screen with a series of menus beginning with File on the left, followed by a "wall o' toolbars" with both text and visual icons—some of which are self-explanatory, some of which are new and intriguing. Then there's the My Notebook area that's organized in a series of folders and sections beginning in this case with General and Side Notes.

Beneath that, you have the main page area. The top is a time-stamped title area, and the bottom is a note-taking area, which looks like a piece of ruled paper. You can vary the appearance of the page area by changing the width of the rules—narrow, college, ruled—and the color of the background. As with most Microsoft applications, you can define and use stationeries.

On the right side, you have page and subpage labels for navigation. On the left side, you see note flag and pen controls.

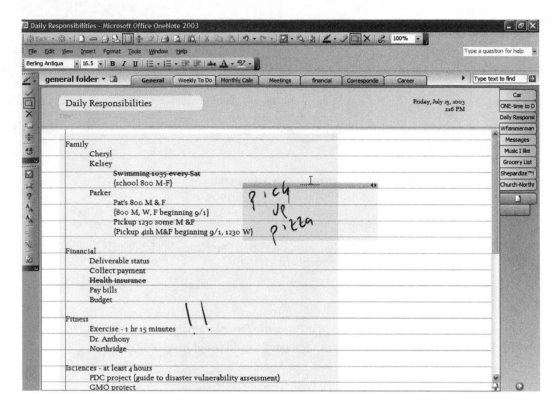

Figure I-3. OneNote main program screen

You'll also see that I've titled this page *Daily Responsibilities* and listed a bunch of, well, errands to do. Those little dots are part of a *handle* that I can use to move that *container* of text around. And I've already done some of the errands, so I've struck them out. You can see that the indents automatically put the items into an outline format.

GUEST: Why wouldn't I just use Microsoft Outlook to keep track of tasks?

FRED: Excellent question. Certainly, you could do that...but for whatever reason, there just don't seem to be that many people who use the very orderly Task feature in Microsoft Outlook. What I can tell you right now is that as soon as I got used to OneNote, I moved all my to do lists into it. OneNote seems to have just the right set of features to make managing lists easy.

GUEST: You wrote some of those notes in handwriting. But I'm not a technology author like you—I don't have a shiny new Tablet PC!

FRED: It doesn't have to be a Tablet PC. You can use OneNote on any modern PC running Windows 2000 or higher. And you can type all your notes. OneNote is very flexible—notes can be typed or can be ink, or images, or even audio. Look, here's a page with an image of a future NASA probe to Titan (see Figure I-4). And see how it brings along the URL!

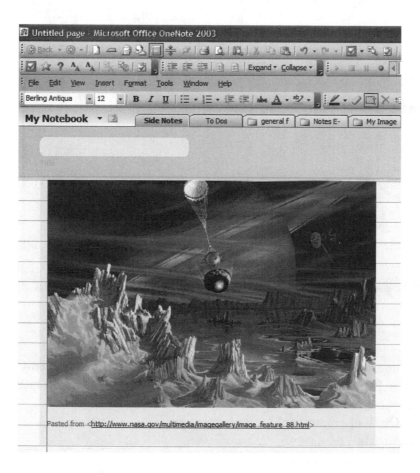

Figure I-4. OneNote page with image inserted, including source URL

And see, here are my notes from Monday's meeting (see Figure I-5).

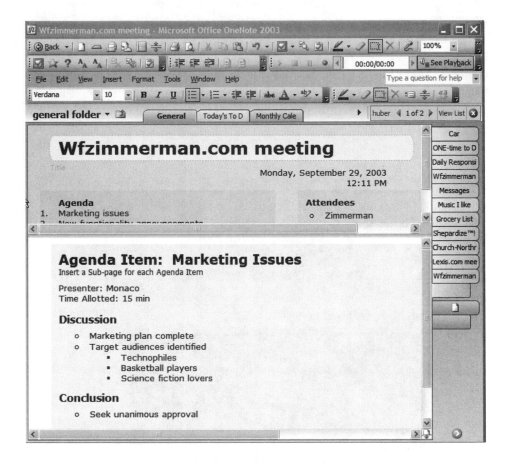

Figure I-5. Sample meeting notes

My notes are automatically synchronized with the audio I recorded using my external mike, so I can go back and verify exactly what my boss said about the last agenda item.

GUEST: Wow. That looks pretty cool. I want to learn more.

FRED: Check out http://www.microsoft.com/onenote.

GUEST: Forget that. I'm ready to buy! Where do I get it?

FRED: Same places you'd buy any other Microsoft software.

GUEST: I've got to run to another meeting. But thanks for showing me the software. I think I get the general idea.

FRED: There's a lot more to it, of course. People have written whole books about this program! But I thought it'd be a good start to show you what the program looks like and tell you a few of the main things it can do.

GUEST: Thank you, Obi-Wan.

In the famous words of William Shakespeare and Bertie Wooster: "Exit, pursued by a bear."[1]

TIP   Before you go much further, it's not a bad idea to familiarize yourself with Microsoft's OneNote Web site at `http://www.microsoft.com/onenote`. There's a wealth of resources available there, of course, but you can ignore most detail for now. I do recommend that you take a moment to flip through the demo, "See OneNote in Action." A picture is worth a thousand words.

I also recommend that you click the Frequently Asked Questions About OneNote link. I recommend this on general principle. Later in the book, I'll direct you to other, unofficial, richer FAQ resources, but this is a good place to make a quick pit stop. It's always a good idea to know where the official FAQ is. It's long—hundreds of questions—so you don't need to read any of it right now, but remember where it is.

Orientation Complete!

Orientations are always a bit of an adventure. I remember that my college freshman orientation included a reception at the president's house, complete with live string quartet, into which I wandered with the price tag still attached to the back of my new beret; a loud, seemingly rather senseless dorm party that I optimistically attended and swiftly fled; a tour of the lovely campus-slash-horticultural park, which turned out to be equipped with labels on every tree; and, mercifully, a sanity-restoring trip to the mystery section of the Swarthmore Public Library.

I hope you're not ready to flee quite yet! It's usually worthwhile to stay the course when at the beginning of a learning process. In the admirable words of the United Negro College Fund, a mind is a terrible thing to waste...and you're about to learn how to use Microsoft OneNote to get more out of your mind.[2]

---

1. Act I, Scene III, *A Winter's Tale*
2. `http://www.bartleby.com/63/75/2475.html`

Summary

I'll use bullet points for my chapter recaps for a couple of reasons:

- Bullet points are a great way of summarizing complex information.

- Microsoft OneNote does a particularly nice job of supporting the use of bullet points.

- Bullet points are the language of love. Okay, they're not the language of love, but they're the language of the office, and they're also the language of the dedicated note taker.

With that, this is a recap of this introduction:

- Microsoft OneNote is a new member of the Office family.

- OneNote runs on any modern PC running Windows 2000 Service Pack 3 or higher.

- The outer shell of OneNote looks similar to most other Microsoft Windows applications, but there are a lot of new controls in the toolbar, and the page behaves in new and unfamiliar ways.

- OneNote is organized into folders, sections, page groups, pages, and subpages.

- OneNote supports alternate forms of input such as ink, speech, and audio.

- It's a good idea to take a guided tour and review the FAQ before diving head first into the program.

In the first chapter, you'll acquire some valuable context—secondary education, so to speak—about the role that note taking plays in our daily lives and the myriad software tools that have been deployed, at one juncture or another, to support us in the task of note taking.

CHAPTER 1

Note-Taking Software Before OneNote

As THE SAYING GOES, "Success has many fathers, but failure is an orphan."[1] OneNote isn't a virgin birth. OneNote occupies a space at the intersection, and the culmination, of a number of interesting and important trends in personal computing software, ranging from fundamental input technologies such as text editing and handwriting recognition to highly specialized niche products such as electronic lab notebooks and electronic course books. In this chapter, you'll explore some of what has gone before so that you have a richer appreciation for where OneNote fits into what's to come.

First, Figure 1-1 gives you the "big picture" of Note-Taking Land. There are, of course, many different types of software, intended to address many different kinds of tasks, from the profoundly esoteric to the profoundly mundane. The note-taking task falls somewhere in the middle—in the general realm of personal productivity. Indeed, note taking is something of a continent to itself...in proximity to many existing categories of software but far from fully mapped by any of them.

In the rest of this chapter, you'll explore how several existing categories of software provide support for note taking. You'll look at software not just on the Windows platform but also on mainframe, Unix, and Macintosh platforms. You'll look at broad horizontal categories such as text editors, word processors, and presentation programs, and you'll look at specialized vertical solutions such as electronic lab notebooks. You'll look at classic application software and at solutions that require only a Web browser to access a server. For each category, I'll touch upon a number of different note-taking scenarios and illustrate the strengths and weaknesses of existing solutions. In this way, you'll build up an almost pointillist understanding of the landscape and why there's room for the innovation that OneNote provides.

Let's begin with one of the most primordial forms of computer software, the text editor.

---

1. Sometimes attributed to John F. Kennedy

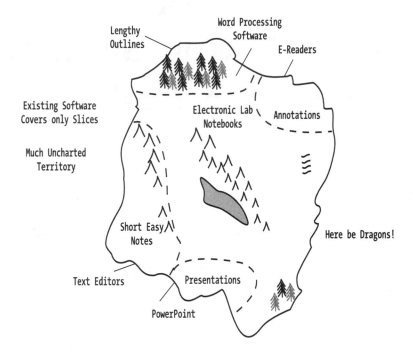

Figure 1-1. Map of Note-Taking Land

Using Text-Editing Programs for Note Taking

Almost since there have been computers, computer professionals have used text-editing programs to take quick notes. A quick survey of computer history shows a few noteworthy milestones along the way.

Very early computers such as ENIAC were primarily calculating machines, but the rapid growth of programming languages brought with them a need to edit programs. The most primordial editing programs edited text one character or one line at a time (thus, they're referred to as *line editors*.)

According to the Computer History Museum's Timeline of Computing History, it was in 1956 that researchers at MIT "began experimentation on direct keyboard input on computers, a precursor to today's normal mode of operation."[2]

For almost every operating system, there have been text editors, and computer professionals have used them to take notes.

---

2. http://www.computerhistory.org/timeline/topics/software.page

The American Standard Code for Information Interchange (ASCII) standard was introduced in 1963. Millions (billions? trillions?) of notes have been taken in this standard, which allows people running different computer systems to exchange and read others' text files.

Even in this world of "infinite diversity, infinite combinations" of textual notes—to quote Gene Roddenberry and Mr. Spock—a few text editors stand out.

Unix Text Editors for Note Taking

In the Unix world, there are a huge variety of text editors, ranging from the simple (such as pico, shown in Figure 1-2) to the extremely powerful (such as emacs). Unix makes it easy to create simple text files that can be easily redirected to the screen, to email, to another program, or to an output device.

Figure 1-2. pico, a simple Unix text editor often used for note taking

Unix users quickly learn to store such files in a simple directory structure and to search that structure using powerful tools such as grep. Notes stored in text files can also readily be manipulated using features in the text editor and combined using Unix utilities such as sed and awk.

Windows Text Editors for Note Taking

In the Windows world, the Notepad accessory (see Figure 1-3) has been part of Windows since release 1.0.[3] It too is tightly focused on creating and editing medium-sized, not heavily formatted, text files.

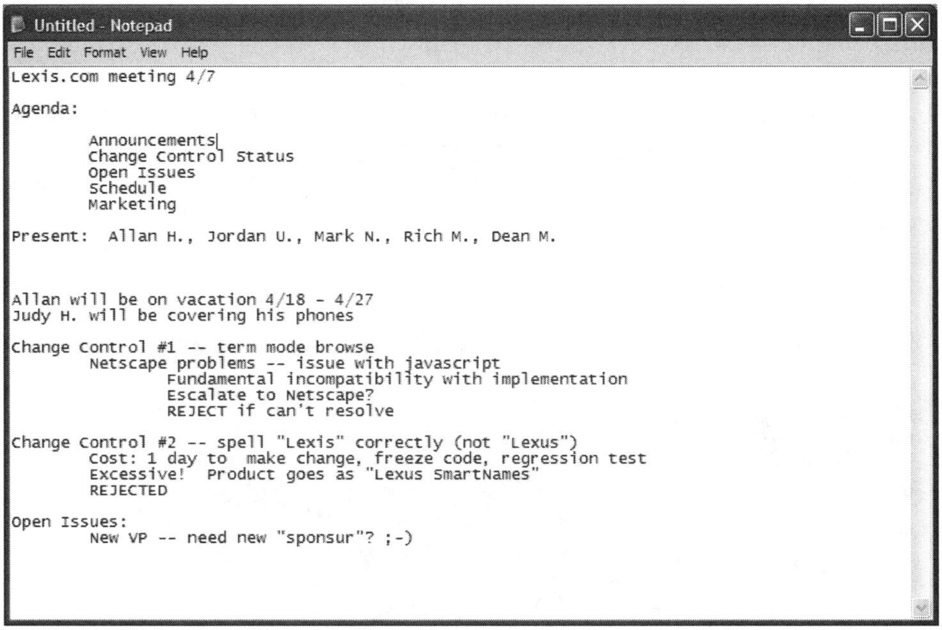

Figure 1-3. The Notepad accessory in Windows

Of course, Windows users may choose from a wealth of alternative text editors.

Macintosh Text Editors for Note Taking

In the Macintosh world, an extremely popular and powerful text editor called BBEdit from Bare Bones Software has been a market leader since 1993.[4] The user interface is similar to Notepad—very clean—but BBEdit has powerful tools to manipulate and change text across many files.

---

3. http://www.microsoft.com/windows/WinHistoryDesktop.mspx

4. http://www.barebones.com/company/history.shtml

How These Tools Compare to OneNote

The availability of these text-editing tools creates an implied threshold: To be successful, new note-taking software such as OneNote must at a minimum be better at note taking than programs such as pico, emacs, Notepad, and BBEdit. Let's think about that for a minute. What does *better* mean in this context?

You can consider a couple of different dimensions. How well tuned are the tools to the task at hand? At the most fundamental level, text-editing accessories such as the ones discussed here exist to meet the needs of software programmers who need a tool that can rapidly create and manipulate clean text. The user interface and feature set are tuned accordingly. To put it in colloquial terms, these text editors don't do a great deal of hand holding. That's not what they're about.

On the other hand, text editors can be darned useful and flexible tools, as anyone who has ever used the programs mentioned previously can attest. For some types of note taking, a text editor may be quite sufficient. What note-taking scenarios are adequately addressed by text editors?

Text Editors Are Good for Some Types of Notes

A text editor is probably going to be adequate to enable you to take notes that are:

- Concise

- Textual

- Formally structured

- Clean

- Searchable

- Discrete

Concise Notes

Text editors are good at the presentation of *concise* information. But if you have to take *lengthy* notes, a text editor may not be the best tool for reviewing the information later because they don't have the page formatting and presentation features that make for high readability.

NOTE   To demonstrate this point, simply look in your My Programs directory for a good-sized README file and then open and print it. I won't even attempt to read more than three or four pages of closely spaced straight text.

Unfortunately, it's fairly common that a beleaguered note taker must take a lengthy collection of notes that must be reviewed later…consider the board meeting that must be transcribed in close detail or the hour-long lecture in school ("Everything I talk about today will be on the exam"). This is one of the reasons, as you'll discuss later, why *word-processing* software has often been used for note taking.

Textual Notes

Another limitation to the text editor is that it is, of course, best at handling text! But note takers quite commonly need to take nontextual notes for the simple reason that people often think, and communicate, in pictures, not words alone. The simple flowchart, the doodle for emphasis, the box around an important point, the sketch of an important object or concept—these are important elements of note taking that are simply outside the scope of text-editing programs.

Formally Structured Notes

Conversely, text editors have some capabilities that aren't needed to support the note-taking task. For example, a primary design objective for text editors is to manage the creation and manipulation of code, which usually is (or should be) *formally structured* text that makes heavy use of indentation, line spacing, and paired symbols such as < > and { }. Some of the resulting features in text editors are quite helpful in note taking, such as the ability to create outline structures and to make text more readable through line spacing.

There's an important distinction to be made, though, which is that note taking is less about *formal* structure and more about *informal* structure, attached hastily to terms and concepts captured on the fly and sometimes ex post facto. For example, a student listening to a lecture may say to himself, "Oh, the three things the prof just mentioned were all part of a group!" and number the items (1), (2), (3). But that's about as far as most of us are likely to go. Few of us have the Mozart-like ability to listen to a meeting or a lecture and translate what you're hearing into blocks of formally structured text.

Clean Notes

Next, let's consider that text editors are focused on entering and producing *clean* ASCII characters. Although some text editors such as Notepad do have basic character and word presentation features such as the ability to change the font, size, and emphasis (regular, italic, bold), they aren't really focused on the task of making the words look different or better. For note takers, making words *look* different can be an important issue. Underlining, strikethrough, double underlining, color changes, circling, highlighting—all these are an important part of the note-taking experience, and most of these are outside the typical "comfort zone" of a text-editing program.

Searchable Notes

Finally, it's important to be able to *search* notes, especially ones accumulated over time. This is something that's difficult to accomplish with paper notes…remember trying to find one particular note taken in illegible handwriting on one particular day in a 13-week class? Your notes may be scattered across multiple folders, multiple notebooks, multiple paper formats, and even multiple states of crinkliness.

There are typically multifile search capabilities built into text editors, but it's not always a highly user-friendly experience. In the Unix world, grep requires some level of enthusiasm for being a power user. In the Windows world, multifile searching can be painfully slow, and, as in the Macintosh world, broadly constructed searches can require the user to open and inspect many documents, a painful task.

Discrete Notes

This brings us to another aspect of note taking for which text editors offer a partial but not complete solution. Text editors are good at taking notes if the notes meet all the previous criteria and are amenable to *discrete* storage and review—in other words, many smaller files that are reviewed independently. If the task is one that requires comprehensive review of a body of notes taken over time (for example, preparing for class or conducting a project postmortem), the text editor is probably not going to be the most convenient tool for that job because of its limitations in terms of document presentation.

In summary, text editors are a useful but *partial* and *not completely in focus* solution to the challenges involved in taking notes on meetings, research, and lectures. Interestingly, as you'll find in the following discussion, the same is true of several other types of software that also offer useful but partial tools to support the task of taking notes. That's one of the fundamental reasons why OneNote, which offers a *complete* and *focused* solution to the task of note taking, is such an interesting and exciting program.

Using Word-Processing Programs for Note Taking

Word-processing programs are also often used for note taking. As the discussion in the preceding section suggests, word-processing programs have a number of strengths for certain aspects of the note-taking task, especially those that involve presentation and review of lengthy notes taken over a long period of time. Word-processing programs have the page formatting and presentation features that make for high readability. Specifically, word-processing programs such as Microsoft Word are good for situations where the notes that will be taken:

- Will be lengthy or will be taken over a long period of time

- Will require comprehensive review

- Will require high-quality, high-precision formatting

- Will be "destructively transformed" into the final work product

- Will be inserted immediately and with minimal editing into the final work product

Taking Notes That Go into Final Work Product

The final two scenarios in the previous bulleted list are new concepts in this discussion of note taking, so let's take a moment to explore them. The first idea, destructive transformation, envisages that notes will be created and then immediately transformed into a final work product. For example, let's say that I'm an attorney preparing a letter for a client. I may begin the process by reviewing the client's file, opening a word-processing document, and banging out a series of points that I want to mention in the letter. Only once I've gotten all the salient facts on the page in rough note format will I go through the page line by line and turn rough notes into nicely phrased paragraphs. I don't need to retain the "notes" I took during the composition phase—I don't keep them because I destructively transformed them into the work product itself. For this scenario, a word processor is the right tool for the job!

The second scenario of inserting notes immediately into the final work product raises a slightly different set of issues. Let's say I'm responsible for taking the minutes of an official meeting and that my only responsibility is to issue a list of action items as bullet points nicely formatted in a Word document. If this is a task I've carried out several times before, I may open a Word template that includes "holes" where the bullet points will go and simply insert the action items directly into those locations in the new document (see Figure 1-4).

WILLYWIDGETS.COM MEETING REPORT

TO: DISTRIBUTION

FROM: W. FREDERICK ZIMMERMAN

SUBJECT: WEEKLY PRODUCTION MEETING

DATE: 7/28/2003

CC: MANAGEMENT TEAM

ITEMS DISCUSSED IN THIS WEEK'S MEETING

cost of Wiki widget

press release

ACTION ITEMS

- Cooper – purchase Wiki manual
- Brown – mail press release to Free Press
- [insert more notes here]

Figure 1-4. Inserting notes into a preexisting Word template

In this case, I don't need to keep a separate document with notes. I simply fill in the missing information straight into the word-processing document. I may check my spelling and formatting when I return to my desk and get ready to distribute the notes; but, basically, the information goes straight from the meeting to final work product without an intervening stop in the form of a notes document. For tasks such as these, the key issue isn't so much the feature/function of the word-processing program as the suitability of the information to quick synopsis.

The approach of inserting information straight into a work product document works fine if the information is simple, easy to spell, easy to format, and doesn't require careful subsequent review. If the information is complex, is unfamiliar, is lengthy, requires extensive formatting, or requires careful review, it'll probably be unwise to try to enter it straight into a word-processing document.

Am...Experiencing...Brain Lock...

Now that I've discussed a couple of scenarios where word-processing programs work well for taking notes, let's talk about where they falter. The nature of note taking is that it requires a division of energy between the act of paying attention to what's being said and the physical act of taking the notes. The more complex the discussion and the more accurate the notes, the more energy required and the more challenging it is to divide that energy. For some of us, like me, it's all you can do to listen and doodle at the same time! Unfortunately, modern word processors are extremely complex—see the "wall o' toolbars" from Microsoft Word in Figure 1-5.

Figure 1-5. Microsoft Word's "wall o' toolbars"

So paying attention to a word processor while taking notes on the fly is quite difficult, and the consequence is often "mission failure." Whilst the user is engaged in navigating among all the menus and toolbars available in Word, she may not be able to absorb or capture important discussions and concepts. Or conversely, the user may create a document that becomes very ragged in appearance. The formatting features of word processors can actually make documents *more* difficult to read if they're applied in a haphazard or error-prone way. (To demonstrate this point to yourself, type a couple of paragraphs in Word, then "accidentally" apply the wrong style.) The peril of "brain lock" is one of the primary reasons why word-processing software, as a category, represents only a partial solution to the challenge of convenient and intuitive note taking.

Personal Experiences with Word Processors for Note Taking

I used Microsoft Word to take notes all the way through law school! Each semester, I'd open a file for each course, and, as I worked my way through the 600 to 900 pages and the 1,000 to 3,000 cases assigned for each subject, I'd use Word's outlining features to create a rolling outline of the entire syllabus, drilling down to the level of the individual case. Most pages were divided into two columns using Word's table feature, and I would put opposing arguments on each side of the table. I would then print the resulting Word documents and use them as my study guide before exams. The printouts were long—maybe 50 to 100 pages each.

In all honesty, this method worked pretty well…my grades improved significantly when I adopted it. But this is far from being a solution that would work for everyone, and it has several undesirable features:

- It kills a lot of trees.

- It only works for a fast typist.

- It is *very* labor intensive.

- The table feature doesn't look especially good when used with imbalanced chunks of lengthy text that stretch over multiple pages.

- As you drill deeper in the outline, the formatting becomes more difficult to read.

- The documents look dog ugly.

I didn't even attempt to use this note-taking method to capture live notes during class. I could never have created outline indents, outdents, body text, or tables while trying to stay a couple of steps ahead of the discussion in class so that I would be prepared if called upon by *The Paper Chase's* Professor Kingsfield. ("Mr. Zimmerman! Please give us the facts of *Pennoyer v. Neff.*")

I used my homegrown note-taking method exclusively for research notes taken while studying at home sitting in front of my computer. I did take notes during class in my own handwriting on lined paper, but they were, in all candor, almost worthless almost immediately. My handwriting is close to illegible, and I usually need almost all my attention to absorb what a speaker is saying.

What *was* helpful before class and in preparing for exams was annotating just about every page of my casebooks with handwritten notes. I was limited by the relatively small (3/4-inch) margins. Even so, these print annotations were extremely valuable. I will discuss the use of word processors for annotation later in this chapter.

Using Presentation Programs for Note Taking

Many of you have spent far too many hours watching PowerPoint slides flicker across the screen as you scribble notes on a pad of paper or perhaps on a printout of the presentation itself. Where do you turn when it's time to take notes that will be used to create, update, or annotate a presentation? In some scenarios, the answer is to the presentation software itself, which represents yet another province of the continent of note taking—a partial but far from complete solution to the general challenge.

If my boss is standing over my shoulder giving me a list of bullet points that he wants incorporated in his presentation next week, where else should I put those notes, except PowerPoint? There's not much reason to put the notes somewhere else and then copy them into PowerPoint—especially considering that if I take notes in a text editor or word processor and *then* copy them into PowerPoint, there's a good chance that my notes won't readily fit into the space available with the larger font sizes typically used in presentations.

If I'm giving a presentation and a good issue is raised about one of my bullet points, where do I record a note of the issue? Until recently, the answer was "in my embarrassed head," or "on a scrap of paper near the podium." That's still the best answer for most people, but Office 2003 does provide a better answer for PowerPoint users, who can now annotate their presentations in digital ink and save the annotations for future reference (see Figure 1-6).

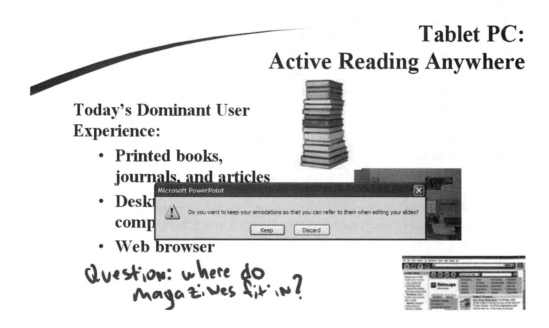

Figure 1-6. Ink annotation in PowerPoint

If I'm sitting in the audience watching someone else present, what are my note-taking options? It depends on whether the presenter has already distributed electronic versions of the presentation. Opinions differ as to whether this is wise. Presenters with a trusting, optimistic view of human nature may distribute the PowerPoint presentation ahead of time so that everyone is on the same page and the questions and dialogue can be as sharp and well informed as possible. Presenters with a cynical, realistic view of human nature may wait until after the live presentation to make electronic copies available so that everyone pays attention during the actual presentation.

If only a printed copy of the presentation is available, audience members have few options. They can either scribble on the printouts or use whatever programs are available on their personal computer. I have already discussed some of the classic options, such as text-editing and word-processing programs. In a subsequent section, I'll discuss some of the newer options that have become available as a result of the advent, several years ago, of Personal Digital Assistants (PDAs) and, more recently, of Tablet PCs.

If the electronic PowerPoint presentation is available, audience members who have personal computers with them have more options. PowerPoint gives users the option to view a Notes page for each slide where they can enter notes (see Figure 1-7). It's a blank half page where minimal formatting tools are available. Experienced presenters use this space to store information that simply is too long or complex to read well on screen…links, citations, detailed text, and so on.

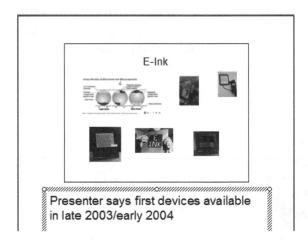

Figure 1-7. The Notes page in PowerPoint

The principal shortcomings of the Notes page in PowerPoint as a mechanism for taking notes are as follows:

- An electronic version of the presentation is often not available when notes are being taken.

- The high-level structure of the notes is tightly bound to the structure of the PowerPoint presentation—each Notes page is bound to a particular slide.

- It's difficult to integrate notes taken during a presentation in a particular PowerPoint file with other notes taken most likely by hand or using a text-editing or word-processing program.

In summary, like many of the other types of programs you've seen, PowerPoint offers a reasonably good solution for certain note-taking scenarios. Where it begins to break down is when the note taking leaves the world of presentations and becomes just a part of a much broader range of note-taking activity…which is, of course, the reality for most people. You spend some of your time taking notes in presentations, sure, but you spend lots of other time taking notes in meetings, in class, and in a wide variety of other settings. A truly successful note-taking program must work for many scenarios and many settings.

Using Personal Digital Assistants for Note Taking

The PDA category has been responsible for a number of important innovations in note taking. By telling this story, I run the risk of dating myself as a "before-the-invention-of-fire" old fogy, but I remember the TRS-80 Model 100 as a pioneering "PDA" that was quite useful for note taking with its lightweight slate-style chassis, clean 8×40 Liquid Crystal Display (LCD), and simple text editor (see Figure 1-8).

Figure 1-8. The TRS-80 Model 100

Another huge milestone for note taking was the invention of the Palm operating system, particularly its handwriting system, Graffiti. As Andrea Butter and David Pogue explained in *Piloting Palm* (John Wiley & Sons, 2002):

> *…Handwriting recognition efforts so far continued to focus on training the computer to read. [Palm founder] Jeff Hawkins took the opposite tack: He would train people how to write. There would be one acceptable shape for each letter of the alphabet, and that was that.*

This made for much more intuitive entry of text on a small, lightweight, stylish handheld device. The Palm OS also offered one-step synchronization of calendar, email, contacts, and to do lists between desktop and handheld computers.

The net effect of these innovations was that Palm devices became an attractive new option for carrying out certain specialized types of note taking. Palm deliberately optimized their tool to be good at its specialties—calendaring, contact information, to do items—and accepted that the tool would not be good at tasks involving lengthy, complex entry of information, such as taking class notes or recording the minutes of a complex meeting. Even so, the Palm OS represented an important "ratcheting up" in user expectations of note taking.

Returning for a moment to the map of Note-Taking Land shown in Figure 1-1, it's as if someone plunked a trio of beautiful Swiss mountain villages named *Calendereich*, *Contactburg*, and *Todoachtung* onto a hitherto undeveloped island off Note-Taking Land (see Figure 1-9). After Palm, people have higher expectations of what a personal computer can do for them in the area of note taking.

I'd be remiss if I didn't also mention the contribution of Microsoft's Pocket PC platform to the general understanding of what a PDA can do for note taking. For those not familiar with Pocket PC, it's Microsoft's version of the Windows operating system, simplified and optimized for a PDA. This is a personal opinion…I'm not sure how widely it's shared…but I believe that Pocket PC has made two key contributions to users' expectations of note taking.

Microsoft would probably tell you something to the effect that Pocket PC is a more powerful operating system than Palm and that Pocket PC versions of Word and other applications are more suited to note taking than the corresponding "word-processor" and text-editing programs in the Palm world. Microsoft might also mention something to the effect that Pocket PC was the first platform that supported a form of the digital ink data type.

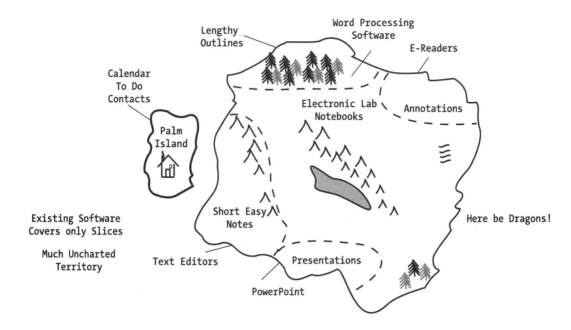

Figure 1-9. Note-Taking Land with Palm Island

I don't work for Microsoft, though, so I'm free to choose a different line of argument. I focus instead on two features that aren't nearly as prominent in Microsoft's strategy pronouncements. The first is a basic feature of a Pocket PC: From launch, all Pocket PCs have been required to offer brilliant color displays. There's no such thing as a black-and-white Pocket PC, and both color text and color images look excellent on a Pocket PC. This means everyone who uses a Pocket PC or sees one in action forms an expectation that a high-end PDA should be able to capture small bits of information and modest-sized images in high-fidelity color. Palm and Handspring swiftly responded to this change in customer expectations by producing a full line of color models. Now, scratchy little black-and-white (or gray-on-green) characters or images on a PDA look painfully ugly and out of style. Because in many users' minds PDAs are all about capturing and accessing small bits of personal information—in other words, taking notes—the net effect is that color and images have become part of the framework of expectations around capturing and accessing both small and large bits of personal information.

The second feature I think has had an important effect on customers' expectations of note taking is a fairly obscure one that many Pocket PC users may take for granted. I'm referring to the Auto-Complete function that watches as the first few characters of a word are entered via the "peck and plink" on-screen keyboard and then recommends several alternate word completions. Suddenly, entering complete words into a PDA becomes dramatically less burdensome. This Auto-Complete feature is a manifestation, or symptom, if you will, of a much broader Microsoft strategy that applications should offer intelligent recommendations based on what they see the user doing.

In applications that use word processing to create formal work product, some users find these intelligent recommendation features intrusive and annoying—especially if they disagree with the correction being offered! That's because in the most common scenarios with those applications, the user is in a setting where he is at his desktop free to concentrate on creating formal work product. It would be wrong to say that any busy professional ever has ample time to do anything in this stressed day and age, but sitting at your desk writing a document is different from being in a meeting or class trying to listen and take notes at the same time. You may have more time available to deliberate on typing and spelling when you're at your desk composing a document than when you're in a meeting taking notes. Thus, the Pocket PC's Auto-Complete feature significantly eases the task of taking notes on a PDA. Once again, the overall trend is that computer software is getting better at supporting note taking, and customers' expectations are rising accordingly.

Using a Tablet PC for Note Taking

November 2002 saw the release of Microsoft Windows XP Tablet PC Edition, the hardware and software platform commonly referred to as *Tablet PC*. Microsoft's target audience for Tablet PC is "corridor warriors," or information professionals who spend much of their time in meetings. Because people who spend a lot of their time in meetings also spend a lot of time taking notes, the functionality developed for Tablet PC has been another development that raises the bar for note taking via computer.

The philosophical underpinning for Tablet PC is what Microsoft refers to as "natural computing." A new layer of software has been added to Windows XP that makes it easier for users to interact with the computer by supporting a new mode of user input: *digital ink*, or scribbles entered via electronic pen on a slate-shaped active digitizer screen. Microsoft has built new software utilities such as Windows Journal, an "electronic yellow pad" application, and enhanced others, such as the Office XP suite, with add-ons to take advantage of Tablet PC's new digital ink capabilities. The 2003 versions of Word, PowerPoint, and Excel were built with "native" support for digital ink, meaning that data entry via digital ink is supported as an integral part of the application, on an equal footing with data entry via keyboarding or Windows speech recognition.

The hardware is lightweight (3.2 pounds or lighter for most models), and every Tablet PC is equipped with a Wireless Local Area Networking (WLAN) card (802.11b or g, which are different types using different frequencies). The universal availability of wireless cards for Tablet PCs has tended to increase Tablet PC users' expectations of being connected to LANs and the Internet, even in highly mobile settings such as impromptu meetings.

Using Wireless LANs

Wireless LAN technology isn't limited to Tablet PC, of course…any modern PC running a recent version of the Windows, Macintosh, or Unix operating systems, equipped with a WLAN card, and possessing the appropriate authentication can connect to any WLAN in the neighborhood. Better yet, WLAN technology is cheap, and it's being adopted rapidly. Many enterprise campuses have WLAN service already, and in some technology-oriented downtowns unprotected WLAN access points can be found on every block. The "viral" adoption of WLAN technology has had a ripple effect on note taking in that it increases the expectation that connectivity should be available in meetings, even impromptu ones held in nonwired meeting places.

Therefore, the trend accelerates that note taking within meetings becomes less about solitary scribing and more about connected information sharing. It becomes less viable to think of a meeting as a group of individuals isolated together in time and space (think *12 Angry Men* or *The Poseidon Adventure*) and more attractive to think of a meeting as a coming together of individuals, each actively connected to a living network (think *Star Trek: The Next Generation* or *The Matrix*). Instead of documenting discussions and decisions reached within a bubble, note takers are reaching out to each other and to the outside world for information to empower the individuals in the meeting and their external "customers."

Using Collaboration Software

Collaboration software has been an active area for innovation in the late '90s and early '00s, and a number of companies have built software such as Lotus Notes, Groove, and Intraspect that's intended to facilitate group interaction in shared workspaces. One strategic goal that's often expressed in this connection is *knowledge management* or the phrase I prefer, *enterprise information strategy.* The idea is to eliminate bottlenecks that impede the efficient flow of information in an organization where it's needed. One type of information that's especially prone to bottle necking is notes taken by individuals or groups—one of the more tangible expressions of "tribal knowledge." There are strong social reasons why this is the case…individuals and teams may be less willing to share information that's informal or "messy."

Accordingly, one of the many goals of collaboration software is to move information gathered during note taking from scraps of paper or word-processor files stored on a stand-alone computer into structured software repositories that can be accessed by an entire enterprise. The tools available in collaboration software are generally pretty robust and, as might be expected, are focused around activities related to collaboration, such as storing, securing, sharing, and publishing information to groups defined with varying levels of granularity.

Because of these feature/function requirements, collaboration software typically involves both specialized server software installed at the corporate data center and a specialized piece of client software installed on every seat in the enterprise. This brings with it some usability and cost issues…collaboration software is Yet Another Piece of Software to Learn (YAPOSTL) for the busy information worker in a corporation (see Figure 1-10).

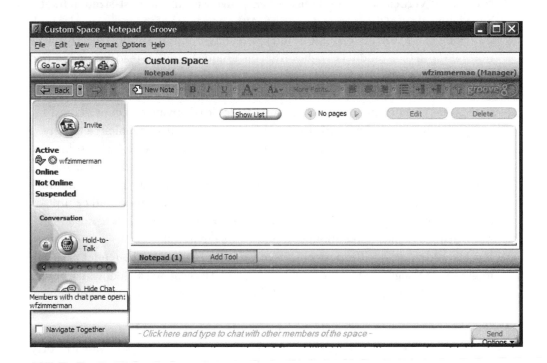

Figure 1-10. You can use Groove collaboration software for note taking.

Because of the inherent complexity in managing the social interaction of groups (Who is part of group X? Who is part of group Y? Do members of groups X and Y both get to see documents A and B, but do members of group Y also get to see document C?), collaboration software does tend to present the user with a lot of decision making. The high-level strength of collaboration software, in terms of its support for note taking, is less in the activity of taking notes and more in "what you do with the notes later."

Note Taking, E-Readers, and Course Books

Textbooks and note taking go hand in hand. Rare is the printed textbook that does not have some form of scribbled annotation by the end of the school year. For this reason, many manufacturers of hardware- and software-based electronic course books and e-readers have devoted some energy to implementing note-taking features in their offerings. This survey of note-taking software would be incomplete without a discussion of the e-reader space.

You can narrow the scope of this survey somewhat by casting a skeptical eye on some of the more marginal players in this field. A number of companies have made significant investments in bringing electronic course book solutions to the market in recent years, but many of them, especially newer companies that offer specialized vertical solutions dedicated exclusively to this modest-sized market, have fallen afoul of the market downturn. Although some of these companies with hardware-based e-reader solutions did interesting things to support electronic note taking in their products, I believe that the unique hardware readers are doomed to be niche products. The fundamental usability logic of buying a dedicated e-reader device and carrying it around *in addition to* a personal computer or multipurpose PDA is less compelling than the fundamental logic of buying a PDA or PC and equipping it with reading software. (Fewer devices = more convenience.) In my view, the market winners in the course book space will be software-based solutions, such as Microsoft Reader, Adobe Reader Mobipocket Reader, and Palm Reader, which run on a large number of target devices. Although there have been demonstrable successes in using PDAs for note taking, many end users would exhibit concern about taking notes in the margin of a PDA-sized e-book or using a PDA-sized display to take notes about complex course material.

I wouldn't exclude the possibility that a Unix or Linux-based e-reader program might become significant in the future. Just as Wal-Mart can sell a Lindows computer for $199, perhaps Linux-based PDAs will also become affordable and commonplace in the next few years.

The analysis in the foregoing paragraphs suggests that there are really only two important e-reader programs for the student of note-taking software to worry about right now: Microsoft Reader and Adobe Reader. Microsoft Reader has had a set of basic note-taking features built in since its first release and added support for handwritten annotations in the version 2.5 release that coincided with the launch of Tablet PC. Similarly, Adobe Reader has some fairly robust commenting features. The fundamental issue with using either of these programs for electronic course book note taking is that their feature sets are optimized for different scenarios. Microsoft Reader is optimized for so-called immersive reading of trade books—in other words, fiction and nonfiction with relatively low levels of graphics and images. Adobe Reader, on the other hand, is optimized to provide publishers with extremely strong control over the appearance of electronically published content. In both cases, the user activities best supported by the programs aren't the same as the tasks required of the student who is most concerned with taking extensive, accurate notes while intensively, actively, and analytically reading a textbook and, most likely, listening to a discussion at the same time.

Word Processing Programs for Reading and Annotation

As I pointed out in the earlier "Personal Experiences with Note Taking" sidebar, annotation is an important type of note taking, especially in the academic setting where it's often important for students to annotate course books and other materials.

Word-processing programs offer a partial but by no means complete solution to the challenge of online reading and annotation. One shortcoming of using word-processing programs for annotated notes is that the documents being annotated must be available in word processing–compatible formats such as Rich Text Format (RTF) or Word. This is by no means always the case. For example, none of my legal casebooks were then available in electronic format. Furthermore, although an increasing number of documents are available in electronic format today, it's often the case that they're available in e-reader formats such as Portable Document Format (PDF) or Microsoft Reader rather than word-processing formats. Although PDF and Reader have annotation and comment features built in, copy protection features can make it impossible to get commercially published e-book text into a word processor for further annotation and manipulation.

Another important shortcoming of using word processors for annotation is that attaching comments to, say, a product requirements document in the middle of a meeting can be a painful process. Live annotation during a meeting almost inevitably slows the meeting significantly and tends to produce loss of nuance and less than optimal word choices. In my estimation there are two fundamental causes of this behavior: the built-in complexity of word-processing software, discussed previously, and the inherent delays involved in translating free-flowing verbal discussion into cogent written format laid atop an already existing word-processing document.

For all these reasons, word-processing programs are by no means an optimal solution to the problem.

If I were doing law school over again today (horrible thought?!), I'd want to have electronic casebooks available to annotate, but I'd probably be out of luck. Only a scattering of electronic casebooks is available, and few professors assign them. Law school is still a print-intensive proposition. My casebook notes would probably still be scribbled in the tiny margins of very thick books. But I'll tell you this— everything else would be in OneNote!

Annotation can also be important in the enterprise productivity space although the scenarios are somewhat less obviously compelling than in the academic space. There's certainly a need for enterprises to "publish" important documents to their end users, and there are scenarios where individual end users maintain annotations to those documents—for example, a developer maintaining personal annotations to a piece of internal documentation or a human resources specialist maintaining case notes on resolutions of matters governed by particular policies. It does seem more likely, though, that these enterprise annotation scenarios would be carried out in productivity software such as Word rather than be published to e-reader software.

There does seem to be some traction for publishing certain types of professional information to e-reader software; for example, product documentation is often made available in PDF, and the consumer market for e-books, although still small in absolute terms, has experienced steady year-over-year growth.

Let's look for a moment at the user scenarios around annotation of e-reader documents in the academic, professional, and consumer spaces. Most of the e-reader software tools discussed previously have annotation features built into them. Microsoft Reader, for example, allows the user to select any words or lines of text and attach annotations in any one of several formats, including text, highlighter, or digital ink. Figure 1-11 illustrates some annotations that a law student or legal professional might make to an e-book version of the Federal Rules of Civil Procedure.

Both the strength and the weakness of this approach are that it's closely tied to the material in the text. This is an advantage if all your notes are closely tied to particular sections of the text (for example, in the scenario where every note is tied to a section of the Federal Rules of Civil Procedure). It may become a weakness if you need to take notes that aren't closely tied to particular sections of the text…for example, if the professor in the same course began to explain the structure of previous exams, where would you put the notes? Reader isn't intended to support free-form notes, and unfortunately, those are often needed in the same user scenario as annotation notes are needed.

When annotating a document in Reader (or in PDF), you also encounter the familiar "decision-making" problem, where the user must make a couple of decisions before she can actually begin taking the note. For example, in Reader, the user must first highlight the text to annotate, then choose which of several methods she wants to use to take notes about that text (as shown in Figure 1-12), and then actually enter the text.

This is too much decision making for someone who is taking notes "on the fly" during class. I know it would've been too much for me!

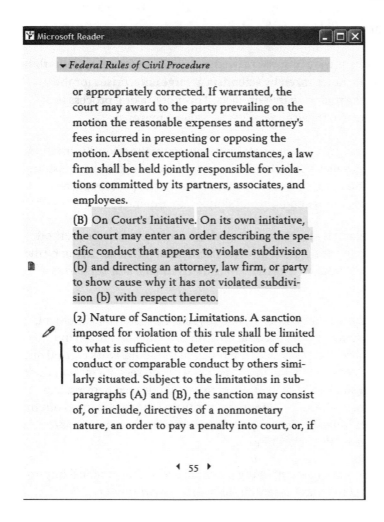

Figure 1-11. A Microsoft Reader version of the Federal Rules of Civil Procedure

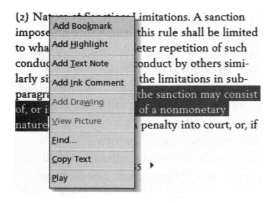

Figure 1-12. Too much decision making before entering notes to annotate text in Microsoft Reader

Using Electronic Lab Notebooks

Electronic lab notebook software is the term used to describe software systems that capture and manage the notes taken by scientists in large enterprises for the purpose of documenting their research projects. This note-taking process is of fundamental importance to those enterprises for several reasons:

- Accurate note taking is a fundamental competency of the scientific method. Most secondary science education in the United States begins with issuing students a lab notebook and walking them through the process of conducting and taking notes about several simple experiments.

- Accurate note taking is also a fundamental value of the scientific method. Unhappily, most scientific fraud involves falsification of notes, driven by the enormous sense of pressure to demonstrate that Mother Nature endorses a cherished hypothesis.

- For better or worse, science now often has a significant hierarchical element, where principal investigators become the hub of a large organized investigation of a complex area of science with much of the actual work carried out by graduate students and young investigators who are seeking to "win their spurs" by working under the supervision of more experienced patrons. Lab notebooks are one of the key methods that verify that the work carried out by these teams does indeed reflect physical reality rather than the stress-induced pressure of high expectations.

- Note taking is a crucial element of the patent process. The practical importance of this point in today's scientific-industrial environment can scarcely be overstated.

Note taking is just one strand of the mighty tapestry (if tapestries can be mighty) that constitutes enterprise Information Technology (IT) in a modern Research and Development (R&D) enterprise, but it's especially important because it's the point of origin for all the value produced by the enterprise. Once created, the research notes are managed in many ways—searching, indexing, reporting, and so on—but without them, there would be no R&D enterprise.

For all these reasons, electronic lab notebook software is one of the more challenging mountain ranges in the world of modern note-taking software, as shown in the map of Note-Taking Land in Figure 1-1. It represents the most challenging and sophisticated user scenario that you'll examine in this chapter.

A number of companies provide electronic lab notebook software. You'll examine a few solutions in this section, not in the pursuit of a comprehensive understanding of the challenges—for that's outside the scope of this book—but rather in pursuit of a representative understanding of higher-end note-taking requirements. The Web site of one provider, Amphora Research Systems, provides a nice high-level summary of the requirements for a successful electronic lab notebook (ELN):

> *Our ELNs are designed to be the natural place for the scientists in a company to conduct and document their research (hundreds or thousands of users, often in different sites and/or countries), even though these might be split into groups with little in common except they all work for the same company.*
>
> *Therefore, we think an ELN should:*
>
> - *Make existing tasks more efficient and minimize time spent on administration.*
>
> - *Be user friendly and flexible, supporting the different scientific disciplines and ways of working found within most companies.*
>
> - *Coordinate and integrate with existing tools in a way that simply isn't possible with paper.*
>
> - *Store and manage knowledge to boost collaboration across departments and geographies.*
>
> *Create patentable records with minimum disruption to work.*
>
> - *Facilitate compliance with external and internal standards.*
>
> - *Archive responsibly so that records can be accessed and understood well into the future.*[5]

The fundamental point about the first four requirements is diversity—these requirements encapsulate a wide range of preexisting methods by which notes are captured in a scientific R&D organization. A moment's reflection will lend credence to the proposition that practitioners in different scientific disciplines (biology, chemistry, physics, medicine) and subdisciplines (organic chemistry, cellular biology, oncology, whatever) most likely have differing preferences as to formats, tools, and methods for note taking.

In one community, spreadsheets may be most often captured in spreadsheets; in another, they might be most often captured in Unix databases, for both historical and logical reasons. Thus, support for scientific note taking in a large R&D enterprise seems to require that the electronic lab notebook system provide a high degree of flexibility and agnosticism. Yet the system must also still provide a central framework

---

5. http://www.amphora-research.com/solutions

that allows the enterprise to manage and share information efficiently. These are challenging requirements to levy on a piece of note-taking software!

Amphora Research meets the requirement by providing a set of Extensible Markup Language (XML) "wrappers" and servers that tie together the information from the enterprise information systems into a consistent, connectable whole. As you'll see in a later chapter, Microsoft has recognized the importance of XML in enterprise automation by building it into the "plumbing" of Microsoft Office 2003. Microsoft OneNote isn't overtly "XML aware" in version 1.0, but it seems likely that Microsoft will move in that direction in future releases.

Drilling into the last three items on Amphora's list generates additional challenging requirements against the enterprise note management system. Anyone who has maintained multiple copies of a document has had just a faint taste of the complexity involved in a scientific enterprise note-taking system!

Another challenging set of requirements are created by the U.S. government's regulation 21 CFR 11, which among other things requires that pharmaceutical companies be able to demonstrate through meticulous audit trails that there has been no deviation from established processes and procedures in testing drugs under development. This means that scientific note takers in these settings must be able to demonstrate an extensive, almost forensic history of the changes made to each document. To understand the complexity that this involves, think about the Track Changes feature in Microsoft Word. Having that feature on adds a lot of visual complexity to reviewing documents, and the average user can't create an "audit trail" that goes back more than a document or two. Now multiply this complexity by thousands or millions of documents containing notes.

I hope you're becoming persuaded that providing support for scientific note taking can be an extremely complex and challenging task! You'll learn later in the book how OneNote is a crucial enabler for a total solution to enterprise support for electronic lab notebooks.

With this, you come to an end of your tour of note-taking software solutions. You haven't seen everything! I know there are great programs that I haven't discussed and scenarios that I've failed to envision. If you're aware of interesting and worthy note-taking scenarios, tools, or research that you think might be of interest to me, please by all means let me know via posting to http://www.OneNoteInfoCenter.com or via e-mail to onenoteguide@onenoteinfocenter.com. I'll try to work them into future publications on this topic! After all, one of the key reasons for this extensive discussion of context is to make sure that you take full advantage of *all* the opportunities available to help make your note-taking activities more productive.

The Personal Knowledge Base

People who have a serious interest in more productive note taking are often also interested in more effective personal information management. In this sidebar, Richard Miller, Ph.D, presents an intriguing view of where personal information management is heading and how note taking fits into that vision.

Dr. Miller is a research scientist in the Alliances and New Technology Research group at LexisNexis, a division of the large professional publishing company Reed Elsevier plc. In previous positions, Dr. Miller managed the usability group for the Structural Dynamics Research Corporation (SDRC) and designed the user interface for the LexisNexis flagship Web research product, lexis.com. His experience has given him a deep understanding of how knowledge workers collect, process, manage, and retrieve information.

Q. Rich, tell us something about how knowledge workers approach the task of taking, managing, and utilizing notes collected in varying settings such as research, class, study groups, and business meetings.

A. First, let's consider why people take notes. I see four basic purposes for note taking:

- To create reminders to do things later

- To capture information from a meeting, class, or other stream of data

- To express an idea or create a new piece of information

- To annotate and complement an existing piece of information

Each purpose is related to enhancing productivity, but the extent to which the information from notes enhances productivity is largely affected by how efficiently the information is integrated into a user's workflow. However, experience and research have shown us that integrating notes into user knowledge bases and workflows hasn't been very efficient. Notes are by definition small pieces of data, so it's easy for them to get lost in the shuffle.

Several factors contribute to inefficiency in the integration of notes into a user's digital repository. Often a piece of information is lost because handwritten notes don't make it into digital form where it can more easily be found and related to other information. Transferring notes into digital form is also an ad-hoc and time-consuming process, so some information stays out of a user's workflow longer than optimal. As the use of portable devices increases, more of a user's notes can be digitized and integrated in a more timely fashion. However, these devices present a bottleneck for some users who find them less natural and more difficult for inputting information. The keyboard is probably the most efficient input device for note taking, but it's not always available.

Methods for integrating notes into a user's digital data repository vary widely across users. Notes may be integrated through a calendar, task list, word-processing document, or other application, depending on how the user thinks that type of information would best fit into their workflow. I often send myself emails as reminders to myself because I know that's a place where I will see it later. If the note is a diagram of an idea, it might be incorporated into an existing work product, such as a word-processing document.

Basically, users attempt to put pieces of information where they are most likely to find it again at the appropriate time and context. When they need to access the information, they will either browse or search in likely candidate locations. The larger the information repository and number of candidate locations, the more likely the user is to perform a search.

Q. Now tell us about your ideas about the Personal Knowledge Base (PKB) and how the note-taking tasks mentioned previously fit into your overall concept of the PKB.

A. The PKB concept, similar to other concepts related to the preponderance of information and the decrease in storage costs, is a vision of an ideal information repository that you can use to improve the design of information-seeking tools. A PKB is a unique, highly organized, and connected repository of information for and about a user. The purpose of a PKB is to support all the information needs of its owner by organizing collected "information objects," relating information to personal goals, and connecting personal data to the outside world.

When such a system exists in a complete and reliable form depends on the rate of continued integration among the current set of disparate data sources that users rely on and interface with today, such as email folders, local and enterprise network folders, workgroup/organization/enterprise portals, Internet browsers, third-party data repositories, handheld devices, cell phones, hard-copy documents, file folders, and so on. The current, evolving system is tolerated by most users but leaves much room for improvement, considering all the time and effort users spend accessing and organizing information.

The following figure shows a conceptual picture of the PKB. The human accesses data from the world of information through his PKB, which is connected to a larger workgroup KB, which in turn is connected to an even larger organization KB. The inner layer in the figure surrounding the core data represents metadata (for example, author, publication, and date of an article) used to organize and present data through the outer layer, which represents a virtually unlimited amount of flexible user interfaces or "views." The PKB is centrally located, secure, and accessible from anywhere using any device. The PKB is constantly evolving and self-optimizing and may use "agents" designed to look for useful information objects that fit into the PKB it in a meaningful way.

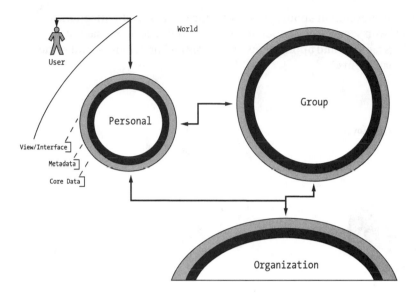

The following figure shows an example of the type of data that may comprise a PKB. This view of a PKB is based on the various roles that the user plays, such as homeowner, family member, community member, employee, and so on.

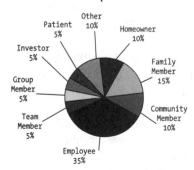

The following figure shows an exploded view of the employee role information, divided into type or purpose of information, such as projects, financial and benefits, and communications. In addition to this type of information, a complete PKB might also have information about a user's identification for authentication, a "digital wallet" with secure information for automated financial transactions, custom settings for tools and applications, user goals and preferences, and some form of personal "agents."

Data for Employee

Benefits of a PKB include less time spent finding and organizing information, more work done for a user through automation, more relevant information presented to a user as it's available, and increased collaboration effectiveness because links between PKBs based on the nature of the relationship between PKB owners. The better organized the PKB, the easier it's to create interfaces or views that serve the user for a particular task in a particular context. Thinking about the various ways in which data should be organized for a given user can shed light on the best tools or applications to create.

Information contained in notes is important to the usefulness of the PKB. Notes provide the glue between other pieces of information in the PKB because they contain a great deal of context for how the PKB information is meaningful and serves user goals. For example, annotations in a document indicate why the document is relevant, notes taken at a meeting help a user better understand and utilize information associated with a project, and a diagram may summarize a concept discussed in an email thread. Notes also are a great source of information about a user's goals and thoughts, allowing for more optimal organization of the PKB and retrieval (by software agents, for example) of more relevant information added to the PKB. In short, the PKB would contain much less knowledge without information from notes.

Q. Of course, many of today's knowledge workers use today's tools to implement a rudimentary version of the PKB on their desktop. What's lacking in today's tools?

A. Yes, every user has some kind of system for storing and organizing their digital information, but most people aren't very good at it, or they aren't very motivated to spend the necessary time and effort. The less organized their information is, the more time they end up spending looking for a given piece of information.

Therefore, they need a lot of help from tools. Today's tools are better than they used to be, but they still leave much room for improvement.

As I mentioned before, users today access information from several different disconnected repositories. These repositories need to be better integrated, allowing users an integrated, flexible view of a user's data, saving time spent browsing and searching separate repositories.

Retrieval of information could be improved by storing information so that it's associated with other related information in a user's knowledge base. User productivity could also be improved by automatically weighting pieces of information, such as notes or emails, in terms of importance to the user's goals (which can be derived from PKB data).

Users also need better tools and devices for capturing information in digital form. Voice input on PDAs and Tablet PCs are great examples of how notes can be easily captured and integrated into a user's knowledge base. PKBs will become more complete as input devices and recognition software improve and become more natural to use.

Q. As is often the case in the world of technology visions and trends, it may be that progress toward fully realizing the PKB occurs as various companies take incremental steps forward, each offering new tools that provide improved support in particular aspects of the overall task flow for various horizontal or vertical collections of end users. What new capabilities do you think are needed in the area of taking, managing, and utilizing notes?

A. In terms of taking notes, the Tablet PC and PDA hardware needs to offer a more natural, paper-like, note-taking experience because the advantage of these devices is taking the first step toward integrating notes into a user's larger knowledge base by automatically digitizing the notes. Currently, the "writing-on-glass" experience that these devices offer seems to lack the tactile feedback that would support frequent note-taking by many users (there are devices available that allow a user to actually write on paper as it's digitized, but I'm not sure how successful these have been).

Many of these devices include a microphone for voice input. This is a feature that should continue to be included and improved because voice input is one of the most efficient methods for taking and digitizing notes.

Once digitized, the next challenge is to convert notes into recognizable text, so voice and handwriting recognition accuracy needs to improve to the point that they require no more than minimal cleanup editing by a user.

In order to derive value from notes, they need to be stored and represented according to their context. This statement has implications for improving tools available at the note-taking event (for example, when a user is taking notes about a particular meeting, if a note-taking tool automatically integrated metadata about the meeting topic, agenda, attendees, and so on, then the notes will be much more understandable and useful upon later review).

In addition, when notes are added to a user's knowledge base, if it were automatically linked to nodes in an index or taxonomy of the user's knowledge base, the notes will have much more value.

Finally, visual representations (for example, charts and diagrams) of a user's knowledge base can help a user understand how notes "glue" various pieces of information together, allowing a user to make connections between pieces of information that may not be made otherwise.

Summary

The purpose of this tour of Note-Taking Land has been to illustrate the point that Microsoft OneNote, far from being the first note-taking program ever, is actually the latest in a long string of programs in many different categories that have supported various end user note-taking scenarios of widely differing nature and complexity. All the solutions you've looked at thus far have significant strengths, but they also have significant weaknesses. You've seen, for example, that many existing solutions are too slow to enter notes because they have *too many* features/ functions and require too much decision making. You've also seen that many solutions seem to have difficulty with "multimodal" note-taking within a single application, for example, switching from annotating a document to taking notes on a meeting to updating a to do list. Conversely, you've seen that a number of new developments in technology, such as the advent of PDAs, WLANs, and Tablet PCs, have made it significantly *easier* for individuals to be digitally empowered as they take notes in meetings and other settings.

Now you're in a position to appreciate what the advent of Microsoft OneNote means to Note-Taking Land! If you'll bear with an unfortunate metaphor for a moment, my first mental image is that OneNote is something like an amoeba or blob that covers a significant portion of the continent—some areas you've already visited, some you've never seen before. To continue along this line of unfortunate metaphors (somewhat like the dinner guest who overstayed his welcome in Hart and Kaufman's classic play *The Man Who Came to Dinner*[6]), you could say that OneNote's presence on the map of Note-Taking Land in this first release is something like an army that has made its first landing and secured a number of strategic locations (see Figure 1-13).

---

6. http://www.pbs.org/wnet/stageonscreen/tmwctd/circle.html

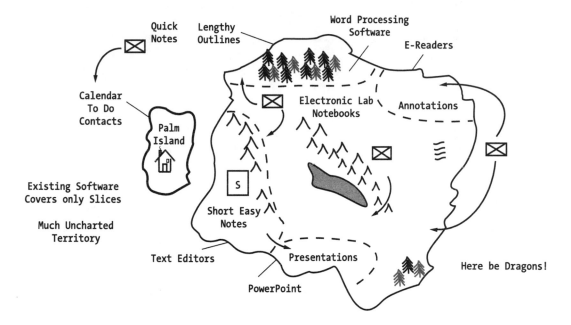

Figure 1-13. OneNote arrives in Note-Taking Land.

You're in the role of the inhabitants of Note-Taking Land who are nervously trying to decide whether OneNote is here to stay and just what your stance should be toward this liberating power. You have basic intelligence about OneNote, gathered in the introduction, and of course you know quite a bit about the topography of your own country, discussed in this chapter. What you *don't* know are the crucial details about the liberating power…just what will each of OneNote's features do? How will they respond if stressed or challenged? How will they interact together? What are their long-term intentions, and how credible are their commitments?

The rest of this book is an extended reconnaissance to ferret out those crucial details. Prepare yourself! In guerilla warfare, every inhabitant of Note-Taking Land is a potentially crucial informant. Your detailed awareness of your local situation and needs is a crucial asset as you put together a picture of how OneNote's capabilities cover the valuable territory of note taking.

CHAPTER 2

Installing OneNote

IN THIS CHAPTER you'll have your first encounter with OneNote. You've learned cnough about OneNote—either from the previous chapter or from elsewhere in your peregrinations through the world of computer software—that you want to see what all the excitement is about. There's no better way than to climb on top of the diving board and take that first header into the pool.

Getting Started

What do you need to do to get started? There are four basic situations, depending on whether OneNote is actually installed on your computer—and whether you know its status! They are as follows:

- OneNote is already installed on a personal computer that you can use, and you know it. In that case, you can skip straight to the end of this chapter, "Verifying That OneNote Is Properly Installed."

- It's already installed, but you don't know it—in which case, all you need to do is find the program!

- It's not installed, but you don't know that for sure.

- It's not installed, and you know that it's not installed.

In the latter two cases, obviously, you'll need to install the software. Before you go to that trouble, though, you may want to see whether the software is already there!

Did OneNote Come with Your Computer?

The easiest way to install OneNote on your computer is to have the manufacturer do it for you before you receive your new desktop, notebook, or Tablet PC. There's a good chance that this will be the case if you buy a computer in fall 2003 or beyond, but you can't take it for granted. The only real way to be sure is to check. If you purchase online, you can inspect the online product information, which usually includes a thorough description of the software that comes with the computer.

CAUTION   Although OneNote is part of the Office family, it's *not* being bundled as part of the default purchase package for Office 2003, so you've got to look for the word *OneNote* in the list of software that you see online or that comes with your computer.

If you purchase by phone or in person, you can ask the salesperson.

 CAUTION   If you're asking about OneNote by phone, make sure the person understands that OneNote is completely different from the Microsoft Notepad accessory that has been part of Windows for years. Don't let them tell you, "Oh, yeah, Notepad comes with every Windows computer." OneNote *doesn't* come with every Windows computer.

Even if the computer manufacturer bundles OneNote as part of your new computer, it may not necessarily come preinstalled. Sometimes manufacturers will leave it to you to install the CD.

Microsoft quite properly reserves the right to decide how OneNote is sold and distributed, and it has the right to revisit those decisions at any time. Unfortunately, if I get too specific about telling you how Microsoft sells and distributes OneNote, I run the risk of becoming wrong soon after this book is printed. For that reason, I will now utilize that famous soothsaying and editorial technique known as "the punt." (This term comes from a play in American football that allows the team with possession of the ball to relinquish control voluntarily whilst allowing itself ample room to avoid being harmed by an unfortunate flow of subsequent events.) Rather than taking the chance of getting the details wrong, I will state some technical information that will help you make the right decision no matter what the circumstances.

It's important to remember that although OneNote is related to Microsoft Office and indeed was added to the Office family with Office 2003, OneNote isn't necessarily bundled with Office 2003. Indeed, when Microsoft announced official pricing for the Office suite in August 2003, OneNote was positioned as always being a stand-alone purchase.[1] (Of course, this may change.) In other words, simply because a computer comes with Office 2003 installed doesn't necessarily mean that OneNote is installed.

Similarly, it's important to remember that Microsoft sells different versions of Office to different audiences. So even if Microsoft begins bundling OneNote as

---

1. `http://www.microsoft.com/presspass/press/2003/aug03/08-19MSOffice2003CompletePR.asp`

part of an Office edition, it might be a mistake to assume that it's in *your* recent version of Office.

It could get even more complicated than that. It might also be a mistake to assume that OneNote has been installed on your computer just because you or your enterprise owns the right to install it. For example, your enterprise might technically have the right to install OneNote, but the enterprise might choose not to include OneNote in the standard "image" installed on employee computers. (It may be hard to believe this, but some enterprise information technology organizations don't rush to support new software packages!)

For all these reasons, the best advice I can give you is don't assume anything. Regardless of whether Office 2003 is installed on your computer, *always check to make sure that OneNote has been installed on your computer.*

TIP   If you're not running Windows 2000 Service Pack 3, Windows XP, or a later version of Windows, you don't have OneNote (and you can skip the following section). OneNote 1.0 *doesn't* run on previous versions of Windows, Macintosh, or Pocket PC.

Is OneNote Already Installed?

The most reliable way to see if OneNote is already on your system is to navigate to Start ➤ All Programs ➤ Microsoft Office ➤ Microsoft Office OneNote 2003. Admittedly, All Programs may not necessarily be the quickest or most convenient way to find a program. If you have a lot of programs installed (as I do), it can be a bit of a challenge to spot one small item on a "wall o' programs." So you'll be glad to know there are a few shortcuts!

If you're keyboard oriented, the fastest way to see if OneNote is installed is to go to the Run prompt (see Figure 2-1) and enter **onenote** in the Open box (see Figure 2-2).

Figure 2-1. The Run prompt in Windows XP

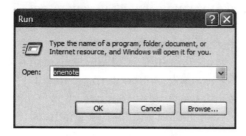

Figure 2-2. Enter onenote in the Open box.

If you're using a computer that someone else has used before (ever!), sharing a user account, or simply sitting in front of a friend's computer for a few moments, you may also see the OneNote icon on the "pinned programs" or "most frequently used programs" section of the Start menu (see Figure 2-3).

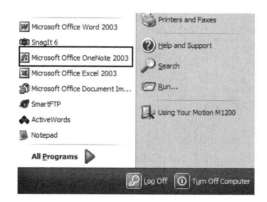

Figure 2-3. The OneNote icon will appear on the "most frequently used programs" section of the Start menu.

 CAUTION   If you're in your own user account and *you've* never run Microsoft OneNote, it will not show up in the "most frequently used programs" area even if the program is, in fact, installed and available on this computer and has been run frequently by other users in *their* accounts. But in that case, the program should be easily visible in All Programs.

Another way to verify that OneNote is installed is to navigate to Control Panel ➤ Add or Remove Programs. If the program is properly installed, it should show up there, as in Figure 2-4.

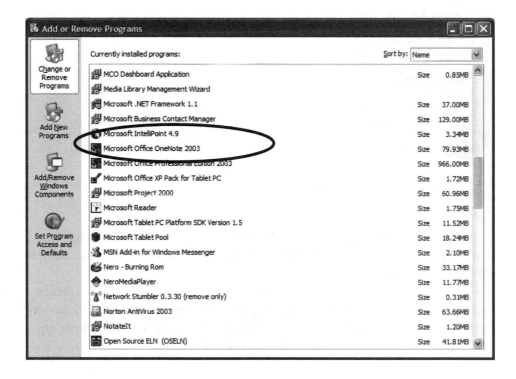

Figure 2-4. OneNote, if installed, should be listed in Control Panel ➤ Add or Remove Programs.

Don't Use XP Search to Find This (or Any!) Program

You may be tempted to use the Windows XP search function to verify whether you have OneNote (see Figure 2-5). My recommendation: Don't!

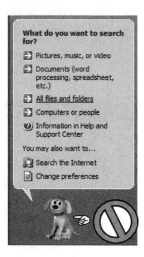

Figure 2-5. Nothing personal, Rover.

One reason not to use XP's search facility is that it's *slow.* On a 20GB hard disk, it took XP 24 seconds to find the first file containing the string *OneNote* and 45 seconds to find an executable.

More importantly, the presence of some files named *OneNote* isn't evidence that you have a properly installed and properly functioning OneNote. If there's any doubt, it's better to start the installation process from scratch. It will remove any corrupted or misplaced files and leave you with a clean slate.

Installing OneNote

Unfortunately, installing OneNote brings you into the messy world of operating system versions, hardware requirements, and complex software environments. The path you take to get to the desired end state may vary quite a bit depending upon your configuration.

System Requirements

I'll discuss system requirements first because if you don't meet the minimum system requirements, you're not going to be able to do the install until you remedy the hardware or software deficiencies.

What Software Is Required to Run OneNote?

You need to have Windows 2000 with Service Pack 3 installed, Windows XP, or later.

 CAUTION   If you have previous versions of Windows installed, such as Windows 95 or 98, you'll *not* be able to run OneNote. In that case, your best bet is to upgrade to Windows XP or later, which you can do by purchasing the software from Microsoft.

Other Operating Systems

Microsoft OneNote 1.0 doesn't run on the Pocket PC operating system, Palm OS, Linux, or Macintosh. The OneNote team is aware that there has been some customer interest in integrating OneNote with Pocket PCs and making it available as part of future versions of Office for the Macintosh. My bet is that OneNote for Pocket PC will be the first to hit the market.

If you're running Windows 2000, you may be saying, "What the heck is a service pack, and how do I know if I have one?" Service packs are updates (a.k.a. fixes) to the Windows operating system. You can tell whether you already have Service Pack 3, or later, for Windows 2000 by navigating to Control Panel ➤ System, which will tell you exactly what version of Windows you're running. If it doesn't appear you have Service Pack 3, by navigating to the Microsoft Windows 2000 page (http://www.microsoft.com/windows2000), selecting Downloads, and selecting Service Pack 4. (Service packs are cumulative and include all previous fixes.) Microsoft's online documentation explains service packs:

> *Service packs are cumulative; each new service pack contains all of the fixes that are included in previous service packs, as well as any new fixes. You do not need to install a previous service pack before you install the latest one. For example, you do not need to install Windows 2000 Service Pack 1 (SP1) before you install Windows 2000 Service Pack 2 (SP2).[2]*

The online download is free, which is fine if you have a fast connection. If not, you must pay a modest fee (around $14.95) to have a CD shipped to you. A detailed README file is available on the Service Pack 3 site—key points are that you can install while running, but you should turn off real-time virus checking first.[3]

---

2. Microsoft Knowledge Base Article 260910

3. http://www.microsoft.com/windows2000/downloads/servicepacks/sp3/ReadMeSP.htm

What Hardware Is Required for OneNote?

Microsoft states several hardware requirements for running OneNote that relate to your Central Processing Unit (CPU), memory, hard disk, CD drive, display, and peripherals.

CPU

You need a personal computer with a processor at least as fast as a 133MHz processor; Microsoft recommends Pentium III or better. This raises a couple of reasonable questions:

Q: If you run OneNote on a Pentium II, will the world come to an end?

A: No.

Q: If you have a computer with a different brand of CPU (say, Athlon or AMD), how can you tell whether it's fast enough?

A: Superficial measurements, such as the clock speed, may be as good a way as any to judge. If you're using a different brand of CPU that has a 600MHz clock speed, then rest assured; it's going to be plenty fast.

Furthermore, Chris Pratley from Microsoft says, "Basically, if it's fast enough to run Windows acceptably, OneNote will not be a problem."

Memory

You need 64MB of Random Access Memory (RAM) plus an additional 8MB of RAM for each application you plan to run simultaneously. As a practical matter, this means you should have at least 128MB of RAM. I almost always have several applications running, and sometimes I have as many as 11 or 12. Because you paid for the book, I will do the math! Ten applications at 8MB each is an additional 80MB, or 124MB total.

It's probably wise not to try to micromanage these numbers too closely. According to a source at Microsoft, "Memory usage as reported by the task manager doesn't always reflect the load the application is placing on the system, especially in Windows XP SP1, which reports much higher memory usage for Office applications than Windows XP gold, or SP2." The bottom line is that you should be sure to have enough memory to run quite a few applications simultaneously. The more memory, the better.

Hard Disk

Microsoft states OneNote's hard disk requirements in the context of its Office 2003 requirements, which are that you need at least 245MB available hard disk with 115MB on the hard disk where the operating system is installed. You can check that you have enough by navigating to My Computer ➤ Hard Disk Drives ➤ Local Disk (which is C: usually) ➤ Properties. Because OneNote can be a stand-alone install, you should be able to get by with less than 245/115 MB, but really, why bother? If you're that low on disk space, it's time to make more room, which you can do either by going to My Computer ➤ Local Disk (or other hard drive) ➤ Properties ➤ General ➤ Disk Cleanup or by purchasing a new hard disk.

CD Drive

This is a show stopper. You must have a working CD drive into which you can put the OneNote installation CD. If for some reason you don't have a working CD drive, be aware that you can borrow or purchase a CD drive that plugs into your computer's Universal Serial Bus (USB) port.

Display

You must have at least an 800×640 pixel resolution display with a Video Graphics Array (VGA) adapter.[4] Only very old monitors have less than 800×640, and VGA is the "classic" or older standard video adapter, so this is a no-brainer.

Peripherals

You must have a working mouse or other pointing device (for example, a trackball or trackpad) to use OneNote at all. Again, this is a no-brainer. However, there's a wrinkle (discussed next)…if you want to use OneNote's ability to capture handwriting, you must have a pen input device.

Optional Hardware

There are two crucial types of optional hardware that you should consider. First, you should consider buying an external microphone. Second, you should consider whether you're interested in using a pen-style pointing device with OneNote. This second category includes, but is not limited to, Tablet PCs.

To use OneNote's audio recording features, you must have a working microphone on your computer. Most modern computers are equipped with an internal microphone. However, this will probably not produce adequate quality results for recording conversations or meetings, and accordingly Microsoft recommends that you purchase an external microphone if you're doing audio recording. Good ones are available for much less than $100 from online and brick-and-mortar vendors.

---

4. http://www.pcguide.com/ref/video/std.htm

Do You Need a Tablet PC?

Because OneNote works really well on Microsoft's Tablet PC platform, there tends to be some confusion about OneNote's relationship to Tablet PC. It's simple: Microsoft Windows XP Tablet PC Edition is *not* required to use Microsoft OneNote.

 TIP   OneNote and Tablet PC are separate products. You don't need one to use the other.

You can use OneNote on any "regular" desktop or notebook computer. You can even use OneNote on tablet-shaped computers that *don't* run Microsoft's Tablet PC operating system. (For example, you can use OneNote on older Fujitsu tablets that run Windows 2000 or XP and were introduced before the November 2002 introduction of Microsoft Windows Tablet PC Edition.)

The key issue is whether you have a pointing device that's suitable for entering handwriting. There's a simple test: Can you write your name legibly with the pointing device? For example, although I love my Microsoft Wireless Mouse with Bluetooth, I have a hard time writing my name with it (see Figure 2-6).

Figure 2-6. My already poor handwriting, entered via a mouse

On the other hand, if you have *either* an electronic pen *or* a touch-screen pointing device, you can enter pen input into OneNote.

If you have a Microsoft Tablet PC that runs Microsoft Windows XP Tablet PC Edition, you'll be able to use the Tablet PC's electronic pen to enter digital ink not just in OneNote but in other "ink-ready" applications, such as Microsoft Office 2003 and Windows Journal, which will accept "native-ink" scribblings. You can also use the electronic pen to enter information into *any* application via the Tablet PC

Input Panel (see Figure 2-7). You can do the same if you have a desktop computer that's running Microsoft Windows XP Tablet PC Edition with an active digitizing pad (usually used for the purpose of software development).

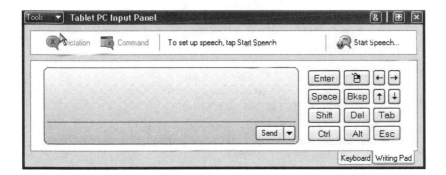

Figure 2-7. The Tablet PC Input Panel allows pen entry into any application, including OneNote.

NOTE   A Tablet PC with electronic pen gives a different (and better) experience than a desktop PC with a digitizing pad for the simple reason that on the Tablet PC what you write appears on the screen where you write it. Conversely, when you write on the digitizing pad, you need to look up at the monitor to see what you're writing, which presents an ergonomic challenge.

If you have a "passive" pen or stylus (just a stick with no electronics to it) and enter information on a touch screen (a screen that responds when you touch it with your finger), then you can also enter information in Microsoft OneNote, but you can't run Microsoft Windows XP Tablet PC Edition, which means you can't enter information via the Input Panel, and most applications won't accept information via pen.

So, summarizing this slightly complicated discussion:

- OneNote doesn't *need* Tablet PC.

- Tablet PC doesn't *need* OneNote.

- If you have an electronic pen and are running the Tablet PC operating system, you can use the pen to enter handwriting in OneNote *and* to control or enter ink in many other applications.

- If you have a passive pen and are running Windows 2000 SP3 or later, you can use the pen to enter handwriting in OneNote, but you can't run the Tablet PC operating system, and you probably can't enter handwriting in most other applications or control them using the pen.

The icing on the cake is that, as I will discuss in Chapter 3, it's very easy to enter Tablet PC's digital ink into OneNote. The combination of Tablet PC and OneNote is a very powerful one.

Troubleshooting Before You Begin!

Experience during the OneNote beta identified a few common situations that may cause problems during installation. It may be worth taking a few simple prophylactic actions before installing.

You may need to turn off antiviral software for the duration of the installation. Some antiviral software thinks you're trying to install a virus. I must report, though, that I was able to do a successful installation with Norton AntiVirus running. It's a shame to turn off antivirus software for any period because you may forget to turn it back on. My best advice: Try the installation first. If you have problems, or if you know from doing other installations that your antiviral software can be problematic during installation, turn it off.

If you're running Windows XP, you may want to upgrade to SP1. This isn't supposed to be necessary—it's not an official requirement—but some people have had problems during installation that were remedied by installing SP1.

Installing OneNote from CD As a Standalone Application

The basic thing to know about installing OneNote from a CD as a stand-alone application is that there's just one CD. If you're installing OneNote together with the full Office 2003 suite, there may be two CDs, one labeled "Office" and another labeled "OneNote." I'll discuss some issues about the complete Office 2003 installation later in this chapter. For now, explore the simpler case first to preserve your sanity.

The first step is to put the OneNote CD in your CD drive with the label up and firmly close the drive door.

 TIP   Make sure you keep the product packaging and documentation handy (do *not* throw them away yet) because you'll need the printed "product key" to get the installation underway. If you don't have the product key, you'll be stopped dead in your tracks.

The most likely scenario is that after you insert the CD and close the drive door, the drive will make a whirring noise for a few seconds as the drive "spins up" and reads off the structure of information on the disk, and then the autoinstall process will begin. If that happens, as it should and most likely will, you can skip the following sections and go directly to "Entering the Product Key: It's *Not* All About You."

The first thing you'll see is a splash screen saying that files are being copied from the CD to your computer (see Figure 2-8). Then you'll see a smaller screen saying "Preparing for autoinstall."

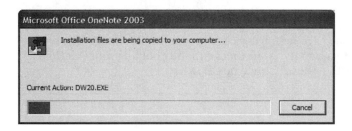

Figure 2-8. The first splash screen

This screen is followed by a larger screen saying "Welcome to Microsoft Office OneNote 2003 Setup" (see Figure 2-9).

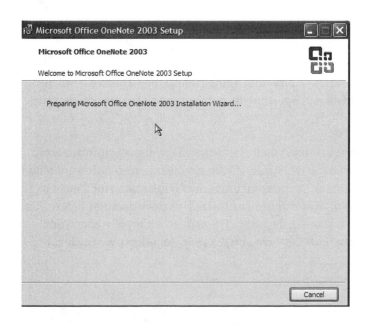

Figure 2-9. Welcoming you to the Microsoft Office OneNote 2003 setup process

Unfortunately, smooth autoinstall isn't the only situation that may transpire—you may encounter other "behaviors," depending on the capabilities of your CD drive and its current Windows settings. Let's deal with those scenarios one at a time.

Can Your Drive Read the CD?

The first question is whether the CD has loaded properly. You can check this by navigating to My Computer and checking whether Windows reports the presence of a CD.

 NOTE   You may have several devices with removable storage. The one you want to focus on is the one that's currently holding your OneNote installation CD. It should be of type CD Drive.

If no CD is present, think positive and eliminate the simple faults first:

- Is the CD right side up? (Usually, this is the labeled side.)

- Is the CD drive properly connected to your computer? In the case of notebook and Tablet PCs with drive "bays" into which CD and floppy drives can be plugged, make sure that the CD drive is firmly seated.

- If the CD drive requires external power, make sure it's plugged in and the power strip is turned on.

- If you've rectified all these possible problems and the CD drive is still not recognizing your CD, try restarting the computer and seeing whether the CD is visible after that.

If none of these actions allows you to "see" the CD, you may, unfortunately, have a more complex problem with your CD drive, which is, also unfortunately, outside the scope of this book. If you're an individual consumer, you'll need to resolve the CD problem via your computer or CD drive manufacturer before you can continue with the OneNote installation. If you're an enterprise user, your system administrator can probably help you do an installation over the local area network.

Did You Have to Cancel Setup Halfway Through?

The phone rings. Your wife calls from upstairs. The boss stops by your cube. The house catches on fire. Stuff happens! You may have to cancel the setup before the installation is complete. In all the installation screens, there's a Cancel button at the bottom right (see Figure 2-10).

TIP It's perfectly okay to cancel the setup at any point. Nothing bad will happen.

 Go For It!

Figure 2-10. Need to cancel? Go for it!

You'll be asked to confirm that you're sure you want to cancel the installation. Go for it! If you do cancel and you leave the installation CD in the drive, you need to know how to resume installation. It's simple and is explained in the next section.

Can You Navigate to the Setup.exe File on the CD?

If you can see via My Computer ➤ Devices with Removable Storage that there's indeed content on the CD, you're not far from beginning the install (or resuming it after canceling). The CD should be named *OneNote*, and you should see a long list of files, including two files named SETUP (see Figure 2-11).

The file you care about is the SETUP file with the Application type. Files of this type have the extension .exe and are also known as *executables*. You should be able to start the install by double-clicking that file or navigating to Start ➤ Run and entering **[DRIVENAME]:\ "SETUP.EXE"**.

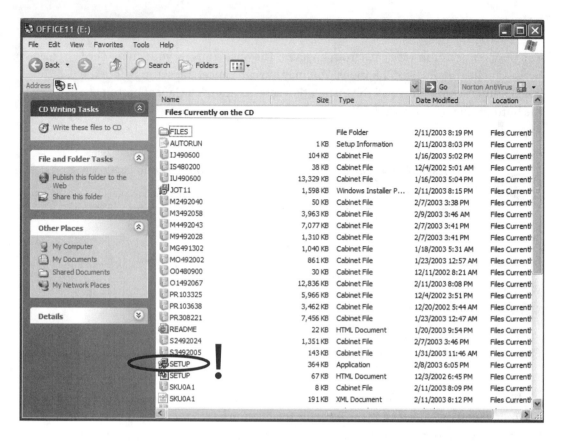

Figure 2-11. The OneNote install CD should have a long list of files that looks something like this.

Entering the Product Key: It's Not All About You

One of my favorite book titles is a story collection by the urban humorist Cynthia Heimel entitled *But Enough About You.* At first glance, it would appear that the product key feature in Microsoft software installation is Bill Gates's answer to Cynthia Heimel: Okay, customer, thank you for beginning to install this piece of fabulous Microsoft software…*but enough about you,* let's make sure that Microsoft's interests are protected.

Product Keys for Consumers

If you purchase the software as a consumer, the product key is usually printed on paper (not digital) and arrives as part of the package that accompanies the CD. Often it's on a sticky label that's attached to the back of the envelope that contains the CD.

Product Keys for Enterprise Customers

If you acquire the OneNote software through your role as an employee of an enterprise that purchases software from Microsoft in volume, you probably won't have a printed product key. Microsoft has moved away from printed product keys for volume customers and prefers to provide them to enterprise system administrators, who typically incorporate the product key in a self-installing routine that can be run either from a custom CD or via the enterprise local area network. Such administrators can obtain product keys by calling Microsoft's network of worldwide activation centers (http://www.microsoft.com/licensing/resources/vol/numbers.asp).

Don't Lose Your Product Key

You'll need the product key if you ever need to install your OneNote software again, which is quite possible, indeed, probable. As a general practice, you should always be prepared to "back out" or uninstall any software that you install in the event that you begin to encounter unusual system or program behavior after the installation. (This is truer for version 1.0 software such as OneNote.) You might also need to reinstall the software if you have unrelated system problems or experience a hard disk failure.

You can uninstall a particular program using the Windows Control Panel ➤ Add or Remove Programs, and you can restore the Windows system itself to an earlier point using Accessories ➤ System Tools ➤ System Restore.

 TIP It's a good idea to keep both a backed-up text file *and* a piece of paper where you store a list of all the product keys that you have installed on your current system.

Entering the Product Key

At this point in the installation process, you'll be asked to enter the 25-character product key that lets the Microsoft installation program know that you've obtained your copy of the installation CD in a legal manner (see Figure 2-12).

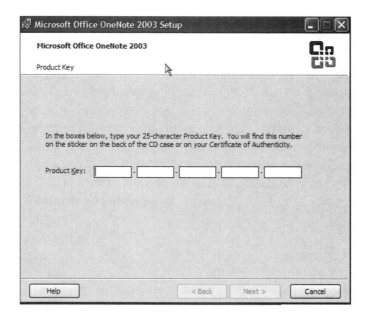

Figure 2-12. Enter the product key here.

You'll be typing into five boxes, each of which contains five characters. You don't need to tab between the boxes; you can just type each five-character group in sequence, and the program will move you to the next box. If you do use the Tab key, you'll have to return to the previous box using Shift+Tab.

If you get an error message asking for a valid product key, retype the product key, paying especially close attention to easily confused characters such as 1 and l. Don't worry about capitalization; product keys are not case sensitive.

If you become convinced after careful checking that for whatever reason the installer is refusing to accept an otherwise valid and properly issued product key, you must contact the company that sold you the software.

TIP When you seem to have an invalid product key and all else fails, contact the company that cashed your check or verified your credit card number—quite possibly a reseller, not necessarily Microsoft.

It is, of course, illegal to obtain product keys via friends or Internet newsgroups, and if you post a message to a newsgroup asking for a product key, you can expect to receive a note from Microsoft asking you to cease and desist.

CAUTION It's against your interest to share product keys with others because the Windows Product Activation (WPA) process keeps track of how many times a given product key has been used to activate a piece of software and enforces a total limit. If you share product keys with others, not only are you breaking the law, you may be making it difficult for yourself to activate newly reinstalled software when you really need it.[5]

Obviously, the justification for product keys is that by preventing theft, they make the entire system of software development and distribution more efficient at bringing high-quality software to power users who are legitimately entitled to it. The reason why the product key uses long, difficult-to-remember alphanumeric strings is to make them more resistant to cryptographic assault (although there have been some indications that WPA can be cracked). It's possible to wish, though, that this step of Microsoft's standard Windows applications installation process could somehow be more user-friendly—in other words, more *about you*.

Entering User Information

Now you'll be prompted to enter your user information (see Figure 2-13). Note that this information will be associated with your use of this version of OneNote in this Windows user account.

---

5. `http://support.microsoft.com/default.aspx?scid=kb;EN-US;293151`

Figure 2-13. Entering your user information

Reviewing the License Agreement

Now you'll be asked to review and accept the standard Microsoft license agreement (see Figure 2-14). Practically speaking, you have few alternatives other than to accept the agreement.

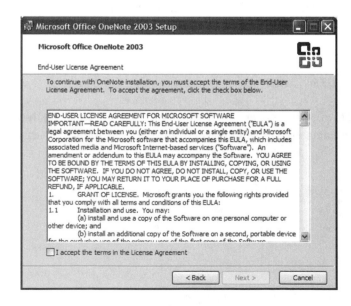

Figure 2-14. Reviewing the license agreement

You can't complete the install unless you accept the agreement by checking the empty box in bottom left (Figure 2-15).

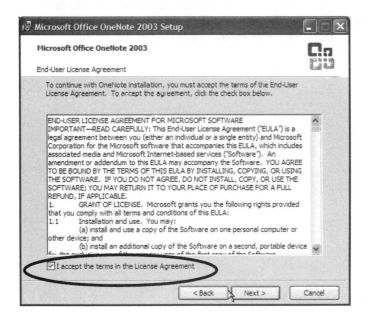

Figure 2-15. Accepting the license agreement

Licensing Agreements

To make sure I address every issue thoroughly for those who are interested, I'll go a step beyond just saying, "There's the license agreement, you have to accept it." If the text of the license agreement really sticks in your craw, this sidebar contains a few thoughts about what you can do to learn more and generate some options for yourself.

Microsoft's Licensing Web site is a good place to start (http://www.microsoft.com/licensing/). That's the place to go for the official answers to your questions.

Consulting firms such as Gartner sometimes have useful perspective on how to get maximum value from Microsoft licenses. See, for example, Gartner's February 2003 report, "Microsoft Licensing Still Causing Headaches."[6] This is stored in Gartner's topic hierarchy under IT Management.

---

6. http://www.gartner.com/DisplayDocument?doc_cd=112984

A search in the Google or Yahoo directories (the list of sites organized by category, not the simple Web pages) will unveil a wealth of perspectives on software licensing, Microsoft, open source, and so on.

As these last two items imply, by far your best options to influence your Microsoft license agreement are either to make your feelings known via a large enterprise or to make your feelings known by considering alternatives.

Selecting the Type of Install

The moment when you're asked to select the type of installation is often one of considerable anxiety (see Figure 2-16). You're presented with four options:

- Typical Install

- Complete Install

- Minimal Install

- Custom Install

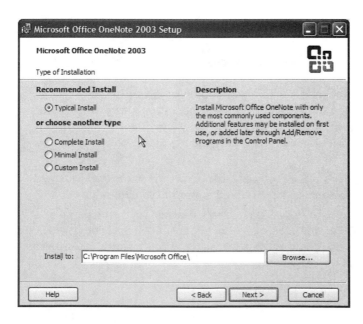

Figure 2-16. Am I typical, complete, minimal, or custom?

And you're also asked where you want the program installed. Unless you have a good reason, accept the default.

The default type of installation is the Typical Install option. How do you know if that's what you want? If you select a typical installation rather than a complete or custom installation, are you missing anything? Conversely, if you're using an older computer or are otherwise performance constrained for some reason, should you select the minimum installation? And is there any reason to consider doing a complete or custom installation?

Let's apply some logic and simplify the decision making. You'll make the easiest decision first.

Where to Install

The default installation location, provided by Windows, is C:\Program Files\Microsoft Office\.

TIP Accept the default location unless you're absolutely sure you have a good reason to do otherwise.

I can think of two fairly plausible scenarios where you might want to install the software in a different location. First, perhaps you're for some cunning power-user reason running or storing multiple versions of Microsoft Office. In that case, it depends on whether you want to have OneNote "go away" when Microsoft Office 2003 goes away. If you want OneNote always available regardless of what other applications you're using, it might make sense to put it somewhere else. Otherwise, keep it with the Office 2003 stuff. Second, it's possible that your system disk is short on space, and you're storing new programs on a second partition or an additional drive. This is a tested configuration and a reasonable option. If you're uncomfortable with storing programs on an additional partition or drive, you can use the minimum install, which only requires 30MB of available disk space.

The bottom line is to try to accept the default location for installation.

Now you can use similar logic to evaluate the four installation options. You'll begin by evaluating the simplest option, the minimum install.

When Should You Do a Minimum Install?

The answer is pretty straightforward: never. Although disk space requirements can be tricky to measure, it appears that you'll save no more than 30MB of storage, or somewhere around 1 percent of the size of a typical hard disk. Almost certainly you can reclaim at least that much storage by emptying your Recycle Bin or your Temp folder. The minimum install offers such a small savings that there's really no reason for anyone to consider the minimum install. Make your life simpler and cross it off your list (see Figure 2-17).

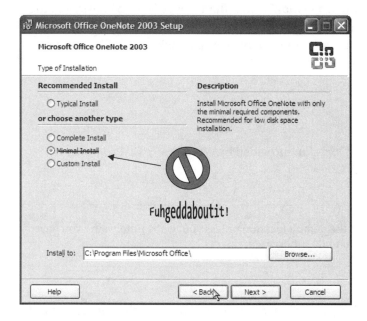

Figure 2-17. Fuhgeddaboudit![7]

And now you can apply some more ruthless logic to get rid of another option, Typical Install.

Why I Don't Like Typical Install

Note the comment next to the Typical Install option that "Additional features may be added on first use or added later through Add/Remove Programs on the Control Panel." I will make a power-user value judgment here: Adding features on first use is a pain.

---

7. In the "leave-no-stone-unturned" spirit of this book, I can't pass up telling you that a Web search turns up an amazing variety of "Fuhgeddaboudit!" resources, including *The Sopranos* online dictionary, the FUHGEDDABOUTIT BBQ Team Home Page, and an actual book, *Fuhgeddaboutit: How to Badda Boom, Badda Bing, and Find Your Inner Mobster* by Jon Macks (New York: Touchstone Press, 2001).

The way that the additional feature installation works is that the first time you select or invoke a feature that isn't supported by the default installation, you receive a message asking you if you want to install the feature. It takes a few seconds for this message to come up, and you must then read it, make a decision, and wait for the feature itself to be installed, which may take 30 seconds or more. In previous generations of Office, you were sometimes required to dredge up a CD that you only used once, months ago, when you first installed the program. In Office 2003, the entire CD image is copied to your hard disk to enable repair of the installation without the CD. This is a significant ease-of-use improvement by the Office team!

There are two primary benefits of a typical install:

- Saving hard disk space—after installation, a typical install uses 61.8MB while a complete install uses about 140MB.

- A sense of comfort from following the designers' advice.

With regard to these benefits, I say this:

- At this writing, hard disk drives seem to cost around $3 per *giga*byte. So by saving 180MB, you're saving about $0.54 worth of disk space. Wow!

- Taking a deep dive into a product is all about *not* following the herd.

Why accept any delay or chance of error? The whole idea of being a power user is to have power features at your fingertips.

TIP   Avoid the Typical Install option and choose the Complete Install option.

Custom Install vs. Complete Install

So you've narrowed down the options dramatically. Should you do a custom install or a complete install?

Let's look at the options that are available to you if you choose to carry out a custom install (see Figure 2-18).

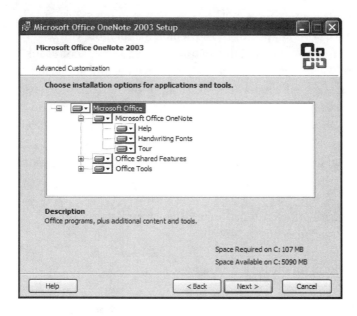

Figure 2-18. Options available in the custom install

OneNote Options Only

If you only focus on the tools available for OneNote, you should be able to understand your options fairly quickly. It looks as if you can choose whether you want to install the following options:

- Help

- Handwriting Fonts

- Tour

If you click the downward-pointing triangle attached to each of these end nodes, a drop-down menu will appear that presents several different modes of installation. In some of the menus, four options are available:

- Run from My Computer

- Run All from My Computer

- Installed on First Use

- Not Available

On some items (Help and Tour), only the first three options are available. The fourth option, Not Available, is itself not available (shades of *Catch-22!*), meaning that you must always be able to activate the feature. Actually, this is reasonable—why would you *not* want to install Help? And, equally to the point, why would Microsoft want to allow you to do so?

Item one is easy: You should always install Help so that it's available immediately the first time it's used. As discussed, any disk space saving is minimal.

Item three is also easy. Even if you're an impatient soul like me who doesn't ordinarily have much patience for online tutorials, you really ought to use the tour, which is available in OneNote via navigating to Help ➤ Get Going with OneNote. The reason? OneNote is a whole new type of program with a new user paradigm. You need the extra reinforcement of a tour that presents the new User Interface (UI) and Microsoft's vocabulary for talking about it.

Item two is more a matter of personal preference. Do you like expressive fonts that look like handwriting? If you do, good news—there are a bunch of them available in OneNote. If you don't care about the handwriting fonts, you can choose not to install them. You're saving a modest, almost minuscule, amount of disk space and making your fonts menu shorter. So you're really looking at minor benefit/minor cost.

To summarize, unless you're severely constrained on disk space, there's probably not much reason to set any of the OneNote custom install options to Install on First Use. The Run All on My Computer will give you a faster learning curve with OneNote, which is what, as a reader of this book, you want.

That was fairly easy. What about the other two sets of options, which relate to the Office suite as a whole?

Office Custom Install Options

Let's expand the Office Shared Features and Office Tools nodes that are available as part of the custom install path (see Figure 2-19).

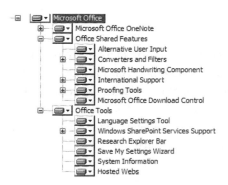

Figure 2-19. Gurk!

Gurk! Suddenly, there are a lot of options.

Office Shared Features

By default, the following Office Shared Features are set to be custom installed:

- Microsoft Handwriting Component (on first use)

- New and Open Office Document Shortcuts (not available)

- Microsoft Office Download Control

By default, the following Office Shared Features are set to be left out of a custom install:

- Alternative User Input

- Converters and Filters

- International Support

- Proofing Tools

Most of these features have fairly self-explanatory names, so I'll just add a few words of additional detail where necessary.

You don't need the handwriting component unless you're planning to enter handwritten text using either a Tablet PC or another type of pen-pointing device or you're expecting to receive handwritten text from Tablet PC users. The handwriting component will enable you to recognize that text and choose among alternatives.

The document shortcuts are available off the Start menu (see Figure 2-20).

These are shortcuts to a number of useful templates in the various Office applications (see Figure 2-21).

Unfortunately, OneNote documents aren't included in this menu in version 1. It would be good if they were included in this menu in a future release.

The Download Control's usefulness is self-explanatory. The only reason to remove this feature is if you prefer to use another download control tool. Some good ones are available via shareware or as part of alternative browsers such as Netscape, Mozilla, and Opera.

Hidden underneath Alternative User Input are the speech recognition features. Like handwriting, you'll probably know if you expect to use these.

Figure 2-20. Document shortcuts

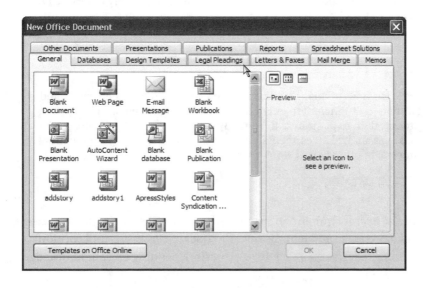

Figure 2-21. Templates for everything except OneNote

Converters and Filters include support for a raft of graphics converters (see Figure 2-22).

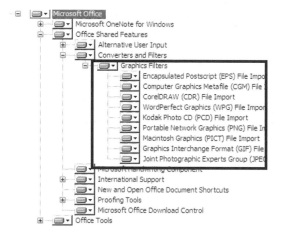

Figure 2-22. A variety of graphics converters

International Support provides you the opportunity to install Universal, Syriac, and Japanese fonts. Again, you know if you need these.

Proofing Tools are available in English, French, and Spanish and include Spelling and Grammar Checker, Hyphenation, Thesaurus, Optical Character Recognition, and Translation modules.

Here I will offer a specific recommendation: At least the first four tools in the appropriate language should be part of any custom install. I firmly believe that commitment to excellence is contagious. High-quality notes will help you produce a high-quality work product.

TIP   Decades of quality research have shown that it's much easier and far more cost-efficient to put quality in at the beginning of a production process than to put it in at the end. By using Microsoft OneNote, you're making a shrewd investment in quality at the front end of your personal process. In other words, don't cut corners!

To summarize my recommendations regarding Office Shared Features: Accept the default custom installs and add the quality-checking Proofing Tools option. Judge the remaining features on a case-by-case basis depending on your knowledge of your own situation.

Office Tools

The following Office Tools are set "on" for a custom install by default:

- Language Settings Tool (on first use)

- Research Explorer Bar

- Save My Scttings Wizard

- System Information

- Hosted Webs

Some of these may be less familiar, so here's a quick word about them:

The Language Settings Tool is most important if you use more than one language on this computer.

Research Explorer is a new, and potentially very important, feature in Microsoft Office that enables you to send queries to Web-based research services. I will go into considerable detail about this feature in a later chapter. For now, install it unless you're for some reason opposed to adding high-quality external information resources to your workflow.

The Save My Settings Wizard will be useful the next time you migrate to another computer, which for some of you may be quite frequent! I seem to break 'em about every six months or so.

System Information gathers configuration information to help in troubleshooting. Why wouldn't you want to make troubleshooting easier?

Hosted Webs allow you to share documents with Office-compatible Internet Service Providers (ISPs). If your ISP is MSN, or if your enterprise or ISP uses Microsoft Web servers, this may be valuable to you. If your ISP runs Unix or Linux servers (as mine does), this will *not* be useful.

Only Microsoft Office Document Imaging is set to "off." There are three sub-options underneath Imaging:

- Scanning, OCR, and Indexing Filter

- Help

- Microsoft Office Document Image Writer

If you do a lot of scanning, you may want to install the Scanning, OCR, and Indexing Filter right away; otherwise, don't.

I strongly recommend that you install Microsoft Document Image Writer. This is a print driver utility that allows you to print documents from any Office application and turn them into either Tag(ged) Image File Format (TIFF) or Microsoft Document Imaging (MDI) compressed document files. Printing documents into TIFF is a good workaround to get documents into OneNote when other methods of pasting fail to format correctly. I'll say a lot more about this in subsequent chapters. For now, install Image Writer.

 TIP   Microsoft Office Document Image Writer is a good way to create images that can be pasted into OneNote.

As for Help? Watson, you know my methods. You should definitely install Help.

Custom Install vs. Complete Install

If you have a newer computer with plenty of space on the hard drive, I recommend doing a complete install.

If you're concerned about disk space, I suggest you use the following settings in a custom install:

- Install all the OneNote options.

- Accept the default settings in Office Shared Features and add Proofing Tools.

- In Office Tools, add Microsoft Office Document Image Writer.

Once you've selected which install mode you want, the installer will proceed to grind away for a while and will finally present you with a screen saying "Setup Complete."

"Setup Complete" (Almost)

The final screen you'll see tells you that the OneNote Setup has completed successfully and will ask you to make two decisions.

(So, the setup isn't really complete! I had to change the heading of this section.)

The Office Update Site

First, OneNote will ask you to visit the Office updates site in your browser so that you can acquire additional components or security updates that may be necessary. It may seem a bit annoying to encounter one more step after a lengthy installation process, but it's worth it. This ensures you have the best and latest version of OneNote with any fixes or improvements made since your distribution CD was burned.

If you agree to go to the Office updates site, you'll be taken via browser to a page that looks something like Figure 2-23.

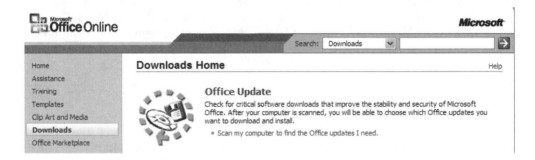

Figure 2-23. The Office updates page

When you follow the link that says "Scan my computer to find the Office updates I need," an automatic process will examine your computer and see whether you need to update your version of Office. If you have a 56.6Kbps-baud modem, this can take up to one minute.

 CAUTION   Under some circumstances, it's possible that the production version of Office Update may get confused if you've previously used the beta version of Office Update. Microsoft recommends deleting (manually!) the file C:\WINDOWS\system32\opuc.dll and the directory C:\Program Files\OfficeUpdate *before* you use the production version of Office Update at http://office.microsoft.com.

Obviously, there are two possible outcomes of running Office Update:

- There are recommended updates.

- There are *no* recommended updates.

I suggest you decide ahead of time just how much time you can afford to invest in being suspicious of Microsoft updates. I certainly recognize that there's a legitimate argument for scrutinizing all updates carefully and deciding whether to install them on a case-by-case basis. The downside is that you need to invest the time to read about the underlying details of the update—especially why it's being issued and what's the problem it's intending to fix. One place to do that is via a search on the update name in the Microsoft Support Knowledge Base, which is accessible via the Microsoft website.

 CAUTION Sometimes Microsoft updates bring a lot of baggage with them. For example, there have been some Windows XP and Internet Explorer updates that are issued to fix **HUGE, GLARING, MASSIVE, EMBARRASSING SECURITY HOLES.** For that reason, it may be illuminating to read the details of why an update was issued. On the other hand, it may simply be discouraging!

Unfortunately, it takes a lot of effort to understand each of these upgrades, and you can't avoid them forever. Unless you want to make a serious investment in understanding the details of each recommended upgrade, I recommend you do the pragmatic thing and upgrade when OneNote recommends that you do so.

Removing the Installation Cache

OneNote will also tell you that during the installation files were copied to one of your disk drives: "These files will be used to assist with Office maintenance and updates. These files can be removed to save approximately 114MB of disk space, but it's recommended that you keep them." If your installation is damaged for any reason (say, human error), the cache helps restore it. I recommend that, unless disk space is critical, you follow Microsoft's advice and leave the installation files around.

Backing It Out

It was 3 a.m. and the new software we had installed in the huge LexisNexis data center—close to five billion documents online—was not working properly. The company's entire sales and marketing force was expecting customers to begin using the new software tomorrow morning. Soon, early-rising attorneys would come to work and begin submitting searches to the research system. We charged those attorneys thousands of dollars a month for access to our service. Yet searches were taking minutes instead of seconds. Neither our customers nor our management team would accept inferior performance. The stocky head of the development team—a former football star at the University of Dayton—shook his head and told the project manager, "We'd better back it out."

With those words, we decided to uninstall the software until we could determine the cause of the difficulty. A painful moment! But it was the smart thing to do. The next morning, with rest and calmer heads, we began problem solving in our test environment. Within a few days, we had identified the subtle cause of the problem and had made the necessary changes. We scheduled an emergency release, and within a matter of days the software was properly installed in production and working like a champ. Our customers never knew there had been a problem.

I spent several enjoyable years at LexisNexis, a leading legal and news publisher that has one of the world's largest information warehouses. When we installed new software there, it was a big deal! There was an entire department that did nothing but manage the release of new software to the online system, and when a new piece of software was ready to be moved to production, it was a major event. Everyone in the development and product team came in late at night and supervised the installation of the software.

You may be thinking, "Sure, that's a big company, running a large, complex data center—they have to be ready to do stuff like that. But I'm just a regular guy running a single computer. I'm not going to go to all that trouble. I'm just going to install OneNote, and if I don't like it, I'll uninstall it."

You're wrong. Anyone who has a modern personal computer is running a large, complex data center! Modern PCs, with their 10, 20, 60, 100GB hard disks, their hundreds of megabytes of RAM, and (not least) their dense, sophisticated software environment—including Windows XP with its 45 million lines of code—are every bit as powerful and complex as huge corporate data centers of previous eras. It's worth your while to think about your computer as your own personal data center and institute some commonsense procedures to make installation of new software less painful.

When you install OneNote, the following best practices will make it easier to "back it out" if necessary:

Prepare properly. For example, read this chapter *before* you install. If you skipped ahead to this spot, skip back to the beginning of the chapter!

Once you've successfully completed the installation and verified that OneNote is present and appears to be working properly, *don't install anything else for a week or so in case there are problems.* I often find that installing one piece of software makes me want to install others, so this may be something of a challenge to your self-discipline. It will be worth it because if you make several system changes at the same time, you'll have the devil of a time figuring out which change caused the problems.

Gradually stress test your system by running OneNote in conjunction with an increasingly "busy" desktop—begin with OneNote by itself, then work up to OneNote running at the same time as a bunch of Microsoft Office applications and, eventually, all your most critical applications.

You probably won't need to back it out—I'm not aware of any known bugs that would make that a likely scenario, and Microsoft has done a good job of making OneNote stable and consistent with other well-behaved applications. But all the same, you must recognize that no software is perfect, and every personal data center has a unique constellation of installed software, not all of which is well behaved.

If you start having severe problems, don't hesitate to do a temporary uninstall. You can probably live with minor blips, such as the cursor changing color or the program occasionally hanging for a few seconds. Consider backing out the software if the program is crashing frequently, performance seems unacceptably slow, or you're losing OneNote data files.

Uninstalling OneNote

Removing OneNote is quite straightforward. The best, and, indeed, as far as I can tell, the only prudent way is to go to Control Panel ➤ Add or Remove Programs. Find Microsoft OneNote 2003—it will be under the Ms (see Figure 2-24). Click Remove. And away you go! It will take a few minutes to complete the uninstall (it took six minutes and 50 seconds on my Tablet PC with a Pentium III CPU).

 CAUTION Back in the good old days before computers became personal data centers, it sometimes made sense to uninstall an application by the surgical method…just going to the directory where the program was stored and deleting all the files. I don't recommend that as a procedure for deleting any Windows application.

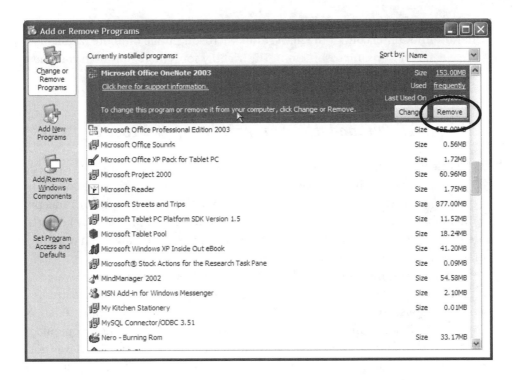

Figure 2-24. After you click Remove, the uninstall will take a few minutes.

After Backing It Out, What Next?

If you're driven to the extreme of doing an uninstall, you'll then have a few basic options:

- Simplify your system by removing third-party add-ons or applications that seem like they may be causing difficulties and then reinstall OneNote.

- Wait for an upgrade or "dot release" to come along and reinstall OneNote then.

- Improve your environment by getting a new computer.

You may find it worthwhile to post a note describing your experience to OneNoteInfoCenter.com or the newsgroup Microsoft.public.onenote (available via news server news.microsoft.com). The friendly souls there may help you find a solution faster than you expect!

Backing It Out and the "Principle of Mediocrity"

As I wrote this section, I questioned whether I should have given you such a drastic bit of "just-in-case" advice—it seemed to run counter to the spirit of a book about a particular software application! On reflection, though, I think it's true to the deeper spirit of the book, which is about how to get the most out of OneNote by taking a "deep dive" into the application. If you're going to take a deep dive, you want to make sure there's water in the tank!

One of the fundamental attributes of taking a deep approach to software is recognizing that the scientific principle of mediocrity applies to software just as well as it applies to the solar system. The principle of mediocrity, simply stated, is that we should not assume that our position is privileged. In other words, Copernicus was more right than he knew when he came to the insight that the Earth was not the center of the solar system. In fact, it now appears likely that Earth is just one of many planets surrounding hundreds of billions of stars in millions of galaxies in a very, very large universe. Yet we do feel that Earth is clearly much more important to us than any other place in the universe!

By the same token, the smartest way of being a power user of any piece of software is to recognize that no matter how cool it is and how special it may seem, it's just one of many, many applications, and there are a lot of ways to do things in the world of computers. It's better to make intelligent judgments with that principle in mind than to press blindly ahead no matter what. If something doesn't work, try something else. Keep that perspective in mind as you take your deep dive into OneNote!

Summary

This chapter offered the following information:

- Check to see whether OneNote has already been installed on your computer.

- OneNote requires Windows 2000 with SP3, or Windows XP or later.

- OneNote doesn't currently run on Pocket PC, Macintosh, or Linux.

- I recommend at least 128MB RAM with Pentium III CPU or better.

- I recommend buying an optional external microphone.

- OneNote *doesn't* require Tablet PC. *However,* OneNote works great on a Tablet PC!

- Don't lose your product key. Don't lose your product key. Don't lose your product key.

- If you can spare the disk space, I recommend the Complete Install option.

In the next chapter, you'll walk through the process of entering your first notes into OneNote—text, images, Web pages, handwriting, and audio!

Taking Your First Notes

IN THIS CHAPTER, I'll walk you through your first extensive session with OneNote. You might compare this to hopping in the pool for the first time and taking a few laps. You're not going on an extremely long swim, and you're not going to brave the rip tides of taking notes "offshore" at a live meeting or class—but you're going to try and practice a few basic strokes, get moving, and have some fun!

First, though, let's make sure you have OneNote installed and running properly.

Launching OneNote

As discussed in the previous chapter, if OneNote is installed properly, it should be accessible in several locations. In Windows XP, OneNote should be visible in the folder reached via Start ➤ All Programs ➤ Microsoft Office. I also discussed how you can tell if OneNote is already installed, which means you know a couple of other ways to launch OneNote. If you see the OneNote icon in All Programs, Frequently Used Programs, Favorite Programs, or the system tray, click it now (see Figure 3-1).

Figure 3-1. The OneNote icon should show up in several places, including All Programs.

If you don't see the icon in any of those places, try the trick discussed in the previous chapter, where you go to Start ➤ Run and enter *onenote*. If none of these ways of starting the program works, I'm afraid you need to revisit the previous chapter's discussion of the installation process.

Once you open the program, you should see the OneNote screen. If it doesn't appear, see the following section, "I Clicked, but Nothing Happened!"

I Clicked, but Nothing Happened!

If you click the icon but nothing appears to happen, you should explore the following possibilities before deciding your installation is broken:

- The program may already be running in another window that you can't see. If you or someone else has previously launched OneNote and then dragged the window to the edge of your monitor screen or minimized the program, it may be hard to see the window.

- You may be looking for a full-sized screen, but the program is launching a Side Note that's only about 2×2 inches.

There are at least two ways you can eliminate these possibilities. First, you can press Alt+Tab to display a list of running applications. You can then use Alt+Tab to cycle through the displayed applications.

Second, you can press Ctrl+Alt+Delete and open the Windows Task Manager. Then go to the Applications tab. If a version of OneNote is running properly, it'll appear under Task and its status will be Running (see Figure 3-2).

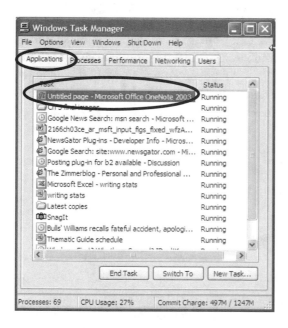

Figure 3-2. OneNote shows up in Windows Task Manager as a task that's running.

TIP　You may see two slightly different versions of OneNote running in the Task list. If your copy of OneNote is set to display the Side Note icon in the system tray, a process called *Microsoft OneNote Side Note* will always be running.

If you're sure you clicked the OneNote icon but nothing is showing up in the Applications tab, you may want to check the Processes tab. Look to see if there's a ONENOTE.EXE or ONENOTEM.EXE (for the Side Note) process listed under Image Name (see Figure 3-3). (If the image name looks a lot like the old-fashioned DOS names for programs, that's because images are simply programs running in different compartments of Windows.) If you see a ONENOTE.EXE or ONENOTEM.EXE process but when you switch to the Applications tab there's no application named OneNote running, it means you're suffering a system error of some kind related to the OneNote application. Don't be unduly disturbed—this happens from time to time even with other well-behaved members of the Office family.

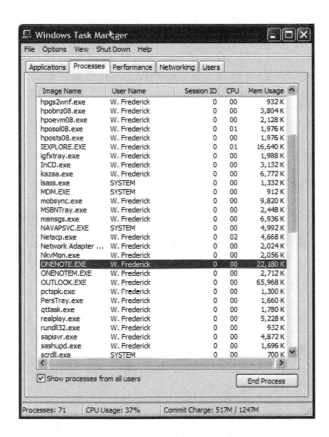

Figure 3-3. Look for processes named ONENOTE.EXE or ONEOTEM.EXE.

In this situation with a "phantom process," your best bet is to shut down and restart. If it continues to occur, do a fresh install or seek technical assistance.

CAUTION If you install OneNote by upgrading from the beta, the OneNote icon may not display in the system tray at first. This means that ONENOTEM.EXE won't be visible in the Processes tab. To fix this, go to Tools ➤ Options ➤ Other, check off the Place Icon in Notification Area of the Taskbar box, exit and restart OneNote, and check the box again.

Understanding the Layout

I'll begin with some basic orientation to the layout of the OneNote page. The layout is *generally* similar to most other Windows applications, and it's *specifically* quite consistent with Microsoft Office 2003 because OneNote is a member of the Office 2003 family. Both of these items are good news. Your knowledge of Windows and Office applications will help you learn OneNote faster.

 NOTE This won't win me many friends in the Independent Software Vendor (ISV) community, but I believe that OneNote being a part of Microsoft Office gives it a huge usability advantage over other note-taking programs. Almost everyone has some experience with the layout of Microsoft Office. That experience will help you understand OneNote.

Furthermore, this won't win me many friends in the Microsoft Office team, but I believe that OneNote being a *new* part of Microsoft Office gives it a huge usability advantage over other programs in the Office family. Basic familiarity with the layout of Office is enough to understand a lot about the layout of OneNote. You don't need to know how to find a configuration screen four levels down! OneNote hasn't had time yet to become so complex that the layout struggles to contain a bad case of "eruptive featuritis."

At the top of the page, there's a *title bar* (see Figure 3-4). On the left side of the title bar, you'll find the OneNote icon, the current filename (Untitled Page the first time you use it), and, followed by a dash, the program name. (Note that *Office* is part of the program's official name.) On the right side of the title bar, you'll note the familiar minimize, maximize, and close icons. The title bar, like most Windows title bars, is draggable.

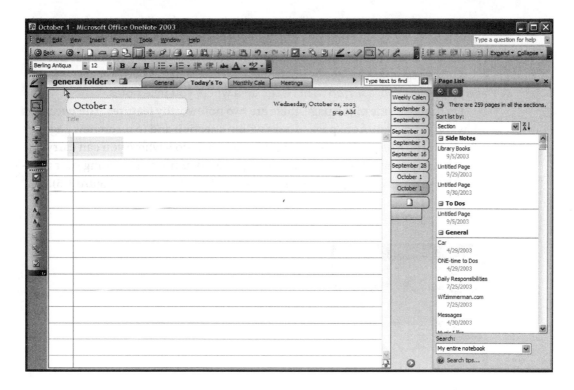

Figure 3-4. The layout of a OneNote page

The next line is the *menu bar*, which begins with the familiar File menu. There are no surprises here—no oddball menu names, just the straightforward and relatively self-explanatory File, Edit, View, Insert, Format, Tools, Window, and Help.

CAUTION　From this point on, the layout of OneNote is, like other Office applications, highly customizable, so details may appear different if you're using an application that you, or someone else, has previously customized.

Underneath the File menu is the usual location of the various toolbars that are available in OneNote. As with most Office applications, there's a place where you can configure which toolbars you see.

Next there's a tabbed display area for *notebook sections*, which can be grouped into *folders*.

There's always a *title area*. I'll discuss this in more detail later, but for now it's enough for you to know that this is a separate area of the OneNote page whose function is, as the name suggests, to capture title information about your notes.

The largest space is devoted to the *page surface*, which Microsoft also refers to as a *flexible 2-D page surface*. This is the area where you take notes.

On the right side of the page, there are two noteworthy features. The *page tabs* allow you to navigate from page to page within a section and to insert new pages or subpages. The *task pane* is a secondary frame or window where you can carry out a wide variety of operations such as creating new documents, searching your notebooks, or reviewing a Page List with previously viewed pages (see Figure 3-5).

Figure 3-5. The task pane appears by default at the right of the screen.

The layout of the task pane in OneNote is similar to the layout of the task pane in other Office applications. Like most objects displayed in Office applications, the location and size of the task pane can be configured at the user's discretion.

Now that you've got the basic lay of the land, you can begin taking your first notes.

Taking Your First Notes

The first thing to understand is that OneNote is capable of taking several different types of notes. In version 1.0, OneNote supports some but not all of the types of content referred to as *multimedia*—for example, you can take notes in the form of images, but you can't take notes in the form of video movies. Specifically, you can enter notes in the following ways:

- By typing them via the computer keyboard

- By scribbling them via pen input device

- By copying to the Clipboard from the browser and from other Windows applications and then pasting them into OneNote

- By recording audio via the computer's built-in microphone or an optional external microphone

Typing Your First Text Notes

The first thing to do is to decide where on the page you want to enter your first notes. There's a fundamental difference between OneNote and a word processor such as Microsoft Word. With OneNote, you can put the cursor anywhere on the page surface (see Figure 3-6) whereas with Microsoft Word, you need to move the cursor forward by inserting content or margins (see Figure 3-7). This is a feature Microsoft calls the *flexible 2-D page surface*. Now that I've done my duty by introducing the term, forget you ever heard it! It's one of those items of marketing mumbo-jumbo that adds more confusion than it removes. Just remember that in OneNote you can put the cursor anywhere immediately, just like on a piece of paper.

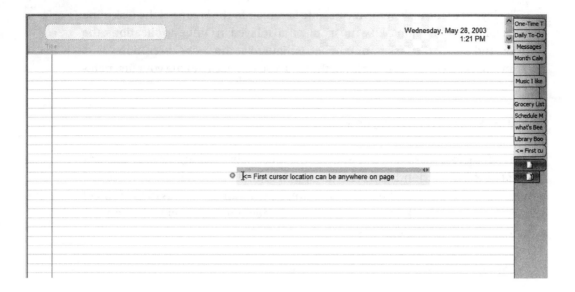

Figure 3-6. In OneNote, you can insert the cursor anywhere on the page, regardless of whether content has previously been inserted elsewhere.

Figure 3-7. In Microsoft Word, you can't just fly the cursor where you want it.

By default, the page appears as a sheet of blank paper, with no lines or rules—in other words, like a piece of typing paper or copying paper, not like a piece of notebook paper. When you move the cursor to a point on the page and start typing, you'll notice that what you're typing appears in a shaded box with a dark bar on top and a small, four-arrowed handle to the left (see Figure 3-8).

Figure 3-8. The text container is a shaded box with a darker bar on top and a four-arrowed handle to the left.

Enter the Container

The shaded box is the *container*. Any time you type text on a OneNote page, it's placed in a container. In fact, any time you enter visual content of any sort (Clipboard, ink, images) into OneNote, it's placed in a container.

Note the two arrows at the top right of the container. If you hover above either arrow, the cursor will change to a double-ended arrow. Then press the mouse button to drag the handle to left or right, the container will resize, and the text you've entered in the container will wrap accordingly. As long as you keep typing by entering text and hitting Enter, the text will stay in the same container. In other words, multiple text notes entered in sequence stay in the same container.

If you hop over to another part of the page to emphasize something different and click a blank new location, you'll create a new container (see Figure 3-9).

Container Pros and Cons

Containers are one of the most powerful and problematic aspects of OneNote. On the plus side, they give you great flexibility in terms of layout. Containers allow you to experience "direct manipulation" of objects on the page. In other words, you can put stuff anywhere on the page without having to worry or think about page margins, tab settings, rulers, paragraph indents, table columns, rows, cells, or any of the other impedimenta of page formatting in Microsoft Word.

On the minus side, containers are a new concept, and they don't always behave quite as you'd expect. As you'll see later in this chapter, there's room for improvement in the way containers handle some kinds of content, such as browser pages, images, and digital ink.

Understanding containers is key to understanding OneNote.

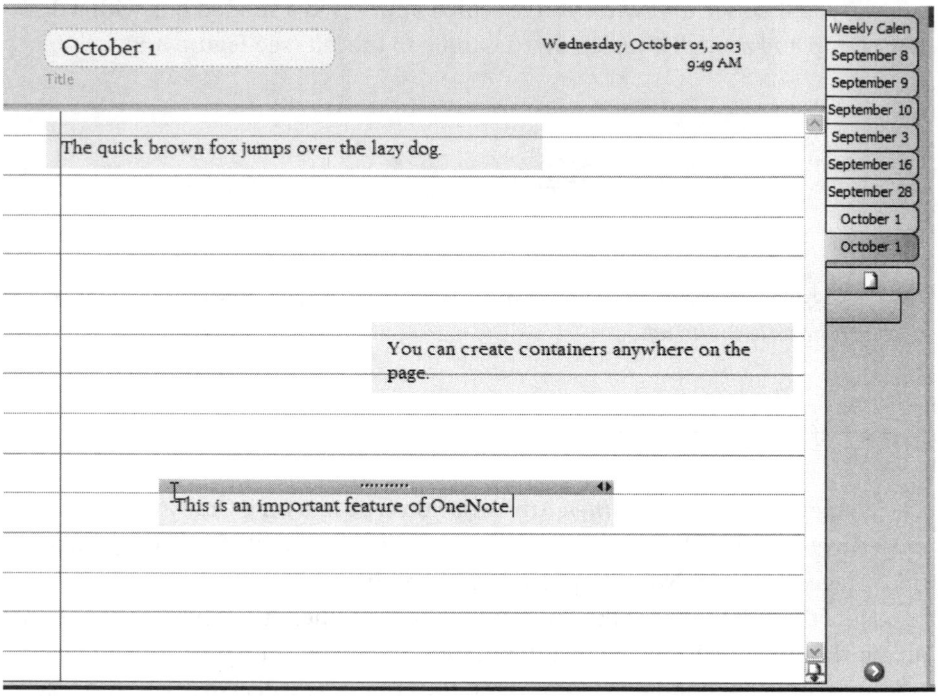

Figure 3-9. You can create containers anywhere on a page.

You can manipulate containers in a variety of ways. You can drag them by the bar at the top of the container to anywhere on the page (something like dragging a difficult puppy by the scruff of the neck!). But a warning: Peter Parker learned when he became the *Amazing Spiderman* that "with great power comes great responsibility." For example, you'll quickly learn that with your power to move containers comes the ability to move a text container and put it on top of another text container so that it becomes unreadable (see Figure 3-10).

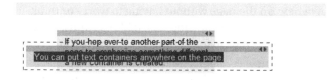

Figure 3-10. Someone has dragged this text container on top of its neighbor, rendering both less than fully readable.

You can't do *that* in Word! Cool.

Selecting Text in Containers

There are a number of little wrinkles about selecting text in containers that you need to understand. For example, when you enter two lines of text, one after another, you'll see that although the two lines together appear to be in a single container, in some ways, they act like they're in two separate containers (see Figure 3-11). Go ahead and enter the two lines shown in Figure 3-11 in your own version of OneNote.

Figure 3-11. Lester Young and Fats Domino appear to be in a single container that's two lines high, but each line of text also behaves like a single container.

Now let's try an experiment. Select the line containing *Lester Young* by inserting the cursor immediately next to *Lester* or by clicking the select cursor next to *Lester*. Then go to Edit ➤ Select ➤ and choose All. You'll see that it's just *Lester Young* that becomes highlighted (see Figure 3-12).

Figure 3-12. Choosing Select All when the cursor is at the top line results in only the top line of text being highlighted.

This is a major difference from Microsoft Word and indeed from many other applications in the Office family. Choosing Select All doesn't select the entire contents of a document! Instead, Select All selects the entire contents *of a container*. In essence, each container *is* a little document.

CAUTION   Select All doesn't select the entire contents of a document.

TIP   Repeating Select All after you've selected the entire contents of a container selects all the containers on the page.

In a manner of speaking, containers are the "quarks" of the OneNote universe. They come in several flavors, including text. As I discuss in more detail in Chapter 5, "Sharing Your Joy," pages are made up of empty space dotted with containers. Pages may be gathered into page groups, and both pages and page groups make up sections, which are part of folders. For now, the important thing to remember is that taking notes with text means creating containers that sit on a page. Editing textual notes means editing the container(s).

Hold on a moment, though! What if you want to edit both *Lester Young* and *Fats Domino*? Well, as mentioned previously, OneNote allows you to treat those words *either* as text residing in two separate containers or as text contained in a single container. If you point the cursor at the *top* of the container that appears to hold both lines of text, you'll note that it turns into a four-directional "move" arrow (see Figure 3-13) and that if you click the top gray bar, you can highlight all the text that's inside the container below it (see Figure 3-14).

Figure 3-13. When you point at the top of the container, the cursor turns into a four-directional "move" arrow.

Figure 3-14. Clicking the move arrow at the top bar highlights all the text in the container and any containers within it.

You can select more than one container by holding down the Shift key while you click each item (the Shift+click combination).

What You Can Do with Selected Text

When text is highlighted in a container, you can copy it or cut it to the Clipboard, just as in other Office applications, by Ctrl+C and Ctrl+X, respectively, which appear on the menus as Edit ➤ Copy or Edit ➤ Cut.

Oops—I didn't want to cut that text (see Figure 3-15)!

Fats Domino

Figure 3-15. I accidentally cut Lester Young.

This is easily remedied via Edit ➤ Undo Typing or Ctrl+Z.

 TIP Undo works just as it does in other Windows applications. You can undo a sequence of editing operations via repeated Ctrl+Zs.

Once text is highlighted, you can change the font in much the same manner as in other Office applications via Format ➤ Font (Ctrl+D), which causes a Font menu to appear in the right task pane. In Figure 3-16, I changed the font of *Lester Young* to Arial.

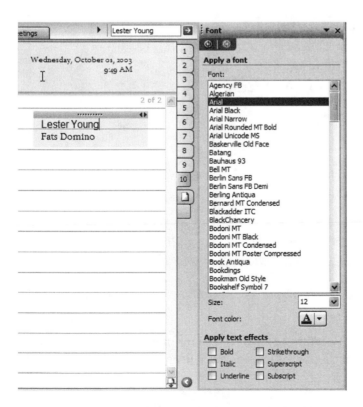

Figure 3-16. The text Lester Young in Arial

Filling Your Container with High-Quality Text

Stalin is reputed to have said that "quantity has a quality all its own." Unfortunately, the adage isn't true of text. Even with text used for note taking, quality matters. Any teacher who looks at a page of notes that's filled with spelling errors will tell you that the student is going to be in trouble on the exam. In a similar vein, decades of quality research by the likes of Edward Deming have consistently reinforced a simple principle, which is that it's much easier and more cost-effective (by orders of magnitude) to put quality in at the beginning of a process than to put it in at the *end* of the process. For these reasons, I strongly recommend you take advantage of the Spelling and AutoCorrect options available in OneNote.

AutoCorrect

AutoCorrect options are available under the Tools menu (see Figure 3-17). The implementation of AutoCorrect in OneNote is similar to its implementation in other Office 2003 applications such as Word.

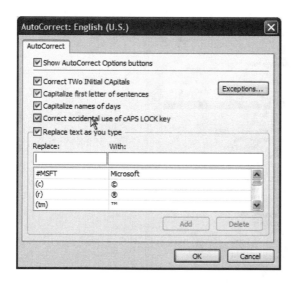

Figure 3-17. The AutoCorrect dialog box is a low-cost way of putting quality in early.

I recommend you select the AutoCorrect options unless you know that you have a specific need that clashes with the functionality of AutoCorrect. If you know, for example, that you're e.e. cummings and you don't capitalize the first letters of your sentences, if you're opposed on grounds of religious doctrine to capitalizing the names of days derived from ancient deities (nix on Thor's Day!), or if you use a lot of technical terms that AutoCorrect (wrongly) tries to fix, then by all means leave those boxes unchecked. Otherwise, keep them checked.

The other noteworthy item in the AutoCorrect dialog box is the Replace/With area (see the bottom of Figure 3-17). This is a great example of a "stealth feature." By default, Replace/With spots and automatically fixes many common errors such as typing *moeny* for *money*. But you can edit, delete, and add new pairs of Replace/With words. This is huge! If you don't like the way AutoCorrect works by default when it finds a particular Replace item, you can either fix it, by providing your own With information, or delete it.

Better yet, you can use AutoCorrect as a sort of "power macro." This works best with relatively cryptic or obtuse strings that you're not likely to input on their own merits. For example, I have set AutoCorrect so that whenever I type the stock market ticker symbol for my previous employer, it replaces *RUK* with *Reed Elsevier*.

 TIP You can make a familiar abbreviation "obtuse" by adding a piece of strange punctuation. For example, I have AutoCorrect set up to replace every occurrence of *#MSFT* with *Microsoft*.

For the note-taking task, this feature is invaluable. In OneNote, AutoCorrect ought to be called something such as *Power Abbreviations* and made quite a bit more prominent. By all means, take full advantage of the opportunity to create useful abbreviations in the Replace/With dialog box. By replacing short mnemonics with long strings, you reduce the opportunity for typing error, thus improving the overall quality and, therefore, the productivity of your notes.

Spelling

Spell checking is a great habit and almost always a good idea. Spell check your notes during quick breaks and learn a little something…it won't kill you! The Spelling pane is available off the Tools menu and can also be invoked by hitting F7 (see Figure 3-18).

Figure 3-18. The Spelling pane

Possible spelling errors are underlined in squiggly red, as in Microsoft Word and other Office applications. OneNote proposes alternate spellings, and you can change spelling of the underlined term, ignore the suggestions, or add the underlined term to the user dictionary.

You can change this to use spelling corrections from other languages if you've installed them.

The Set Spelling Options dialog box, also available from Tools ➤ Options, provides you with the option to ignore words in uppercase and with numbers. These options are set to Ignore On by default, and I recommend you leave them that way unless you're lucky enough to live and work in an environment that's mercifully free of acronyms. You're also presented with the option to hide spelling errors (which is off by default). I recommend you leave this option off unless you need to share your .ONE file with a fussy superior.

TIP   Squiggly red underlining doesn't print.

Research

The Research pane is one more way of making sure you've high-quality text in your container, but it's too advanced a subject for this early chapter, so I'll discuss it in more detail in a later chapter.

Manipulating Text

You can make a lot of changes to text in OneNote. Let's begin by exploring some of the options available from the Format menu. In particular, you're going to look at the submenus List, Bullets, and Numbering because these are particularly important to entering text notes. (I'll discuss Note Flags, Section Color, and Column Size in a later chapter.)

Using Lists

Making lists is a huge part of taking notes, so it should be no surprise that OneNote is really good at making lists on the fly. The first thing that will jump out at you, if you're familiar with making lists in programs such as Microsoft Word or in Hypertext Markup Language (HTML), is that making a list in OneNote requires no decision making.

By contrast, the fundamental unit of text in Microsoft Word is the indented paragraph. When you start typing, the words appear as sentences in an endless paragraph. When you hit Enter, a new paragraph begins. Of course, you can change the indenting so that successive paragraphs appear as lists, but the point is that some minimal decision making and setup is required, unlike OneNote.

Similarly, the fundamental unit of text display in HTML is the paragraph, whose beginning is indicated by <P> (and, for sticklers, is terminated by a </P>). It's easy enough to create unnumbered lists using the <UL></UL> construct, with list items identified by <LI> (see Listing 3-1). As anyone who has ever typed simple HTML can attest, though, typing lists in raw HTML gets old fast—especially as soon as you start editing, rearranging, and moving list items.

Listing 3-1. Editing HTML Lists Gets Old Fast

```
<UL>
<LI>List item #1</li>
<LI>List item #2</li>
<LI>List item #3</li>
</UL>
```

By default, OneNote enters items in list mode. The fundamental unit of text is a line of text that's aligned flush left. When you start typing, you're typing lists. Each time you hit Enter, you're creating a new list item. Let's type a list of great jazzmen, in no particular order: Dizzy Gillespie, Arturo Sandoval, and John Coltrane (see Figure 3-19).

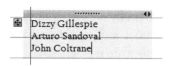

Figure 3-19. A simple list of three great jazzmen

Now let's mention two of Sandoval's recent albums, *The Essential Jazz Trumpet* and *My Passion for Piano*. Start a simple outline by hitting Tab at the beginning of the line to create a second level of outlining (see Figure 3-20).

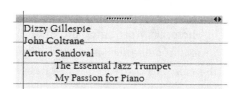

Figure 3-20. A simple list outline with a second level of indentation

Formatting Lists

Now let's take a look at how you can format the list using the Format ➤ List command (see Figure 3-21). The list formating controls appear in the task pane, located by default on the right side of the screen, with the List drop-down selected.

Figure 3-21. The List task pane

You can control the horizontal spacing, which is the number of inches that the margin for the second level is indented from the first level. The default, 0.5 inches, is quite reasonable. You can also control the vertical spacing that occurs *before* the list, that occurs *between items* in the list, and that occurs *after* the list.

The most likely reason that you'd want to control vertical spacing before and after the list is to avoid having items in the list "squinched" together with other bunches of text. There's an extensive body of print design knowledge that suggests text with a reasonable amount of white space is easier to read than text without white space.

NOTE Look at magazines and newspapers that you enjoy reading. Although the knowledge base is often held in ad-hoc and intuitive ways, the layout of today's books, magazines, and newspapers represents the cumulative readability innovations of publishers over hundreds of years. If you want your notes to be easy to read when it's time to review, emulate some of the commonsense "best practices" that you see in printed materials.

If you don't care about the appearance of your list (or at least you don't care right now), you can skip ahead to the next section on lists with multiple levels.

If you maneuver the cursor into different locations in the container that holds the "great jazzmen" information, you'll notice that the List pane changes in response, graying out some of the dialog boxes at certain times. For example, if the cursor is on a second-level item, the entire List task pane is grayed out (see Figure 3-22).

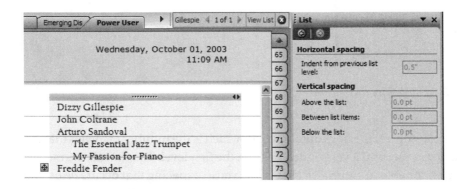

Figure 3-22. When the cursor is on a second-level item, you can't change any of the list spacing parameters.

The reason for this is that the "list" in question begins with Dizzy Gillespie and ends with Freddie Fender. The second-level item, in this case, isn't part of a separate list. Certain commands only make sense for certain types of items in a list. For example, changing the horizontal spacing via Indent from Previous Level makes no sense when only first level items in a list are selected, where there *is* no previous level. The same logic applies for changing the vertical space before and after a list (see Figure 3-23).

Figure 3-23. Certain parameters are unavailable when only first-level indented items are selected.

Note that you can change the line spacing between first-level items, without changing the spacing between second level items (see Figure 3-24).

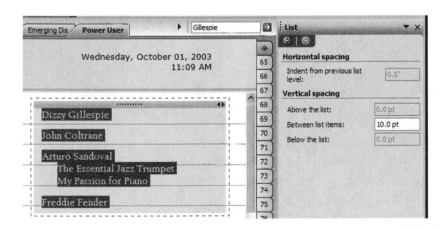

Figure 3-24. Line spacing affects items at all levels

You can enter line spacing values in points or inches; OneNote will automatically convert inches back to points and display accordingly.

Formatting Lists with Multiple Levels (a.k.a. Outlines)

A list with multiple levels is, of course, also known as an *outline*. The phrase *also known as*, or *a.k.a.*, is most commonly used in the criminal justice system to identify a criminal by his alias—for example, "James Dean, also known as John Dillinger." Those with vivid memories of painstakingly creating pencil outlines for early essays and term papers may find the use of a term from criminal justice very appropriate when referring to an outline (see Figure 3-25)!

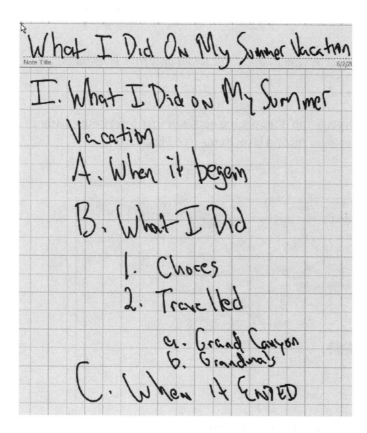

Figure 3-25. A re-creation (using Windows Journal) of the first time I prepared an outline for an essay

You've seen OneNote handle outlines with one and two levels. What's next in this series? The obvious guess is the correct one. Where OneNote allows lists with one or two indented levels, it also allows lists of three, four, five, and more levels. You can build additional outline levels by simply hitting Tab as you go to the next line. Conversely, you can return to a previous level ("outdent") by hitting Shift+Tab. The maximum number of levels depends upon the page size and the horizontal indent spacing. Practically speaking, anything beyond ten levels is ridiculous (see Figure 3-26).

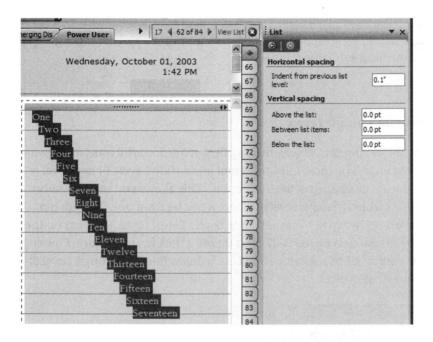

Figure 3-26. I made a ridiculous outline with 17 levels so you don't have to prove to yourself that you can!

An outline with 17 levels should be more than enough for almost any note-taking challenge. Consider that even substantial books usually manage to get by with only six or seven levels: parts, chapters, sections, and two or three levels of sub-sections. Remember, it could be worse! The most hierarchically complicated data in the 3 billion+ documents in the LexisNexis database has 13 levels of hierarchy. You should never take notes that complex!

Note-Taking Usability Tip

Keep the number of levels as low as you can.

The way to keep the number of levels low is to keep your top two levels relatively "flat." For example, if you have three list items at the first indent level, each of which is the "parent" to three second-level items, you have a total of only nine first- and second-level parent nodes to which you can attach notes that belong in deeper levels of the hierarchy.

Conversely, if you have 20 list items at the first indent level, each of which is the parent to 20 second-level items each, you have a total of 400 parent nodes off which you can hang subsequent notes.

Viewing Lists with Multiple Levels

In addition to formatting lists, OneNote also offers some powerful tools for viewing lists in different ways. The most important tool is the Hide Levels Below Level n command, which is available via the View menu. This allows you to show only those levels of a hierarchy above level n, where n can be from one through ten. Only Hide Levels Below Level 1 through Hide Levels Below Level 5 appear on the View menu by default (see Figure 3-27), but there's a trick to show more. Pressing Alt+Shift+1 is equivalent to selecting Hide Levels Below Level n through Level 9. Alt+Shift+0 shows all levels.

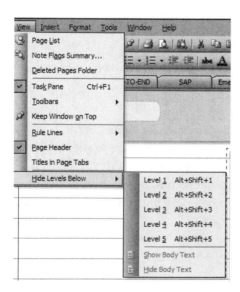

Figure 3-27. Hide Levels Below Level n is available from the View menu.

Using Body Text

If you've used Microsoft Word's outlining features, you're probably already familiar with the concept of body text. In a nutshell, body text is discussion that belongs "underneath" an outline level. Specfically, body text is information that's too complex to be reduced to a one-line outline heading. You might think of the outline as the skeleton and the body text as the muscle (or, for some of us, the fat). In books, a paragraph such as this one is body text (see Figure 3-28).

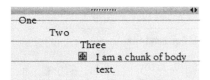

Figure 3-28. Body text hangs off level three of this outline.

You can convert outline headings into body text via Edit ➤ Make Body Text.

Using the Outlining Toolbar

If you expect to do any significant amount of outlining, I recommend you go to View ➤ Toolbars and turn on the Outlining toolbar (see Figure 3-29).

Figure 3-29. The Outlining toolbar is checked as active.

For the cost of a little extra "busyness" on your screen, you get a handy set of controls for manipulating outlines (see Figure 3-30). Table 3-1 describes the controls on the Outlining toolbar.

Figure 3-30. The Outlining toolbar occupies a small amount of space.

Table 3-1. Controls on the Outlining Toolbar, Listed from Left to Right

Function	Keyboard Equivalent
Decrease Indent	Alt+Shift+left arrow
Increase Indent	Alt+Shift+right arrow
Make Body Text	Ctrl+Shift+0
Show Body Text	
Hide Body Text	
Expand...Levels 2 through 5, or All	
Collapse...Levels 1 through 5, or All	

Using Tables

One question that arose frequently regarding the OneNote beta was, "Does OneNote support tables?" The short answer is that no, OneNote 1.0 doesn't support tables in the sense of allowing the explicit definition and insertion of a formal table structure. There's no Insert Table command, and there's certainly nothing like the elaborate feature set that's available in Microsoft Word. There is, however, a useful workaround that relies upon OneNote's outlining features to create a simple table (see Figure 3-31).

Table caption

Novelist	My favorite book	My least favorite book
David Brin	Earth	Kiln People
Frank Herbert	Dune	ChapterHouse Dune
George R.R. Martin	A Storm of Swords	Not applicable

Figure 3-31. A simple table in OneNote

Follow these steps to create a simple table in OneNote:

1. Create a text container.

2. Type the table caption, and center it between the margins using the Center command, Ctrl+E. (Unfortunately, the Center command isn't visible on default menus, so if you often use tables, you'll want to add the Center button to the Formatting toolbar. I'll describe how to do this in a later chapter.)

3. Use a carriage return (the Enter key) if you want to create vertical spacing.

4. Enter the table column headings by tabbing across the top line of the column. Underlining the headings will enhance the visual appearance of a table.

5. Enter the content of subsequent rows using the Tab key to control which content appears in which cell.

That's all it takes to build a table.

To rearrange rows, simply cut and paste. Unfortunately, there's no easy way to cut and paste columns.

 TIP   If you need to create a table in OneNote, try to make sure you have the order of the columns correct and leave the lengthiest content for the right side of the page. You won't be able to rearrange columns as easily as in Word.

Pasting Tables into OneNote

You can paste simple tables from Microsoft Word cleanly into OneNote (see Figure 3-32).

Function	Keyboard Equivalent
Decrease Indent	Alt-Shift-Left
Increase Indent	Alt-Shift-Right
Make Body Text	Ctrl-Shift-0
Show Body Text	Not available
Hide Body Text	Not available
Expand .... Levels 2 through 5, or All	Not available
Collapse ... Levels 1 through 5, or All	Not available

Figure 3-32. This table looks pretty good in OneNote.

However, the table isn't an Object Linking and Embedding (OLE) object, so you can't edit it using Word's table features, and it can't be automatically updated via linking to the original document, so once you paste it into OneNote, it's staying there as is.

Alas, complex Word tables don't paste extremely well. For example, if you've relied upon Word's formatting capabilities to squeeze words into cells or make some of the columns narrow, the table probably isn't going to look good when pasted into OneNote.

If you need OneNote to retain and present information from a complex table, your best bet is probably to select the Paste As Picture option on the Paste dialog box.

Using Bullets

Bullets are the corporate drone's friend. For those of you who've been dwelling in a cave in recent years or otherwise isolated from the world of making presentations to managers with short attention spans, the "bulleted list" has become an inescapable and indispensable tool for summarizing short lists of "action items." "Bulleted lists" are just like regular lists except that they have, yes, bullets attached to them. I'm talking about typographical bullets, which make a list look like this:

- Item 1

- Item 2

- Item 3

The key benefit of using bullets is that they make lists more readable. Think of yourself as a busy corporate chieftain too important to peer at your own poorly formatted notes.

There are a couple of ways you can add bullets to a list in OneNote. One of the simplest is to start typing the list and then use the Add Bullets control in the Formatting toolbar (see Figure 3-33). This method adds bullets to current list items at the same level of indentation. Bullets will also be added to any future items at the same level *or below* (see Figure 3-34). You can add bulleted items to a bulleted list by hitting Enter and then just typing. A bulleted item will be added at the beginning of the current line. You can add bulleted levels at deeper levels of indentation by hitting Enter and then hitting Tab once for each level of indentation you want to add. Note that this assumes that the Auto Bullets setting in Tools ➤ Options is on, which it is by default; I'll discuss changing options in Chapter 7, "Integrating with Other Microsoft Tools."

Figure 3-33. The Add Bullets control

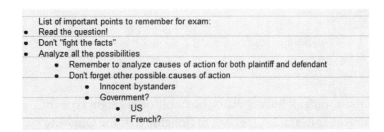

Figure 3-34. After applying the Add Bullets control, all subsequent list items in the container appear with bullets.

If you want to have maximum control over the format of your bulleted list, you should navigate to Format ➤ Bullets. The Bullets pane will appear. You're offered what I can only characterize as a truly excessive array of different-looking bullets (see Figure 3-35). I say *excessive* because a key design goal of OneNote is simplicity and ease of use, and this seems like a classic case of giving the user too many options for no good reason.

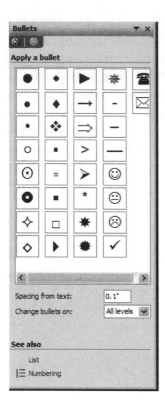

Figure 3-35. A whole lotta bullets

In Microsoft Word, the default bullets dialog box only offers eight types of bullets, all pretty simple in appearance. It's hard to imagine that the OneNote product requirement said "the user must be able to select from up to 34 different kinds of bullets, including smiley faces and snowflakes." More likely, the product requirements said "the user must be able to choose from a variety of different bullets," and some energetic person at Microsoft took a forklift into the bullet warehouse and brought 'em all out.

Let me ease your mind by reminding you of a basic point: Bullets are a typographic convention *intended to increase readability*. Don't get caught up in the fun of choosing lots of stylistically different bullets unless it helps you read the bulleted content.

With that homily in mind, let's explore the rest of the Bullets pane. At the bottom of Figure 3-35 you see that the pane allows you to change the spacing between the bullet and the accompanying text. The default value is 0.1 inches, and this is a pretty reasonable value. You don't need to consider changing it unless you have increased the accompanying font size to very large or very small.

You can also see in the Bullets pane that there's a control allowing you to select at which level bullet changes are made. The OneNote approach is an interesting (and, some would argue, inferior) implementation of a functionality familiar from Microsoft Word, where you're able to define a nested hierarchy so that different levels of a bulleted outline receive different types of bullets. It *does* appear that this layout technique can improve readability, so it may be worth trying in OneNote. As Figure 3-36 suggests, however, "less is more"—choose your styles carefully.

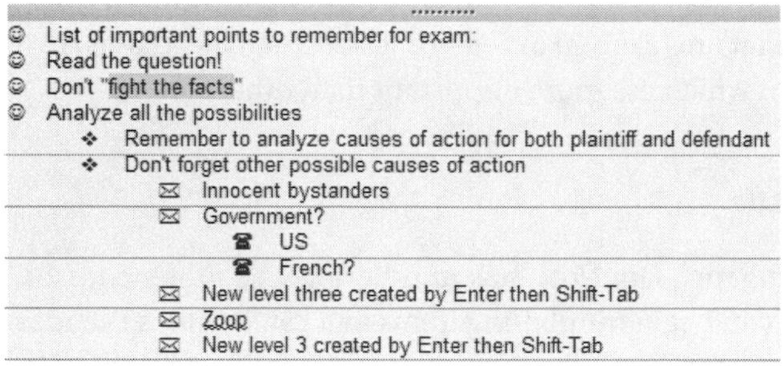

Figure 3-36. Varying bullet styles can improve (or detract from) the readability of a bulleted outline.

Individual bullet style is persistent; in other words, the last bullet style selected will be the next bullet style used unless you explicitly change it. By contrast, the way Microsoft Word handles bullets allows you to set things up as a nested scheme of bullet styles so that level-three bullets always use a particular style, regardless of the style of the bullet you entered most recently. This isn't a bad or stupid design decision by Microsoft—in fact, persistence is often a good thing in user interface designs and is unfortunately often neglected. The OneNote implementation simply reflects a different user scenario—maybe expecting more "in-the-moment" layout decision making by the user—and perhaps some version 1.0 resource limitations.

The fact that in OneNote bullet style persists at the individual level, not as a description of a nested scheme, also has an unfortunate consequence in that the next time you create a new container and populate it with bulleted text, you'll be back to the default bullet scheme. You won't have the benefit of the pretty nested bullet scheme you just set up in the previous container.

The moral of this story? Don't obsess about bullet styles in OneNote. Keep things simple and stick to the default values wherever possible. Remember, bullets are about making the text *next to them* more readable.

Using Numbering

Bulleted lists and numbered lists ought to be close friends, but in fact there's an inherent tension between them. That's because numbering implies a sense of priority and precedence whereas bulleting implies "all these items are pretty much equally important, and we'll do them all. Probably." So the numbered list is often at odds with the bulleted list.

You, however, can afford to take a statesmanlike posture. Both bulleted and numbered lists are important tools in your note-taking toolkit. The information you're recording probably needs to be numbered if it's sequential—that is, if it describes steps or actions that are taken in order—or it's normative—that is, if it describes actions, some of which are more important than others.

How to Start a Numbered List

Fortunately, your note-taking tool, OneNote, has numbering well under control. There are several ways you can begin numbering items in a list. Perhaps the most elegant, and my favorite, is to start by typing the number one followed by a period and space—1. You'll see OneNote do a little shimmy as it turns on automatic numbering for that item and all other items at the same level of indentation. The next time you hit Enter, you won't have to type 2. OneNote will do it for you.

NOTE This assumes that Auto Numbering is turned on in Tools ➤ Options, which it is by default. I'll discuss how to modify options in Chapter 7, "Integrating with Other Microsoft Tools."

If you create a simple numbered list, you'll see that by default the second-level items are designated with an *a* and *b* (see Figure 3-37).

1. LeBron James
2. Darko Milicic
3. Carmelo Anthony
   a. Championship mentality
   b. Can create his own shot

Figure 3-37. A simple numbered list

Now let's say you decide that you want to insert some additional second-level items. You can simply go to the appropriate place in the outline, hit Enter and Tab, and start typing. New numbered items will be inserted using the default numbering scheme. Let's further suppose that you want to modify the numbering scheme for these new second-level items. When you navigate to the Format menu and select Numbering, the Numbering pane will appear (see Figure 3-38).

Figure 3-38. The Numbering task pane appears in the same location as other task panes.

Modifying the Numbering Schemes

Numbering schemes exhibit the same behavior with regard to persistence as bullet styles do; namely, numbering schemes are defined and persist at the level of the individual indentation level. You can't define a multilevel nested scheme as in Microsoft Word. As in the Bullets pane, you can select at which indentation level you want the changes to apply. On the plus side, it's easy to tweak the numbering style associated with individual outline items; on the minus side, this makes it easier to produce lists with inconsistent numbering (see Figure 3-39).

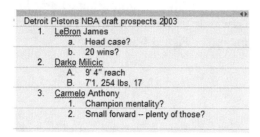

Figure 3-39. This numbered list has inconsistent second-level numbering. But the Pistons don't care!

Customizing Number Formatting

Once you've selected a numbering scheme for a particular indentation level, you can also tweak the formatting of that number scheme. For example, let's say you decide to modify the way you format the numbered items in Figure 3-39 because it turns out that NBA Commissioner David Stern, overcome by a bout of egalitarianism, wants you to refer to draft picks as A, B, and C rather than 1, 2, and 3. You'll click the Customize Numbering Format link at the bottom of the Numbering pane, and a new pane will appear (see Figure 3-40).

You're greeted by a wealth of options for how to customize the formatting of the simple numbered item A. You can present it as A), as A>, as A., as A >, and so on...down to such obscure variations as A_ and A/. The question is, why would you want to bother? It looks as if someone has taken a forklift into the Microsoft punctuation closet and come out with a large selection of Bill's hand-me-downs. Again, the key is readability; keep your numbering system simple.

At the bottom of the Customize Numbering task pane are some additional controls that enable you to adjust the positioning of the numbers themselves, in terms of spacing from the text and alignment (left or right). The default spacing of 0.1 inches is quite reasonable and shouldn't be tweaked unless you're using very small or, more likely, very large text. Ditto for the default right alignment.

At the bottom of the Customize Numbering task pane you can also change the starting number of a list. The bottom line with this feature is that "you'll know if you need it." Sometimes it just doesn't make sense to start a list with #1 and #2 because you know those items have already been taken care of.[1] But in some situations you may need to force two items in a list to have the same number (see Figure 3-41).

---

1. Winston Churchill's famous response to an editor's margin note: "This is the sort of bloody nonsense up with which I will not put." (http://alt-usage-english.org/excerpts/fxprepos.html)

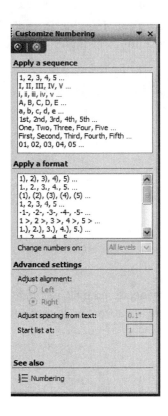

Figure 3-40. The Customize Numbering pane

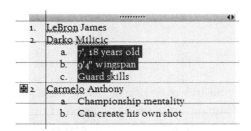

Figure 3-41. Two major items on this list are tied at 2.

OneNote tries to be smart about forced numbering—if you drag the "forced" item 2 to the top spot in the list, it becomes item 1, as it should (see Figure 3-42).

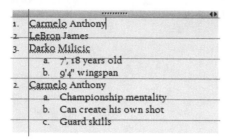

Figure 3-42. The numbering attached to Carmelo Anthony is set to begin at 2.

If you copy item 1 and paste it into the spot formerly occupied by *2. Carmelo Anthony* (see Figure 3-43), it'll now have be numbered as 4 because it no longer has the special numbering property "starts at 2" attached.

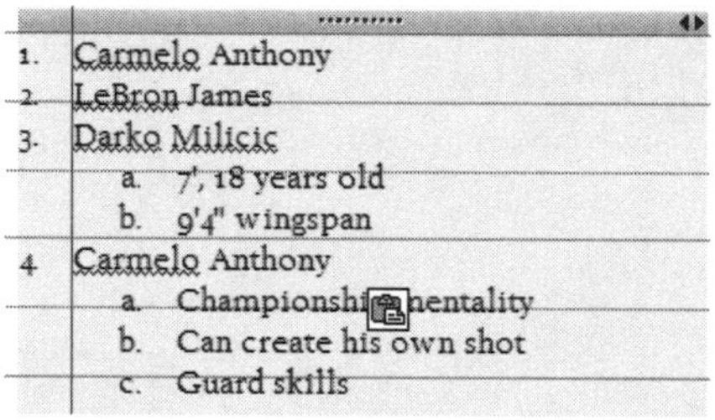

Figure 3-43. Carmelo becomes item 4.

Because these distinctions are pretty subtle and, to be honest, cause me a fair amount of heartburn, I always try to avoid "forcing" numbering whenever I can. This is a forgivable limitation in a product that's intended as more of a work-in-progress note-taking tool than as a final presentation tool—and, to be fair, I encounter the same type of problems when I use forced numbering in Microsoft Word and PowerPoint, which *are* intended as final presentation tools. Forced numbering is usually more trouble than it's worth. The best advice is to use bullets, or, better yet, add a marginal note—something that OneNote makes very easy to do! Simply place the cursor next to your original list and add a container with an appropriate comment (see Figure 3-44).

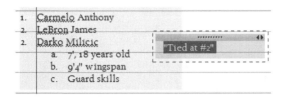

Figure 3-44. Rather than worrying about forced numbering, just "roll with it" and add marginal notes.

You should consider anything that interferes with speed and simplicity, the cardinal principles of efficient note taking, suspect. So if you're experiencing undue complexity or heartburn with numbered, bulleted, or outlined lists, pause for thought…is there a simpler way to get across your message? One simple way to add a dash of feeling to your notes is the judicious use of typography and fonts. Thus, the last aspect of text formatting that you'll consider will be familiar for many of you with experience using other programs, namely, the Format ➤ Font command, mentioned briefly a few pages ago.

Applying Fonts

OneNote follows in the footsteps of other Microsoft Office programs with regard to font formatting. The Font pane is available via the Format menu and contains no major surprises (see Figure 3-45).

Figure 3-45. Straightforward controls for manipulating fonts

There's a "picker" control that allows you to choose a font for the currently selected text, and there are checkbox controls that allow you to apply styles, including bold, underlining, italic, strikethrough, superscript, and subscript.

The only mildly surprising feature was the relative profusion of fonts available in Office 2003. If you chose the complete install, as I recommended in Chapter 2, "Installing OneNote," this will include several "handwriting fonts." There are several nice new serif and sans serif fonts in this Office package.

As I've emphasized throughout this chapter, readability should be your watch word, and judiciousness and parsimony shouldn't be far behind. Don't go hog wild! Use only a couple of fonts. Professional layout designers establish a small set of approved fonts and the situations in which they'll use them.

For example, there's a considerable body of research that suggests sans serif fonts are easier to read on screen. (*Sans serif* is French for "without feet," with the feet being the tiny appendages that extend horizontally from the major up and down strokes of letters such as l and p.) So you might choose to standardize on, say, Arial or MS Reference Sans Serif for any note taking that may later be reviewed on screen by you or others.

Similarly, it's well established that serif fonts tend to look "nicer" and less plain when printed, and it's also well understood that each font communicates a different emotional tone, ranging from the archaic to the authoritative to the elegant. Fonts also have technical properties that may be significant—for example, Times New Roman is usually among the most efficient in terms of displaying a large number of words per page. So when taking notes that will later be printed and circulated, it might be reasonable to choose to standardize on a particular serif font such as Times New Roman or Palatino Linotype.

Font sizes from 8 to 72 are available via a picker. Many familiar printed publications are in 10- or 11-point text for optimum readability. For materials that will be projected on a screen, 18-point text is about the minimum that will be readable.

Fonts are usually applied to whole bodies of text—paragraphs at a minimum. Font styles such as bold, italic, underline, strikethrough, superscript, and subscript are usually applied to individual characters, words, or sentences. A full range of font colors is available using a picker. Judiciously applied, font styles can be extremely useful in communicating nuances of meaning in your written notes. Don't overuse them because too much emphasized text becomes difficult to read.

Shortcut keys are available for font styles. Bold, italic, and underline are represented by the usual Ctrl+B, Ctrl+I, and Ctrl+U shortcuts, respectively. Strikethrough is toggled on and off by holding down the Ctrl key and the hyphen character (-) at the same time. Superscript is toggled on and off by holding down Ctrl, Shift, and the plus character (+) at the same time, and subscript can be toggled either by holding down Ctrl+Shift and the equal character (=) or by holding down just Ctrl and the equal character (=). (It may be easier to remember that it's Ctrl+Shift+plus for superscript and Ctrl+Shift+equals for subscript.)

I find strikethrough particularly useful as a way of communicating that a noted action has been completed and my responsibility for that action has been eliminated. In Chapter 7, "Integrating with Other Microsoft Tools," I'll discuss how you can add strikethrough and other commands to your default toolbars.

You can superscript and subscript individual characters, but, of course, you can't do both at the same time. In Chapter 8, "Using OneNote in Your Profession," I'll discuss in more detail how some users have handled scientific equations and formulas in OneNote.

Setting Paragraph Alignment

You can align paragraphs left, right, or centered, but the controls to do so are somewhat obscure. The right and center controls *don't* appear by default on the Format menu and submenu or on the Formatting toolbar. You can make them appear using the Customize ➤ Buttons control on the right side of the Formatting toolbar (see Figure 3-46).

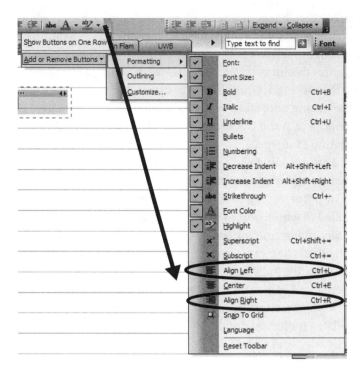

Figure 3-46. You can add Align Left and Align Right to the Formatting toolbar.

TIP   You can align a paragraph left, right, and between the margins (centered) using shortcut keys Ctrl+L, Ctrl+R, and Ctrl+E, respectively.

Summary of Text Note Taking

You should now have all the tools you need to enter text notes in OneNote. This quickly summarizes the most important concepts:

- Text goes in containers. You can have any number of containers on a page, and you can put any container in any location.

- Take advantage of spell checking and AutoCorrect to enter high-quality text faster.

- Simple outlining, bulleting, and numbering are easy using OneNote.

- Changing fonts and changing font styles is also easy.

- Remember, it's all about readability! Too much clutter and too much variation in style will make your notes difficult to read, thus frustrating your prime customer, yourself.

Now that you have a thorough understanding of how to enter text notes, it's time to break out of "Flat Land" and enter the multimedia world of data imported from other applications.

Entering Application Data into Your Notes

A great deal of OneNote's power comes from its ability to put all sorts of information into its containers, including information from other applications such as Microsoft Office and Internet Explorer. In the following sections, you'll begin exploring the types of data that can be imported *into* OneNote from other applications. (I'll defer until Chapter 6, "Sharing Your Joy," most discussion of exporting data *from* OneNote *to* other applications.) The most straightforward and fundamental mechanism for importing data into OneNote is the Clipboard, familiar to almost everyone as "copy and paste" functionality.

Copying and Pasting from the Clipboard into OneNote

The process is straightforward: Highlight a chunk of content in another application, hit Ctrl+C or select Edit ➤ Copy for Copy or hit Ctrl+X for Cut and then paste into OneNote via Ctrl+V or Edit ➤ Paste. The details of what happens next vary considerably because of a number of subtleties involved in the operation of the Clipboard.

One important thing to know is that when you paste a document into OneNote, you may be offered up to five different ways of doing it. A small Clipboard icon will appear at the bottom right of the pasted material. If you click this icon, you'll be presented with several choices:

- Keep Source Formatting

- Match Destination Formatting

- Match Outline Format

- Keep Text Only

- Paste as Picture

- Set As Default Paste

These are fairly self-explanatory in intent, if the actual behavior may be a bit more complex. I'll discuss wrinkles of how these options work with major applications as you move forward in this chapter.

Copying from Word into OneNote

When you copy from Word into OneNote, OneNote preserves those **fonts** and <u>formatting</u> features from Word that are also available in OneNote. It does this even if you've selected the Match Destination option in the Paste dialog box (see Figure 3-47)!

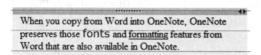

Figure 3-47. OneNote preserves Word formatting.

Furthermore, if you paste content into a OneNote outline, it preserves that structure (see Figure 3-48).

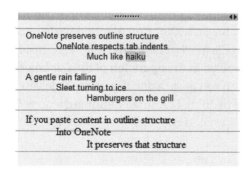

Figure 3-48. OneNote haiku

Dragging and Dropping from Word

You can drag and drop a selected chunk of text from an open Word window into an open OneNote window (see Figure 3-49).

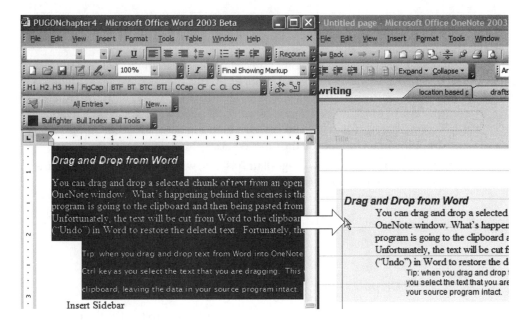

Figure 3-49. Dragging from Word to OneNote

What's happening behind the scenes is that the selected text in the source program is going to the Clipboard and then being pasted from there into the target program. Unfortunately, if you simply select the text and drag, it'll be cut from Word to the Clipboard, forcing you to do a Ctrl+Z (Undo) in Word to restore the deleted text. Fortunately, there's a better way!

TIP When you drag and drop text from Word into OneNote, or vice versa, hold down the Ctrl key as you select the text you're dragging. This will copy the text to the Clipboard, leaving the data in your source program intact.

Note also that you must be careful about the exact location where you deposit the text you're dragging into OneNote. OneNote will create a container for the text and put its left corner exactly where you put your cursor. If you're hasty, this can result in the container being located fairly far from the normal left margin, which means you have to drag it back where you want it.

Drag and Drop Challenges on Tablet PC

I find that when I use my Tablet PC, especially in portrait mode, by necessity I keep the windows maximized most of the time. This means that opportunities for dragging and dropping are much less frequent. In fact, to drag and drop requires some awkward window configurations with half-sized windows in each major application. But the folks at Microsoft talk about the convenience of dragging and dropping into OneNote all the time! What's a Tablet PC user to do?

The best option is to take advantage of the taskbar, which normally resides at the bottom of the screen (although you can move it to the side using the controls built into Windows).

Dragging and Dropping Using the Taskbar

You can drag text from Word (or any other application) onto the OneNote program icon sitting at the bottom of the screen in the taskbar (see Figure 3-50).

Figure 3-50. The OneNote icon is visible on the taskbar.

There's a wrinkle, though. You can't just drag it to the icon and release. No, that would be too easy! If you drag it to the icon and release, you get the error message shown in Figure 3-51.

Figure 3-51. The taskbar warning

So you need to learn to drag the text (selected with the Ctrl key) to the OneNote icon at the bottom of the icon and then pause for a moment, keeping the mouse button pressed. After the pause, OneNote will "automagically" appear, and you can drop the text anywhere you want on the OneNote page.

No Direct Importing RTF and OLE into OneNote

Word users may wonder if they can directly import familiar Word file types such as Rich Text Format (RTF) into OneNote. The answer is "no"—version 1.0 of OneNote has no special import capabilities and can't import RTF, text, or other types of Office files. Of course, you can open content in Word, copy it, and paste into OneNote.

Word users may also wonder if they can open or embed Word and other Office files inside OneNote, as they can with other Office applications using OLE technology. (Figure 3-52 shows the Insert ➤ Object command in Word for those who know what Word does but not necessarily what everything is called.)

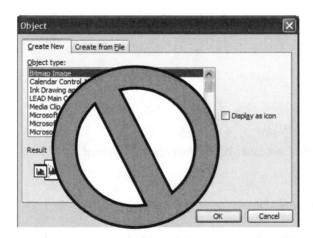

Figure 3-52. No equivalent of this Insert ➤ Object dialog box from Word is available in the first release of OneNote.

The Office Clipboard Not Available into OneNote

Unfortunately, the Office Clipboard—the Clipboard on steroids that shows up to 24 recent Clipboard entries—isn't available in the first version of OneNote. This means you can only paste the most recent Clipboard entry into OneNote.

Office Clipboard Is Available from OneNote

The good news is that information you copy or cut while in OneNote *is* available in the Office Clipboard in other applications such as Word 2003. So if you copy several items in OneNote, they'll all be available in Word or other applications that run the Office Clipboard. For example, in Figure 3-53, the five type items available in the Office Clipboard in Word 2003 are all copied from OneNote, including drawings, handwritings, and outlines.

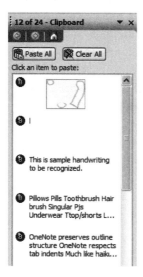

Figure 3-53. Pasting multimedia from OneNote to the Office Clipboard

Moving Images into OneNote

You can move images from many Windows applications into OneNote. The key issue is whether the images are displayed discretely as objects on the page that can be selected individually or whether they're displayed as an integral part of the application user interface. Try to select the image using your mouse or pointing device. If you can select it, try your mouse's right-click feature (see Figure 3-54).

Figure 3-54. You can right-click to copy a picture.

You'll know that you're in good shape if you see the Format Picture command on the menu. If you can copy the picture, you can paste it into OneNote!

The Paste As Picture Menu

The Paste Picture menu, which you see when you've placed an image in the Clipboard, is logically enhanced by the addition of the Paste As Picture command and, even more logically, trimmed by the removal of the Keep Text Only option because there's no way to turn a picture into text (see Figure 3-55).

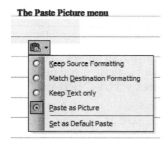

Figure 3-55. The Paste As Picture menu item

The radio button options on the menu do require some explication because at first glance it may seem they relate only to text formatting. In fact, these commands do cause changes in OneNote's behavior when you paste images. The first important choice is whether you want to paste into a standard container or as a picture. If you choose Paste As Picture, OneNote will put the image into your current page as a picture, without any container around it. You *won't* be able to add other content to the container that holds the picture. You will, however, be able to move and resize the picture and add or remove vertical space from its vicinity (see Figure 3-56).

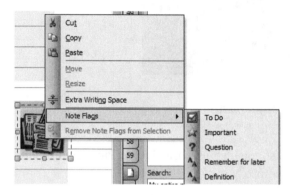

Figure 3-56. The picture menu includes Note Flags

The Move command works as you might expect—drag the picture anywhere you want on the OneNote page. Remember that OneNote gives you direct control over page layout—you can put the picture *anywhere* you want on the page, including on top of another picture or on top of a container or containers. The Insert/Remove Space command works just as it does in other settings, with the simple exception that this is an easy way to give yourself a little white space around an image you've just inserted.

 CAUTION No, you can't use Insert/Remove Space to split an image in half by "inserting space" in the middle of it. To edit a picture, you need to copy it into an application that can edit pictures, such as Microsoft Paint.

The Resize command allows you to change the height or width of the picture by dragging using arrows from the center of the image holder (see Figure 3-57).

Figure 3-57. Resizing the height of an image

You can preserve the aspect ratio (height:width) by dragging from the corners of the picture (see Figure 3-58).

Figure 3-58. Resizing an image while preserving its aspect ratio

TIP Your control over height, width, and aspect ratio is implicit. You can't specifiy explicit values. This is consistent with OneNote's intuitive model of direct control over page layout.

Moving Information from Your Browser into OneNote

As you carry out research on the Web, you may want to take part or all of a Web page and put it into a page in OneNote. You have several ways to do this, each with its own advantages and disadvantages—and none of them is quite perfect in OneNote version 1.0!

The first and most straightforward method is to select the relevant portion of the Web page in your browser and paste it into OneNote. OneNote automatically puts the content into a container and presents you with a Paste dialog box so you can format the pasted text on the OneNote page. Unfortunately, there are a few disadvantages to this method. Most importantly, the results aren't What You See Is What You Get (WYSIWYG)—OneNote often does quite a bit of reformatting with the pasted content. The problem I've noticed most often is that HTML pages that rely on tables for layout—in other words, almost every "designed" nice-looking page (see Figure 3-59)—seem to lose most of their table structure when pasted into OneNote, resulting in a long procession of navigational items down the left margin of the OneNote page (see Figure 3-60).

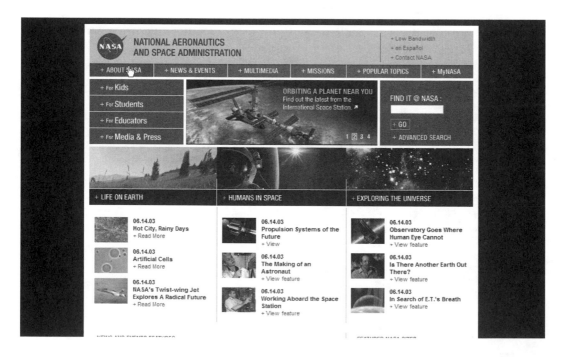

Figure 3-59. A NASA Web page that uses tables to organize content and images, viewed in Internet Explorer before pasting into OneNote

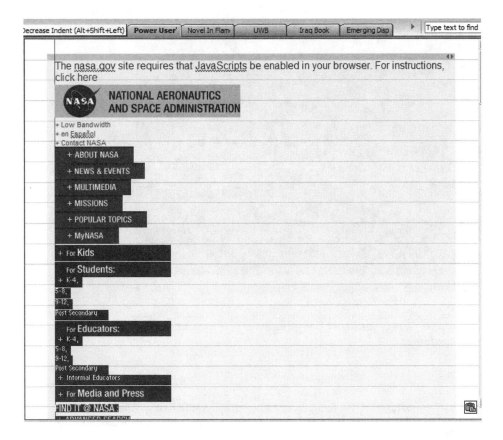

Figure 3-60. The table structure now stretches along the left margin.

 TIP   Be judicious in selecting only the minimum amount of the Web page that you need. In practice, I find this usually translates into one image plus some adjoining text.

Flagging URLs

If you copy any selected content from Internet Explorer and paste it into OneNote, the target program considerately adds a note at the bottom indicating the Web address—the Uniform Resource Locator (URL)—from which the Web page was posted (see Figure 3-61).

Pasted from http://www.nasa.gov/multimedia/imagegallery/image_feature_54.html

Figure 3-61. The originating Web address is provided at the bottom of the new container.

⚠ **CAUTION**   URL flagging doesn't work if you're using other browsers such as Netscape and Opera. Selected content is simply pasted into OneNote without the URL.

All the selected content is pasted into a container in OneNote. There's white space above and below the URL, and you can type into that space (see Figure 3-62).

The line of white space above the URL is useful in case you want to add some additional comments to remind yourself of the circumstances in which you viewed the page. Beware, though, that you can't type on the "phantom" white space to the right of the image. In essence, it's part of the image. This is actually a useful feature because it means that when you resize the container, the image stays in scale and preserves its proper (original) aspect ratio. This is almost certainly the right behavior for a note-taking program because it's hard to imagine a scenario where squishing your notes like a funhouse mirror will help you.

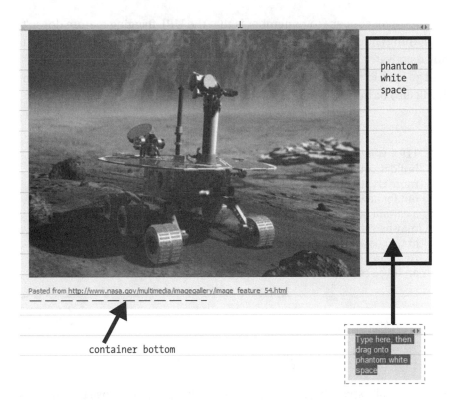

Pasted from http://www.nasa.gov/multimedia/imagegallery/image_feature_54.html

phantom
white
space

Type here, then
drag onto
phantom white
space

container bottom

Figure 3-62. White space around the image

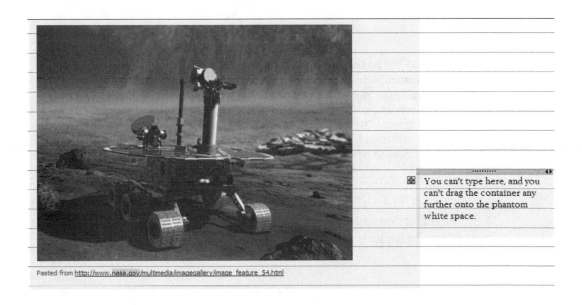

You can't type here, and you
can't drag the container any
further onto the phantom
white space.

Pasted from http://www.nasa.gov/multimedia/imagegallery/image_feature_54.html

Figure 3-63. You can't drag the container onto the phantom white space.

One important concept to remember is that the URL flagging feature doesn't change anything about the way URLs work. In other words, OneNote isn't going to magically reactivate a broken URL. If you paste content from Internet Explorer today and go back to the same page in your browser tomorrow and find it broken, the link will also be broken when you click it from inside OneNote.

 TIP Watch out for "dynamic" URLs, in other words, Web services that build unique URLs every time you log into the service. (The longer and more cryptic the URL, the more likely it is to be dynamic.) Also watch out for news sites, which tend to move news into archive locations after a certain period of time. To be able to return to a particular page, you may need to truncate the URL to the "top" of the site (for example, http://www.nytimes.com) and then use the site's navigation features. Be aware that many news sites require you to pay for access to archived content.

Paste As Picture from the Browser

If the phantom white space bothers you, it's probably better to choose the Paste As Picture option, which doesn't create any phantom white space around the borders of the image—you can put your text anywhere you want, as close as you can get to the image.

 TIP If you choose Paste As Picture and type directly onto the image immediately after you've pasted it into OneNote, you'll accidentally erase the image! You're typing onto highlighted content, and, as in most other Microsoft applications, the effect is to replace the highlighted content with the new content. If you make this error, there's a simple workaround—do a Ctrl+Z (Undo) to restore the image, then type your container *next to* the image, and drag it where you want it.

The major downside of Paste As Picture from a browser is that, even if you're using Internet Explorer, URL flagging isn't available.

Copying from Opera and Netscape into OneNote

Opera is a browser program offered by a third-party software manufacturer independent from Microsoft. Some people like Opera because it offers high performance—renders HTML pages quickly—and offers some useful features such as maintaining multiple browser windows from startup. Unfortunately, I can't recommend it for use with OneNote.

Aside from the fact that URL flagging isn't available, there's another major limitation when copying from the Opera browser into OneNote. If you "select all" in Opera, it selects all the text on the page—but none of the images. There's a rather poor workaround—you can use the Save With Images command on Opera's File menu, then open the file in another browser such as Internet Explorer, and copy into OneNote. But that undercuts the whole benefit of copying from the browser to OneNote, so why bother?

Netscape, of course, is the innovative browser company that was acquired by America Online (AOL) and is now a property of AOL Time Warner. At one time, Netscape had a dominant share of browser usage…but according to most independent reports, its share has shrunk to a single-digit percentage. And the spring 2003 "treaty" between Microsoft and AOL Time Warner, in which Microsoft granted AOL Time Warner a seven-year license to continue to use Internet Explorer in its AOL access software, seems to have sealed Netscape's fate. Nevertheless, there are still significant bodies of Netscape users, particularly in academia, which is a natural market for OneNote.

Copying from Netscape into OneNote yields a somewhat different experience than copying from Opera. In a nutshell, it works somewhat better than Opera but not as well as Internet Explorer. Unlike Opera, images do come along when you copy a chunk of context including images and paste into OneNote. As with any non–Internet Explorer browser, URL flagging isn't available. Unfortunately, when you point at an image and right-click, Netscape doesn't have a Copy command available (Internet Explorer does). This means you can't do a quick copy and paste into OneNote as you can in IE. For these reasons, I still can't recommend using Netscape in conjunction with OneNote.

Importing from PowerPoint into OneNote

Are you a PowerPoint Ranger? In some organizations, the Microsoft presentation tool is so ubiquitous that it's the primary means for communication. (*PowerPoint Ranger* is a derogatory term coined by the U.S. military to describe someone who is better at presenting than at doing; a Google search on the term will provide some entertaining background.) Even if you aren't a PowerPoint Ranger, it's pretty hard to escape having the occasional 3MB PowerPoint presentation forwarded to you by a friendly colleague!

To the extent that there's a "typical" PowerPoint presentation, it usually involves a series of slides (a *deck*) with slides that contain varying mixtures of simple bulleted text, images, and tables. And, as suggested in the previous paragraph, a PowerPoint file storage system makes for pretty large files—even a relatively brief presentation can swiftly approach 1MB.

You may not want to keep the entire presentation around, and you may want to put the key pieces of relevant information into your own organizational system, rather than leaving them in the context of someone else's presentation. So what's the most efficient way of getting information from PowerPoint into OneNote? You have several choices.

Pasting a Slide from the Deck

One option is to drag and drop slides from PowerPoint's Slide Sorter view onto the OneNote icon on your system taskbar. When you do this (remembering to pause briefly above the taskbar), OneNote will become the active (front) window, and when you drag the cursor into OneNote, it'll change to a boxed plus sign and arrow that casts a shadow to indicate that you can now paste (see Figure 3-64).

Figure 3-64. The cursor indicates that you can now paste.

One interesting wrinkle is that the current slide will be pasted as an image about a quarter of the size of a full PowerPoint page. This was a good design decision by Microsoft because it keeps the information readable but doesn't overpower the layout of your current notes page. What's a little more frustrating is that if you drag a complete slide to OneNote, it's automatically pasted as an image—there's no way to "disentangle" the text once it's part of a slide image.

 CAUTION If you select two or more slides in PowerPoint and paste them into OneNote, only the first slide will come along. This is an expected behavior because PowerPoint only puts one slide on the Clipboard in this situation.

If you want to move text from PowerPoint to OneNote as text, you must select it as text in PowerPoint.

Pasting PowerPoint Text into OneNote

Because both PowerPoint and OneNote deal with a lot of outlined text, it's good news that the structure of PowerPoint bulleted text is preserved when pasted into OneNote. There are a few issues you should remember, however.

PowerPoint font sizes are usually bigger than OneNote fonts. Text that looks "normal" in PowerPoint is going to look large when pasted into OneNote. A rule of thumb is that PowerPoint text smaller than 16 points is too small for most people to read when projected on a screen. Books, magazines, and printed text are usually in 10- or 11-point type. Accordingly, if you want the text pasted from PowerPoint to look like the text nearby it, you should select the Paste option for Match Destination Formatting. Otherwise, the text will look too big (see Figure 3-65).

Figure 3-65. Match Destination Formatting will make the size of pasted text consistent with neighboring text.

There are two other ways you can get the pasted text to be the same size as the nearby text. One is after the fact, "the old-fashioned way," by selecting the pasted text and using the Format ➤ Font command to adjust font size and other properties. This has the advantage of preserving the outline structure. The other way to make pasted PowerPoint text look like text nearby is "before the fact," by selecting Keep Text Only. This has the significant disadvantage of losing the outline structure (see Figure 3-66).

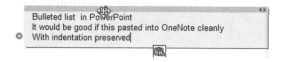

Figure 3-66. The Keep Text Only option destroys PowerPoint's outline structure.

Pasting Tables from PowerPoint

PowerPoint presentations frequently contain tables or charts, sometimes created using PowerPoint's basic table functions, more often created using Word or Excel. Because OneNote has only rudimentary support for tables in version 1.0, it won't allow you to paste tables in their native format. You must convert the table to an image.

Pasting Images from PowerPoint

You can select images in PowerPoint and paste or drag them directly into OneNote. Oddly enough, if you select a good-sized image from a slide and paste it into OneNote, it may be bigger than the image of the slide itself. This is because slide images are reduced by a larger fraction than stand-alone images when pasted into OneNote.

If a small- or medium-sized image is displayed on the blank content layout option in PowerPoint, it'll have white space surrounding it, in which case the white space will accompany it into OneNote (see Figure 3-67).

Tablet PC Ink on PowerPoint Slides

PowerPoint 2003 allows Tablet PC users two ways of using digital ink during slide preparation: inserting new drawings or writings and annotating (writing over) existing content.

If you've *inserted* ink drawing or writing on your PowerPoint slides, you can select that ink and paste it into OneNote as a picture. You *won't* be able to select and manipulate it as ink in OneNote. You can also select ink along with images or text in PowerPoint and paste the whole thing into OneNote as a single image.

If you *annotate* a PowerPoint slide using ink, you can drag the entire slide, including ink, into OneNote as an image. You can select the annotation and paste it into OneNote.

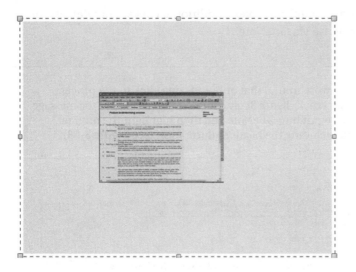

Figure 3-67. White space in PowerPoint, white space in OneNote

Moving Information from Email into OneNote

All modern email programs make it easy to save an email message for future reference. There are several places you can save such messages:

- An ever-growing and rarely zeroed-out Inbox server, residing either on the computer or on a mail server, most readily accessible via an email program

- A mail subject folder ("From the Boss," "UltraWideBand"), similarly located and accessible

- A document file, accessible via a word-processing program

All of these methods work reasonably well for some scenarios, but as you all know, these methods all tend to falter when there are too many messages in the store or there are a wide variety of topics stored. Conversely, you may have already found that OneNote is a good place to store useful FYIs. If you want to put email into OneNote, what are the best methods?

As usual, copying selected text to the Windows Clipboard is a straightforward and useful first cut. But there are some disadvantages. In some email client programs, such as Microsoft Outlook, you can't select both the message header and the message body in the same operation. This is a major problem because it means that in order to get the information into OneNote with necessary context such as the sender information and when it was sent, you have to perform two copy and paste operations, requiring several additional clicks. That defeats the whole purpose of ease of use via OneNote!

 TIP There's a workaround that only adds one click to the process. Simply use your email client's Reply command to respond to the message that you want to put into OneNote and then highlight the original message text, including the header information (see Figure 3-68).

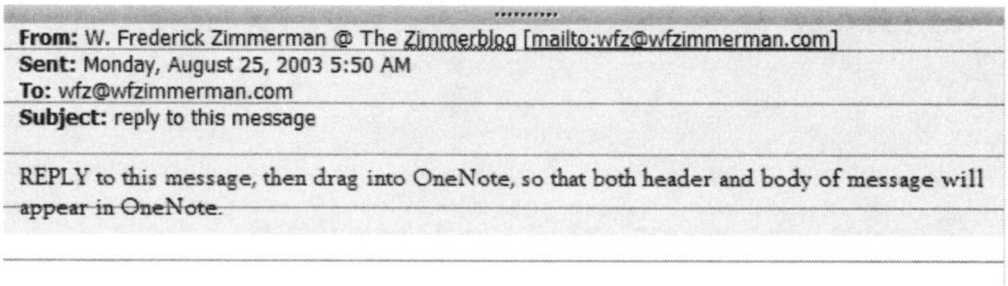

From: W. Frederick Zimmerman @ The Zimmerblog [mailto:wfz@wfzimmerman.com]
Sent: Monday, August 25, 2003 5:50 AM
To: wfz@wfzimmerman.com
Subject: reply to this message

REPLY to this message, then drag into OneNote, so that both header and body of message will appear in OneNote.

Figure 3-68. Reply to the message to capture important header information.

Moving Information from Usenet Newsreaders into OneNote

I was a frequent visitor to the Usenet newsgroup news:Microsoft.public.onenote during the research for this book, and I often wanted to copy useful news postings into the OneNote section I devoted to notes for this book. But just as with copying email messages, there was a significant problem. In some news client programs, such as Outlook Express, you can't select both the message header and the message body in the same operation. Again, this is a major problem because it means that to get the whole message into OneNote, you have to perform two copy and paste operations, requiring several additional clicks.

TIP   Reply to the message that you want to put into OneNote and then highlight the original message text, including the header information. If you want to preserve the unique news message ID for reference or citation purposes, you need to use Reply Group or Reply All.

Another workaround is to use your Web browser to access a Web-based newsfeed such as the one at groups.google.com.

Entering Audio Notes

Using OneNote, you can create audio recordings of meetings, lectures, and other events. Even better, the audio recording is synchronized with your written notes.

Until now, audio recording features have been largely confined to special-purpose programs. This is the first time that such powerful audio recording and synchronization features have been embedded in version 1.0 of a "note-taking" application intended for general ("horizontal") audiences. This is an area where OneNote is a truly innovative—indeed, revolutionary—application, in that it provides easy-to-use, computerized help in carrying out an important task that previously was so difficult as to be the province of specialized professionals such as court recorders.

So what do you need to get started? As discussed in Chapter 2, "Installing OneNote," you probably don't need special hardware to experiment with OneNote's audio recording features. Most modern computers have an internal microphone.

TIP   To verify whether you have an internal microphone, XP users should go to Control Panel ➤ Sounds and Audio Devices ➤ Audio. If you have a sound recording device, you'll see it in the drop-down list in the middle of the page.

An internal microphone is probably enough for you to experiment with OneNote's audio features, but if you're serious about making recordings and being able to understand them later, you'll probably want to get an external microphone. The "Buying External Microphones" sidebar provides some brief hints about how to buy one.

Buying External Microphones

The crucial issue is to understand what sort of microphone you need. (And, depending on your situation, you may need to buy more than one.) It's important to remember that OneNote records sound and synchronizes it with your notes, but it doesn't do speech recognition of a room full of people talking, and it's not going to produce a word-by-word transcript of a meeting for you. Therefore, the determining issue in how "much" sound quality you need is your preference as a listener.

If most of the meetings you want to record occur in your office at your desk, you may be able to get by with a computer desk microphone. These are quite inexpensive. Make sure you get a Universal Serial Bus (USB)–connectable device because this gives you the option of plugging into an inexpensive multiport USB hub, thus giving you more flexibility with your single microphone port.

You should consider a headset with speech-quality microphone if you plan to use Windows' speech recognition capabilities with any program, including OneNote. Eliminating background noise significantly improves the quality of speech recognition.

If you want to record a speaker who is far from where you're sitting (for example, a lecturer), you may want to consider a high-end solution—a two-way wireless radio that can be connected to your portable computer via a USB or microphone jack.

Software Issues Specific to Audio

It's worth repeating that there are some software requirements specific to the audio recording feature of OneNote. You must have Windows Media Player (WMP) 8 or above and DirectX 9.0a or above. If you haven't previously paid attention to your Media Player software, be aware that this is Microsoft-provided software to play audio and video files.

If you use media player software from another provider (for example, RealPlayer from Real Networks, it's quite possible that you haven't updated your version of Windows Media Player. You can verify that you have WMP by navigating to the Start menu and inspecting your list of available programs. To verify that you have the correct version, launch the program and then select Help ➤ About link to verify.

 TIP Remember that WMP is an application that normally displays a browser-like window inside it. You want to look for the Help menu on the outer, topmost WMP window (see the following figure).

DirectX is a group of Application Programming Interface (API) technologies intended to help Microsoft and Independent Software Vendors (ISVs) provide a high-quality multimedia gaming experience. It's an underlying infrastructure technology that's part of Windows, not an application to carry out a particular task. You can find out what version of DirectX you're running by going to Start ➤ Run and entering *dxdiag* followed by Enter. This launches the DirectX Diagnostic Tool, which is part of Windows. The version number is displayed on the System tab (see the following figure).

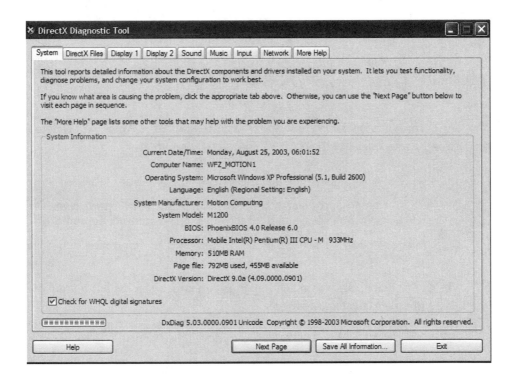

OneNote's simple audio recording tools are concentrated in two places. On the Tools menu, there's an Audio Recording submenu (see Figure 3-69).

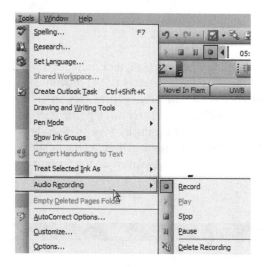

Figure 3-69. The Audio Recording submenu

The commands available are simple—Record, Play, Stop, Pause, and Delete Recording. These work like those on a standard tape recorder.

 TIP   There's approximately a three-second pause between when you click Record and when OneNote actually begins capturing the audio.

When you click Record, a small audio link icon appears in the left margin of your OneNote page (see Figure 3-70).

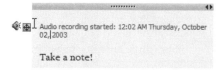

Figure 3-70. The audio link icon appears to the left of your notes.

It's important to understand that this is a *link* from your OneNote container to the corresponding place in the audio file that's being created as your record. While you're recording, OneNote will create a new audio link icon each time you create a new line in a new container (see Figure 3-71).

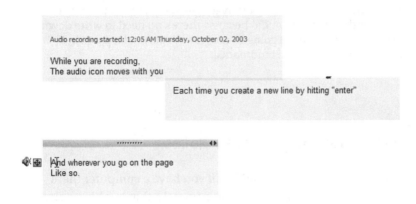

Audio recording started: 12:05 AM Thursday, October 02, 2003

While you are recording,
The audio icon moves with you

Each time you create a new line by hitting "enter"

And wherever you go on the page
Like so.

Figure 3-71. The audio icon moves to follow your current note.

You can remove the audio links from one particular container in OneNote by using the Remove Link to Audio command on the Audio Player menu. I'll discuss how to remove all the audio links from a particular page or file in the next chapter.

There's also an Audio Playback toolbar, which covers much of the same territory as the Audio Recording menu but also provides some crucial visual feedback (see Figure 3-72).

00:15/11:52   See Playback

Figure 3-72. The Audio Playback toolbar

This toolbar contains six major elements. The first four elements, on the left, are buttons for Playback, Stop, Pause, and Record. The next item is the audio gauge, which is always available on this toolbar. The number on the right is the length of the recording in hours and seconds, and the number on the left is the time played so far. The thermometer moves to the right as the recording plays back. Finally, there's the See Playback command, which becomes active only when you're playing a recording. (Otherwise, it's grayed out.) When See Playback is active, OneNote will select and highlight the notes that were taken at the same time as the portion of the recording that's currently played. In other words, the audio icon and the selected note container move to follow the playback, just the icon moves to follow your notes when recording as in Figure 3-71.

 TIP　If you're recording a conversation and want to synchronize your written notes, take lots of notes. Chris Pratley of Microsoft points out that the notes needn't be particularly long—in fact, they can be just "labels" for the section of audio because there's no need to write down what's being said. If you're going to navigate to particular spots in a recording, you need lots of landmarks.

Entering Your First Handwritten Notes

You can enter handwritten notes into OneNote if you have a computer that's equipped with a pen-style pointing device. Unfortunately, that last bit requires some explanation.

Devices That Will Input Handwriting

If you're running OneNote on a Tablet PC—a device bearing the Microsoft Tablet PC brand name and running Microsoft Windows XP Tablet PC Edition—you're good to go.

If you're running OneNote on a computer that's running Microsoft Windows 2000 Service Pack 3 or Microsoft Windows XP or above *and* is equipped with a pen-style pointing device, you'll also be in good shape. In this scenario, the following are true:

- The PC can be any type of PC—desktop, notebook/laptop, or a previous-generation tablet computer (shipped before the Nov. 7, 2002, launch of Microsoft Windows XP Tablet PC Edition).

- The PC *may* be equipped with an active electronic pen such as the Wacom models, but it may also be equipped with a passive stylus such as those on some previous-generation tablet computers.

- The pen-style pointing device may be part of the computer (physically attached or "hangared," as in some of the Tablet PCs), *or* it may be a desktop accessory where the user writes onto a pad that sits on the desktop.

In fact, you actually *can* enter drawings into OneNote with a standard mouse. The reason you need a pen-style device is an ergonomic one, not a technical one. The OneNote software isn't looking at your device drivers to see if you have a pen as opposed to a mouse, and if you turn Pen Mode on in OneNote, the program will treat the cursor input as a drawing whether it comes from a pen or a mouse. The problem is that unless you're using a pen-style device, your experience will not be very ergonomic—so much so that no reasonable person would bother with it.

The bottom line is that if you have a pen-style pointing device of any kind, and a computer running OneNote on Windows 2000 SP3, Windows XP, or later, you can use Pen Mode to enter drawings into OneNote. A Tablet PC is the best choice, but it's *not* a requirement.

 TIP As mentioned elsewhere in this book, OneNote version 1.0 doesn't work on Pocket PC, and at this writing there's no way to read native .ONE files in a Pocket PC. This was one of the most common user requests during the beta, so Microsoft definitely has this on its radar screen. I'll discuss options and future possibilities in a later chapter.

Using Your Special Pen

Everyone wants an edge—can OneNote be yours? When I was in junior high school, one of my two best friends was a brilliant guy who later wound up first in his class in Harvard Law School and a clerk to Supreme Court Justice John P. Stevens. Steve worked fantastically hard and was extremely quick on his feet, but whenever I think of Steve, I also think of his special pen. He had an edge, you see…a special four-color pen that allowed him to take notes in black, blue, green, and red just by pressing a little selector at the top of the pen. If you have the right hardware—a pen-style pointing device—Microsoft OneNote gives *you* a special pen.

Your pointing device can act like a pen, an eraser, a regular mouse, or a "magic wand" that adds and removes space from a page. These settings work whether you're controlling a mouse-style pointing device or a pen-style pointing device. (In other words, you can make your mouse act like a pen or make your pen act like a mouse. Isn't that helpful?) For practical purposes, the only time you want to make your pointing device act like a pen is when it *is* a pen. If it's a mouse, it's not going to be much good as a pen.

You can control the pen's behavior using the Drawing and Writing Tools command on the Tools menu (see Figure 3-73) or via controls on the Standard toolbar (see Figure 3-74).

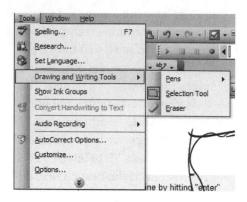

Figure 3-73. The first submenu off Drawing and Writing Tools lets you choose the function of the pen "tip."

Figure 3-74. Pen controls toward the right of the standard toolbar

Now that you've selected the pen's function, you need to pick one of three particular types of pen—thin felt tip, thick felt tip, or highlighter. For felt tips, the colors black, blue, green, and red are available. For highlighters, you may choose from yellow, turquoise, green, and pink, relatively translucent colors more suitable for highlighting existing text.

In other words, my friend, you have *three* special pens! Unfortunately, in the first version of OneNote, that's all you have. You can't select other colors or customize the pen thickness—features that are available in today's versions of Windows Journal for the Tablet PC. Those features can't be terribly hard to implement, so it seems like a safe bet that some future version of OneNote will include improved support for pen input. You'll learn more about this in the last chapter.

If you don't have a preference, I recommend you start with the black or blue thick felt tip. I find the thicker writing easier to read. But if you already know that you like thin tip or different color pens, go with what you like.

Using Rule Lines

I also recommend you go to the View menu and turn on Rule Lines before beginning to write, for two reasons. The first reason, a simple one, is that most people find it easier to write neatly when there are horizontal lines on a piece of paper (also known as *rule lines*). I'll explain the second reason as you move forward.

The Rule Lines submenu gives you a choice of Standard, Narrow, College, and Wide Ruled pages, as well as Large and Small Grid. Again, if you don't have a firm preference, go with more space to write rather than less.

Creating Drawings

OneNote can tell the difference when you're entering handwriting or when you're doing any other type of scribbling, which it calls, inclusively, *drawings*. I'll talk about drawings first because anyone who is using OneNote with any type of pen-style pointing device on Windows 2000 or Windows XP or above can enter drawings.

TIP   Handwriting and handwriting recognition are only available for people who are using Microsoft Windows XP Tablet PC Edition on a Tablet PC. OneNote treats handwriting entered on non–Tablet PC devices as drawings. The quality of ink entered as a drawing in a non–Tablet PC device will be less than on a Tablet PC because the sampling rate of a passive stylus device may be as low as 40 per second, whereas Tablet PC's sample rate is 133 per second.

When OneNote sees a user doing a drawing, it automatically puts the drawing in a special type of container (see Figure 3-75).

Figure 3-75. Drawing container with triangular dot arrays

You can identify drawing containers by the small triangular array of dots in each corner. If ink is treated as a drawing, it can be resized by dragging the top, bottom, left, or right sides of the container.

Switching Between Drawing and Handwriting Modes

For Tablet PC users, OneNote provides two modes for entering ink—drawing and handwriting—and switches intelligently between them by default. If you begin writing letters on a horizontal baseline, OneNote assumes you're writing handwriting and puts it in a text container. Anything else, and OneNote assumes that you're doing drawings. You can tell OneNote that you're doing only one kind of ink entry or select the ink and toggle back and forth between drawings and handwriting.

If you know that you're going to be doing a lot of drawing in the current OneNote page on your Tablet PC, you can switch OneNote's Pen Mode to Create Drawings Only (see Figure 3-76).

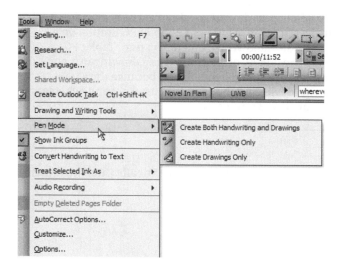

Figure 3-76. The default is Create Both Handwriting and Drawings.

 CAUTION Pen Mode must be in "pen." If you're using select or erase mode, the handwriting/drawing options will be grayed out.

The downside is that if you start doing handwriting, you'll find that individual letters are put inside one or more drawing containers each, which is far from helpful.

If you know you're going to be doing handwriting only, you can switch Pen Mode to Create Handwriting Only. There's a downside to this choice. OneNote is going to get confused if you write so much as one smiley face or draw a long arrow for emphasis (see Figure 3-77). It'll put those objects in handwriting containers, which is far from helpful, and when you paste those objects, it'll try to recognize them as text.

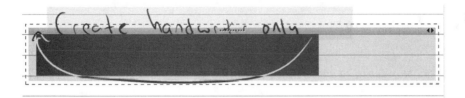

Figure 3-77. Getting confused in Pen Mode...Create Handwriting Only

Once the object in the container is selected (either by clicking or by the Select commands available off the Edit menu), for Tablet PC users a tiny drawing icon becomes visible when you hover near the size handle in the top left of the container. This handle lets you treat the ink either as a drawing or as handwriting (see Figure 3-78).

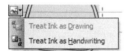

Figure 3-78. Ink is already in drawing mode, so Treat As Drawing is grayed out on this Tablet PC.

On the whole, it's probably best to stick with OneNote's default, Create Both Handwriting and Drawings.

Now, write your first bit of handwriting and see what happens. Basically, your scribble appears on the OneNote page with a four-cornered handle (see Figure 3-79).

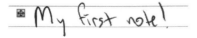

Figure 3-79. My first note, with handle

If you look closely, you can see that there's a shaded area behind the writing. This represents the ink container. If you continue to use your pen, you can scribble on top of what you've already written. If you click the container *with the mouse*, the container handle will appear (see Figure 3-80).

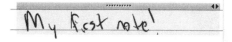

Figure 3-80. Handwriting with container handle

In short, ink is treated as just another form of input.

Writing Guides

If you use the Tools menu to turn on Show Ink Groups, a rectangle called *writing guide* will appear as you enter handwriting. The writing guide is a shaded area with four rectangle corners that covers the entire vertical space between the nearest two rules and extends a couple of inches to the right (see Figure 3-81).

Figure 3-81. The writing guide

TIP   Writing guides are turned off by default. You must use Tools ➤ Show Ink Groups to turn them on.

As you write more, the rectangle extends with you so that your pen is always writing in the shaded part. What's going on? The answer is simple:

- Microsoft OneNote puts everything in containers, including handwriting,

- Microsoft OneNote automatically expands containers so that they're big enough to hold whatever you're putting in them, including handwriting.

You may find that it requires a little extra coordination to make sure that the handwriting stays inside the guide.

TIP You *don't* need a guide in order to enter handwriting. Guides help you stay on the "straight and narrow." Guides are there to help you, not the other way around.

If you find the guides irritating or obtrusive, you can make them lighter or darker by navigating to Tools ➤ Options. Under Display, you can adjust the lightness or darkness of the guides in either landscape or portrait mode (see Figure 3-82).

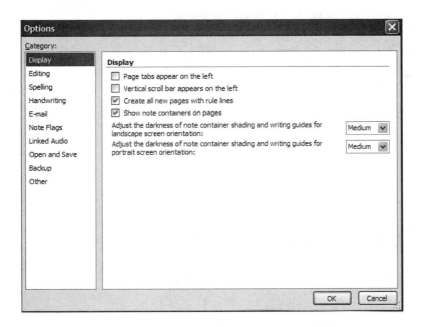

Figure 3-82. The default darkness setting is Medium.

I recommend adjusting both settings to Lightest.

You can also adjust the way the writing guides behave as your pen moves toward the right margin. The default setting assumes that you tend to write long lines that go all the way to the far side of the paper, so the writing guide for the *next* line doesn't appear until you get near the far edge of the first line. But if you take lots of notes that involve short lists, it might work better for the writing guide for the next line to appear almost immediately to help you move on to the next item. This feature removes a barrier that might otherwise stand in the way of fast, intuitive note taking.

Why Use Writing Guides?

Writing guides in particular and the treatment of ink in general were heavily discussed and controversial during the OneNote beta. Many Tablet PC users were frustrated because they expected to be able to freely scribble ink on a blank piece of paper as in Windows Journal (see the figure), and instead during the OneNote beta they found themselves writing inside cramped little rectangles. OneNote's support for ink improved considerably over the course of the beta. With Tools ➤ Show Ink Groups set to off, the ink flows much more freely.

There are two fundamental reasons why handwriting appears inside writing guides:

- Handwriting, just like every other type of content, is stored inside rectangular containers in OneNote.

- Studies show that handwriting recognition is considerably more accurate when the user stays aligned with his baseline.

However, Microsoft became keenly aware that customers were frustrated with writing guides during the beta process and made a number of improvements as production neared. As a result, writing guides work considerably better in the Release to Manufacturing (RTM) version of OneNote than they did in the beta.

Pressure Sensitivity

If you're using a Tablet PC with a pressure-sensitive electronic pen, you'll note that when you press harder on the stylus, the ink stroke becomes darker. This is a useful feature, especially in note taking because pressure is an important emotional cue in handwriting. You can tell just by scanning over old notes where you became excited by the variations in your handwriting pressure (see Figure 3-83).

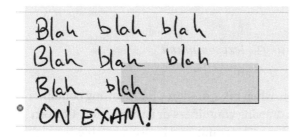

Figure 3-83. "This is important!"

You can turn off pressure sensitivity by checking a box in the Handwriting section of Tools ➤ Options. The cost, of course, is that you lose some nuances. The benefit is that you make file sizes smaller. The size saving is probably not very significant unless you're planning to make a regular practice of mailing or posting notes to users who have slow connections.

Handwriting Recognition

Handwriting recognition in OneNote is only available on Tablet PCs because it relies on Tablet PC's handwriting recognition engine. If you don't care about the detail, you can skip to the next section!

OneNote can attempt to recognize handwriting using the Convert Handwriting to Text command, which is available off the Tools menu (see Figure 3-84).

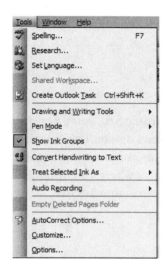

Figure 3-84. The Convert Handwriting to Text command

The command is only available when ink stored in a handwriting container is selected. If the ink is contained in drawing containers or isn't selected, Convert Handwriting to Text will be grayed out. The command is also available as a right-click option off a selected handwriting container. If the ink is contained in drawing containers, you can select the ink using the selection marquee and change it to handwriting via Treat Selected Ink As Handwriting.

TIP　You can't change drawings to handwriting via right-clicking; only the hammer and wrench icon or the menu command will do.

The quality of handwriting recognition is the same as Tablet PC standard, which is to say pretty good but not perfect. If you concentrate on writing clear, fully formed letters, you can probably get pretty good results. If you're sloppy, like me, you may not get very good results.

 TIP   Treat ink as ink. One of Microsoft's key mantras for Tablet PC is "treat ink as ink," which means to keep your digital scribbles as scribbles, just as you would keep paper scribbles as scribbles. Only convert ink to text when it's essential.

Ink that's converted to text is displayed in a simple font by default (see Figure 3-85).

Figure 3-85. Recognized text

You can, of course, change the font after it's displayed, just as you can change any other text that's entered into OneNote.

 TIP   You can't "train" the handwriting recognition engine on your own handwriting because there's no "training" function built into the Tablet PC recognition engine. The closer you are to the millions of samples that the Tablet PC engine has successfully recognized, the better it'll do, which implies, "Don't be an outlier." (An *outlier* is a statistical term for data points outside the main cluster.) You'll get better results if you reduce unique flourishes or idiosyncrasies in your handwriting.

Selecting Ink

You can select ink with your special pen in much the same way as with your mouse. Switch to select mode via Tools ➤ Pen Acts As ➤ Select or by tapping the selection marquee (the dashed rectangle). Try drawing a rectangle around some ink with your pen—see how it becomes selected (see Figure 3-86).

Figure 3-86. I drew a rectangle around this text with my pen.

You can also "wave" your pen over the ink to select it. Right to left seems to work a little bit better than left to right.

The Select All and Select Page commands are also available via the Edit menu. Note, however, that Select Page doesn't work on the individual container level, so you can't do anything to your ink containers while the entire page is selected (see Figure 3-87).

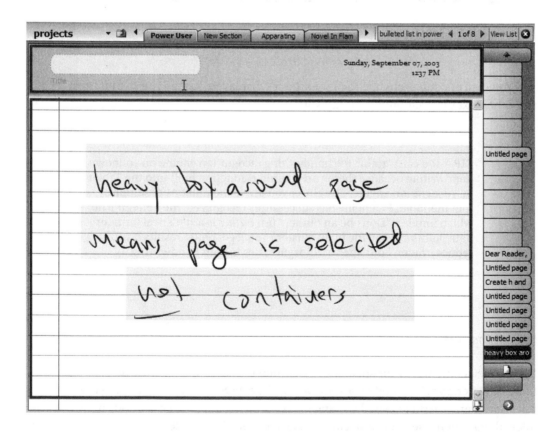

Figure 3-87. Note that individual containers aren't selectable when the page itself is selected.

Consult the appendix for details on the wide variety of keyboard shortcuts related to selection.

Erasing

Your special pen has an eraser, too. The Eraser function works pretty much as you might expect once you invoke it from Tools ➤ Pen Acts As ➤ Eraser or the toolbar icon, with only a couple of minor subtleties. First, the Erase function isn't a "paint-brush" feature that erases a particular swath of bits but doesn't touch anything outside of its path. It's more like an intelligent wand of death that "kills" any ink stroke it touches. For you, this is good because it means you need only hit an ink stroke with a glancing blow.

TIP Don't try to Shift+click or use the Edit ➤ Select command while you're using the eraser. Shift+click will shift the pen into select mode, Select All simply won't work, and Select Page selects an entity (the page) that isn't erasable. If you want to select multiple items and then erase them, do just that.

Inserting/Removing Space

Finally, your special pen can insert or remove blank space from a page. Of course, you invoke the "spacer" function via Tools ➤ Pen Acts As, via keyboard shortcut Ctrl+J, or via the toolbar icon (see Figure 3-88).

Figure 3-88. The Insert/Remove Space icon on the toolbar

The spacer icon appears on the screen as a large, unique-looking cursor. If you drag it upward, it removes white space, which you can visualize by watching the mega-sized shaded arrow shrink (see Figure 3-89).

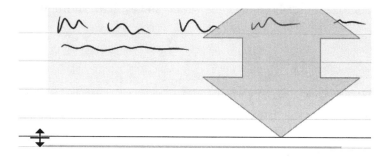

Figure 3-89. The large, shaded arrow shrinks as you move the cursor up.

Conversely, as you move the cursor down, the shaded arrow grows, and you insert white space.

 TIP You can create space by selecting containers and drag them right, left, up, and down.

If you're near the bottom of the page and you want to add space, you can add space one line at a time by clicking the down arrow in the vertical scroll bar. There's a better method, though, which I recommend: Clicking the small "make page grow" icon in the vertical scroll bar at the bottom right corner will automatically add half a page (see Figure 3-90).

Figure 3-90. The "make page grow" icon in bottom-right corner

To insert space on the left or right side of a page, you can move the Insert Space cursor to the left or right margin, where it becomes an inward-pointing arrow (see Figure 3-91).

Figure 3-91. Inserting space on left side of page

Saving Automatically

The last thing you'll do in this chapter is to save the work you've already done.

Congratulations! It's all taken care of. You don't need to do anything. OneNote has an Automatic Save feature and has been saving your work every 30 seconds since you started experimenting with it. Everything you've put on any page is still there, unless you deliberately deleted it. OneNote is also creating automatic backup files as you go.

This is a conscious design choice by Microsoft; the idea was to emulate paper. The design goal is to give you the feeling that once you write a note down, it's there forever.

In Chapter 5, "Sharing Your Joy," I'll discuss how to do "conscious" saves and how OneNote backs up your work. For now, you're done.

Exiting OneNote

You can exit the program by clicking the red X at the top right of the open window, by selecting File ➤ Exit, or by pressing the X key when the File menu is displayed (see Figure 3-92).

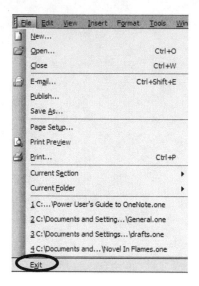

Figure 3-92. How to exit OneNote

TIP Remember, you don't need to save before you exit!

The next time you launch Microsoft OneNote in the standard manner, you'll return to *exactly* where you were working when you exited, unless you launch a Side Note using the system tray icon or the shortcut key combination Start+N.

Summary

In this chapter, you learned the following facts:

- Entering information into Microsoft OneNote is all about containers.

- You can place containers anywhere on a page. Containers can even overlap each other. There can be any number of containers on a page.

- Containers can hold text, images, pasted HTML, and handwriting.

- For each type of content that can go in a container, there are a variety of controls that allow you to manipulate and format the content.

- You can drag information from other Windows applications into a container.

- You can link containers to audio files.

Now that you've seen how to get content into OneNote, you'll spend the next chapter exploring how to organize and manage your growing body of notes.

Organizing Your Notes

IN THIS CHAPTER I'll discuss how you can organize and manage your growing collection of notes. Chances are that you've already begun doing that in a small way. Chapter 3, "Taking Your First Notes," covered a lot of ground, and you probably didn't confine yourself to just one page of test notes! Just to be on the safe side, though, let's begin with a discussion of how OneNote creates and organizes new pages.

Understanding the Organizational Structure of OneNote

As discussed in the previous chapter, OneNote is all about putting *containers* on *pages*. Containers can hold all kinds of different stuff, and you have complete control over where the containers reside on the page. Similarly, pages can hold all kinds of containers, and you can have any number of pages. OneNote provides a structure into which pages are poured, but you can modify that structure and move pages around with a great deal of flexibility.

The following is a quick introduction to the overall organizational structure of OneNote.

- Containers hold the following:

  - Text

  - Images

  - Hypertext Markup Language (HTML) pasted from HTML pages

  - Handwriting

  - Links to audio files

- Pages hold one or many containers.

- Pages can be either regular pages or *subpages*.

- Both pages and subpages can belong to a *page group*.

- Pages and page groups belong to *sections*.

  - By default, OneNote prefabricates several sections for you, including Side Notes and Deleted Items.

  - You can create any number of sections.

- Sections are placed in *folders*.

  - You can create any number of folders.

Now, let's walk through the process of using this structure.

Getting Started

The organizational structure of OneNote is visually represented in several ways in the program, such as through My Notebook (see Figure 4-1).

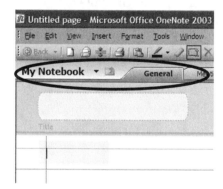

Figure 4-1. My Notebook

TIP This line is a cleverly compressed version of a typical hierarchical outline. In other words, when you look at the line *My Notebook*, realize that although it may appear "flat" and as if it only contains a single level of organizational structure, it actually contains multiple levels of organization.

If you click the caret to the right of My Notebook, you'll see the outline structure revealed (see Figure 4-2).

Figure 4-2. My Notebook expands into an outline structure.

The top level of the structure is My Notebook, and underneath it are two sections—General and Meetings—that OneNote establishes for you by default.

Within each section, there are pages and subpages. Within each page, there are containers, holding text, images, handwriting, pasted HTML, or any combination thereof, plus links to audio files.

Using Note Flags

Note flags are an important feature that lets you add a layer of navigation and searchability to any of your notes at the container level. OneNote provides five predefined types of note flags:

- To Do

- Important

- Question

- Remember for Later

- Definition

In Chapter 7, "Integrating with Other Microsoft Tools," I'll discuss how to customize these note flags and add others for a maximum of nine. You can attach these note flags to any container via the Format ➤ Note Flags command (see Figure 4-3) or via the keyboard shortcuts Ctrl+1 through Ctrl+5.

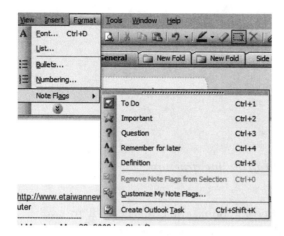

Figure 4-3. Default version of the Note Flags submenu

Each note flag comes with a corresponding visual cue that's displayed *inside* the container to which it's applied. By default, the cues for the predefined note flags, in the order listed previously, are a checkbox, a star, a question mark, yellow highlighting, and green highlighting. You can customize the cues.

TIP   Use note flags liberally. They provide a great opportunity for you to add fine-grained organizational structure to your notes at the container level. It's crucial that you put them in as you go along because without flags to find, this feature loses most of its value.

Using the Note Flags Summary Pane

This summary pane is one of OneNote's coolest features. It's a bit hard to discover. You can reach it via View ➤ Note Flags Summary or via the Tools ➤ Research command, which opens the task pane. Ctrl+F1 is a useful keyboard shortcut that also opens the task pane. Then use the task pane drop-down list to select the Note Flags Summary pane (see Figure 4-4).

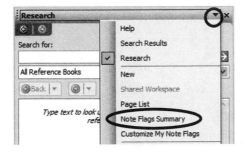

Figure 4-4. Reaching the Note Flags Summary pane

Another way you can reach it is via the small icon of a magnifying glass and checkbox on the Standard toolbar (see Figure 4-5).

 TIP   If the icon doesn't appear to be visible, make sure you've extended the OneNote window as wide as possible on the screen. The narrower your screen width, the fewer buttons you'll see. The icon should be visible by default within a screen display that's 800 pixels wide.

If you're using someone else's computer or user account and the Note Flags Summary pane doesn't appear, see Chapter 6, "Customizing OneNote," for a discussion of how a user can customize the OneNote menus and toolbars.

It's easy to customize the Standard toolbar so that the icon always displays, and you'll do so in Chapter 7, "Integrating with Other Microsoft Tools."

Figure 4-5. The tiny but powerful toolbar icon for the Note Flags Summary pane

The Note Flags Summary pane gives you a great way of pulling together all the fine-grained organizational structure you've added to your notes via note flags (see Figure 4-6).

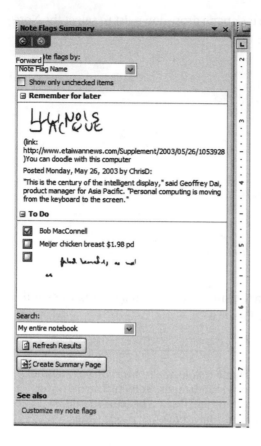

Figure 4-6. The Note Flags Summary pane

Grouping Note Flags

The Note Flags Summary pane gives you a tool to organize all the metadata you've applied to individual containers. You can group note flags by the following:

- Note flag name

- Section

- Title

- Date

- Note text

For example, grouping by note flag name allows you to view all the containers where you've applied the Remember for Later or To Do note flags. In the example in Figure 4-6, it appears I've applied the Remember for Later note flag to a handwriting container reading *Illinois Jacquet* (the name of a jazz musician I like) and to an article at www.etaiwannews.com about intelligent displays. I also added the To Do flag to call Bob MacConnell (done) and to purchase chicken breast at Meijer for $1.98 a pound.

CAUTION If you can't read your own handwriting (such as in Figure 4-6), flags don't solve the problem!

If I check the Show Only Unchecked Items box, only unchecked To Do items will show up (see Figure 4-7).

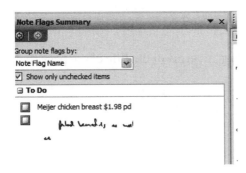

Figure 4-7. Unchecked To Do items only

I'll show each of the grouping options in a figure because I think these are hard to visualize by naked brainpower alone.

Grouping by section organizes the note flags in terms of your OneNote sections (see Figure 4-8).

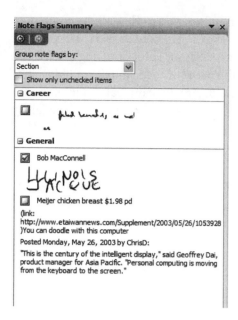

Figure 4-8. Note flags sorted by section

Grouping by title organizes the note flags in terms of the title of the page that owns them (see Figure 4-9).

Figure 4-9. Note flags sorted by the title of the owning page

Grouping by date organizes note flags into categories such as Today's Notes, Yesterday, This Week, Last Week, and Older Notes sections (see Figure 4-10). (This is particularly useful for those who manage their To Do items on a first in, last out basis.)

Figure 4-10. Note flags sorted by date

Grouping by note text organizes note flags in ascending alphabetical order based on the content of the associated container (see Figure 4-11).

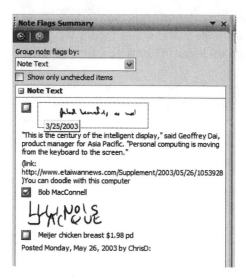

Figure 4-11. Note flags sorted by container text

Searching for Note Flags

You can adjust the Note Flag Summary pane to find note flags by various date options; within a selected page group, page, section, or folder; and within your entire notebook (see Figure 4-12).

Figure 4-12. Searching for note flag options

TIP   If you add new notes or note flags during a session, you may want to click Refresh Results to keep the display of note flags up-to-date.

Creating a Summary Page

Perhaps the coolest feature available on the Note Flags Summary page is the ability to create a summary page, which lists all your flagged note items from throughout your notebook on a single, printable sheet (see Figure 4-13).

Monday, June 30, 2003
2:07 AM

Title

Remember for later
ILLINOIS JACQUE
(link: http://www.etaiwannews.com/Supplement/2003/05/26/1053928687.htm)You can doodle with this computer
Posted Monday, May 26, 2003 by ChrisD:
"This is the century of the intelligent display," said Geoffrey Dai, product manager for Asia Pacific. "Personal computing is moving from the keyboard to the screen."

To Do
☑ Bob MacConnell
☐ Meijer chicken breast $1.98 pd

Figure 4-13. A summary page of all items with note flags

Wow! This is creating a level of personal organization that simply didn't exist before and emerges out of your day-to-day note taking. *This* is the true power of OneNote.

Using Page Tabs

You can organize and navigate to particular pages within a section using the page tabs (see Figure 4-14).

Figure 4-14. Page tabs

By default, this is located to the right of the screen, but you can change it to the left side by going to Tools ➤ Options ➤ Display.

There are three basic controls on the page tab tool. The first, logically enough, is the page tab. In Figure 4-15 there's only one selected page tab because only one page in the General section is selected. Note that the page tab is labeled with the text in the title area, *Page Title Here*.

The next important control is the New Page button, which is visible in Figure 4-15 as the small page icon in the middle. When you click this icon, you'll add a new page to the current section.

Figure 4-15. A new page (designated by the Page Title Here text) has been added to this section.

Setting the Page Tab Labels

Note that until you put text in the title area, the page tab label for the new page is simply *Untitled Page*. If you leave the title bar blank, the content in the first container on the page provides the page tab label (see Figure 4-16).

Figure 4-16. Page tab label based on page content

The change to the page tab label takes effect only when the page is autosaved by OneNote. By default, that occurs either when you leave the page or every 30 seconds, whichever comes first. (You'll learn more about saving later in this chapter.) The page tab label is assigned on the basis of physical proximity to the title bar area rather than chronological priority. In Figure 4-17, I entered the text in the bottom container first, but the text nearer the title bar takes precedence in determining the page tab name.

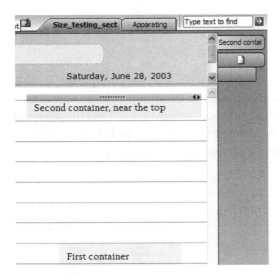

Figure 4-17. First in place, first in page tab

Creating New Subpages and Page Groups

The third important control on the page tab bar visible in Figure 4-15 is the New Subpage button, distinguishable from the New Page button by its smaller size and the absence of the page icon. Logically enough, when you click the New Subpage button, you create a new subpage that "belongs" to the current or *primary* page. You can create any number of subpages belonging to the same original page. You can't create "subsubpages"—in other words, there are only two levels of hierarchy within page groups—the primary page and any subpages.

The subpage shares the same page header and title area information as the primary page. It's as if there's a window from the subpage that looks directly into the title area of the current page, and the subpage doesn't have its own title area. Even if you have 20 subpages and one primary page, they share just one title area.

If you make a change in the page header or title area of one subpage, it's reflected in the page header of *all* the other subpages and the primary page. For example, in Figure 4-18, I've created a primary page called *Things to Check Out* and have inserted two subpages.

Figure 4-18. A primary page with two subpages

If I go into subpage 1 and insert some text in the title area of subpage 1—say, *Library Books*, which is page 2 of the three pages in the group—watch how that change ripples through the entire page group (see Figure 4-19). Now the page tab label for the primary page reads *Library Books*, and *Library Books* is displayed in the title area in pages 1 of 3, 2 of 3, and 3 of 3.

Figure 4-19. Changes in the title area in the subpage ripple throughout the page group.

OneNote exhibits the same behavior if you type anywhere in the page header.

Creating a Page Group from Existing Pages

You can also create a page group solely from existing pages. The way to do this is to select the pages you want to group by holding down the Ctrl or Shift key and then selecting Edit ➤ Group Pages (see Figure 4-20).

You can also group pages via the right-click menu (see Figure 4-21).

Let's create a page group using two adjacent pages and watch what happens (see the second and third pages of Figure 4-22, DVDs to Check Out and Library Books).

The most recent page selected, Library Books, turns orange.

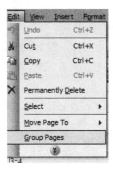

Figure 4-20. Group pages

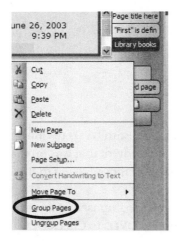

Figure 4-21. The right-click menu when pages are selected

Figure 4-22. Creating a page group from two adjacent pages

TIP   In OneNote, when the color of an object turns orange, it means it's the actively selected item.

Now you can use the Group Pages command. Something a bit surprising happens (see Figure 4-23).

Figure 4-23. The new page group

There's a new subpage underneath DVDs to Check Out. Both DVDs to Check Out and its subpage are dark blue. The subpage has all the content that was on the page Library Books. But the page tab label *Library Books* has moved down to the next page. What's going on?

Here's what happened: Library Books was a page group composed of three pages—the primary and two subpages. When you grouped DVDs to Check Out and the first page of Library Books, that Library Books page 1 became a subpage of DVDs to Check Out and part of a group owned by DVDs to Check Out. A subpage doesn't have its own header; it shares it with the primary page. So, the *Library Books* header disappeared from the Library Books primary page 1 (now DVDs subpage 2.) *And* the Library Books page group, previously composed of three pages sharing a page header, became two pages sharing the same page header.

 TIP   *Voilà!* A page group shares a single page header. A page that joins another page group loses its original page header. It's part of the new page group now.

Understanding That Order Matters

Sequence matters when you create a page group from existing pages. The first page in the sequence of pages that you select is going to be the primary page of the new group. You can't designate a page in the middle of a group as the primary page. In other words, page groups have only one possible shape, the "overhanging little *r*" (see Figure 4-24).

Figure 4-24. Page groups always have the shape of a little r.

The shape of the page group as a whole can never be shaped like an *E* or an *F* or anything else. It's always shaped like an *r*, with the top primary page forming the arch of the *r* and the stack of subpages forming the vertical stroke.

Understanding That Mergers Obliterate Fine Structure

If you merge several page groups, the effect is to obliterate the fine structure you established in each of the individual groups (see Figure 4-25).

Figure 4-25. Several page groups, each with a primary page, some with subpages

You're going to be left with one page group, shaped like an *r*, with a long list of subpages (see Figure 4-26).

Figure 4-26. One page group with a long list of subpages

Moving and Copying Pages Within a Section

To move a page within its section, select its page tab—it'll turn orange—and drag the page tab a fraction of an inch to the right or left. This feature requires very good motor control! A small (very small) triangle will appear to the right of the page tab at the line separating two page tabs (see Figure 4-27).

Figure 4-27. The small triangle is the insertion point.

The cursor will become a double-headed arrow. As you drag the selected page triangle up and down, you're moving the point at which the selected page will be inserted. Release the cursor, and the page will be moved to the new insertion point.

NOTE   It's possible to release the page at its current location, in which case nothing happens.

If you press the Ctrl key during the drag operation, you'll see a boxed plus sign appear. This signifies that the move has become a copy. A copy of the selected page will be inserted where you release the cursor.

Moving and Copying Pages to Other Sections

The drag and drop approach will *not* work to move pages to other sections. One way of moving pages is to select the page or pages that you want to move and then activate the right-click menu (see Figure 4-28).

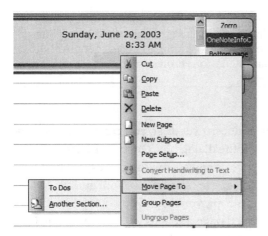

Figure 4-28. The Move Page To right-click menu

You want to select the Move Page To right-click menu, which will display at least one option—Another Section. Clicking there brings up yet another hierarchically organized outline of all the possible target sections (see Figure 4-29).

Figure 4-29. The Move or Copy Pages dialog box

This profusion of pop-up dialog boxes isn't one of the most appealing experiences in the OneNote user interface, but to be fair it's comparable to that experienced in other complex Windows and Office applications. To select a target section for the pages you're moving or copying, navigate through the outline, expanding folders as necessary.

TIP   The fact that you'll sometimes be dealing with this compressed version of the OneNote folder hierarchy is a good reason to keep your personal information architecture fairly simple. You'll learn more about this in Chapter 8, "Using OneNote in Your Profession."

If the section or folder that you need doesn't yet exist, you can create it using the "create" buttons in the bottom part of the dialog box. Once you select a destination section, you can complete the move or copy using the corresponding buttons. If you do a move, OneNote will close the "source" section, and you'll find yourself in the "target" section. If you do a copy, you'll still appear to be in the "source" section. In either case, the selected page or pages will appear as the last page in the target section at the bottom of the page tab list.

The part of the Move Page To submenu above the line lists sections that have recently been the destination of page moves—in Figure 4-28, it appears that I recently moved a page or pages into To Dos. By all means, use this option whenever you can because it saves you several clicks and reduces the cognitive effort to navigate through an outline structure.

TIP   There are usually multiple ways of accomplishing a task in Office applications. Remember, you can also move a page to another location by cutting or copying and then pasting the page.

Ungrouping Pages

On those occasions when you want to ungroup pages, select any *one* of the pages you want to ungroup and choose Ungroup Pages from the Edit Menu or the right-click menu. For example, when I select any one of the four pages that are part of

Library Books (see Figure 4-30) and choose Ungroup Pages, the result is to make all four pages primary pages, none of which are part of any page group (see Figure 4-31). Because every page has to have a page header, they all inherit the same header that they previously shared.

Figure 4-30. Ungrouping pages

Figure 4-31. Each page inherits a page header.

 CAUTION   Removing one page from a page group ungroups the entire page group. A Microsoft spokesman points out the workaround by saying, "If you want to ungroup just one page, drag it out and move it somewhere else."

Ungrouping has no memory. In other words, if you group a bunch of pages (see Figure 4-30) into a new group with a primary page called *Library Books* (see Figure 4-31) and then ungroup them, they'll have a new, totally ungrouped structure with all primary pages called *Library Books* (see Figure 4-32), not the initial structure in Figure 4-30 that included pages called *Xylophones* and *Gifts*.

Figure 4-32. Ungrouping has no memory of previous structure.

TIP   Undo (Ctrl+Z) *does* have a memory. You can get back to a previous structure if you're willing to retrace all your edits to get back to that point.

Using Sections and Folders

Now that I've discussed how to move and organize pages, subpages, and page groups, it's time to turn your attention to the next two higher units of organization in OneNote, sections and folders.

TIP   Sections are contained within folders. Folders are a higher level of organization than sections.

When I was first exposed to OneNote, it took me a while to grasp the relationship between sections and folders in OneNote. There were a couple of reasons for this, which I'll explain because otherwise you may follow the same path.

First, there was no a priori concept in my head that folders were bigger than sections. In fact, if anything, my experience with paper folders predisposed me to think of the folder as the basic unit of organization for a project. Wrong! In OneNote, the section is the basic unit of organization for projects. Related sections are grouped into folders.

Second, I was directing my attention toward the horizontal view of the OneNote folder structure (see Figure 4-33).

Figure 4-33. Horizontal view of OneNote folder structure

In this visual representation, the differences between folders and sections aren't glaring although, admittedly, the presence of a folder icon in the folder tab is a pretty big clue (see *New Folder* toward the left side of Figure 4-33).

The best way to avoid this cognitive confusion is to focus on the vertical view of the OneNote hierarchy contained in the drop-down list next to My Notebook (see Figure 4-34). I found I understood OneNote much better when I looked at this visual representation.

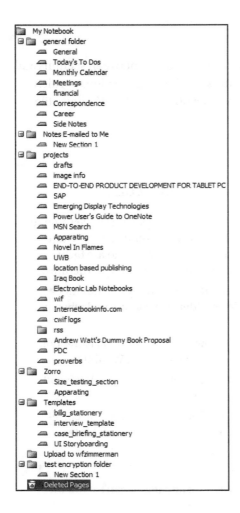

Figure 4-34. Vertical view of the OneNote hierarchy

When you click that drop-down caret, the drop-down view is presented in the familiar hierarchical format, which makes it clear that folders contain multiple sections and can be expanded. You can also see that sections can be parallel to folders—see, for example, that at the top of Figure 4-34, General and New Folder are at the same level of the hierarchy. A folder can contain both folders and sections—see, for example, the section To Dos and the folder Folder Within a Folder, both contained within New Folder.

NOTE   My Notebook is a folder that contains both folders and sections.

Finally, if you really want to understand the relationship between sections and folders, explore the "OneNote and the Windows File Structure" sidebar, which goes into detail about the relationship of OneNote objects to the Windows file structure.

OneNote and the Windows File Structure

The relationship between OneNote and the Windows file system is in fact simple and logical, but it isn't obvious from within the OneNote user interface. Quite properly, the designers of OneNote sought to insulate users—who are busy taking notes—from having to worry about filenames and directory structures.

Here's how it works: OneNote files are, by default, stored in My Documents ➤ My Notebook. My Notebook is a new Windows folder that was created when you installed OneNote.

Each folder in OneNote corresponds to a Windows folder within My Notebook. The name of the folder in OneNote is the name of the folder in Windows.

Each section in OneNote corresponds to a Windows file. The type is Microsoft Office OneNote Section and .ONE is the file extension.

When OneNote sections are contained within a folder in OneNote, the corresponding .ONE files are located within the corresponding Windows folder.

TIP   For this reason, two sections in the same folder can't share the same name.

Section files created by OneNote, such as General and Meetings, don't belong to folders unless you move them there, and therefore they reside in the top level of My Notebook, at the same level as any folders you may create.

As an example, look at the following figure, where within OneNote I created a new folder called, brilliantly, *New Folder*. I moved the To Dos section into New Folder.

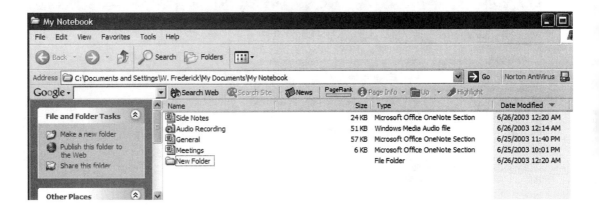

That folder is now represented in the corresponding Windows file structure.

Audio files created when you record a discussion with OneNote are stored in the same folder as the section to which they belong. The type is Windows Media Audio file and .WMA is the file extension. They're located parallel, not subordinate, to the file to which they belong.

As an illustration, I made a brief recording in the Side Notes section, with the result that an audio file is now stored in the same folder as the Side Notes file. Note that if you're only looking at the Windows file structure, there's no way of telling whether the audio file is associated with Side Notes or with General or Meetings.

When you publish a copy of a OneNote file by using Save As A Single-File Web Page, it's saved as a Mime-Embedded HTML (.MHT) file, and henceforth that file is visible in the Windows file system. (You'll learn more about publishing and .MHT files in Chapter 5, "Sharing Your Joy.")

What Happens If You Start Monkeying Around in My Notebook?

If you copy a .ONE file and leave it in the same Windows folder where you copied it, such as in the following figure:

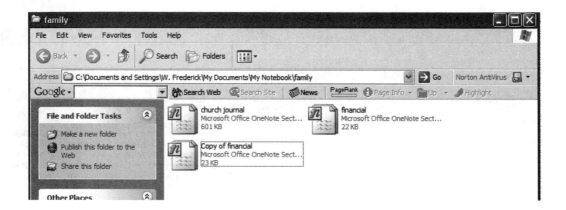

then a corresponding new section will show up in the folder view within OneNote, as in the following figure.

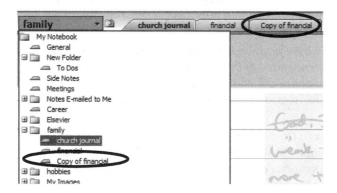

If you delete a .ONE file from the Windows file, it'll no longer show up the next time you launch OneNote.

When you open a section during a OneNote session and are actively making changes in it, the Windows file system considers the corresponding .ONE file "open" until you stop making changes *plus* five additional minutes of inactivity or until you close OneNote. (I'll discuss how to change this default duration in

Chapter 7, "Integrating with Other Microsoft Tools.") If you try to delete an open file within Windows, you'll receive an error message that the file is open and in use by an application.

If you rename a .ONE file in Windows, you're renaming the section in OneNote.

If you create a new folder in My Notebook, it'll be visible the next time you launch OneNote. If you rename a folder—which was created by OneNote—in Windows, you're renaming the folder in OneNote.

If you put a non-OneNote file inside a folder in OneNote, it'll be invisible when you're in OneNote. You can't see it, and you can't access it.

Note that this is true even if the file is of a type (Windows Media Audio or Mime-Embedded HTML) that's sometimes visible within the My Notebook file structure.

.WMA and .MHT files stored in My Notebook must be created in OneNote if they're to be visible in OneNote. This is because OneNote creates additional metadata that's required to tie the .WMA or .MHT files to their OneNote source.

NOTE   .MHT files created using Windows Journal on the Tablet PC can't be viewed directly using the first version of OneNote, even if they're stored in My Notebook. A workaround is to open the files in Internet Explorer and then copy and paste into OneNote.

Inserting New Sections and Folders

Inserting a new section is easy via the Insert menu (see Figure 4-35).

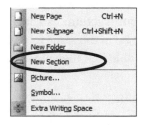

Figure 4-35. Inserting a new section

The keyboard shortcut is Alt+I+C. The new section will appear to the right of the insertion point (see Figure 4-36).

Figure 4-36. A new section appears to the right of the insertion point.

There appears to be no hard limit on the number of new sections you can insert or on the number of sections that can inhabit a folder.

Naming New Sections

The new section will be inserted immediately after the current section, and by default the title will be *New Section 1*. If you've already inserted *n* New Sections in the same folder and have not renamed them, the title will be *New Section n+1*.

If you insert new sections near the same time in *different* folders, OneNote doesn't worry about the potentially duplicate names. However, OneNote does care if there have been sections with duplicate names in the *same* folder. If you've already created a section named, say, *Test* in a particular folder, OneNote won't allow you to add another section called *Test* in that folder unless you delete the underlying section file, TEST.ONE.

By closing a section name, you can hide a section so that it no longer appears in the horizontal tab, but the .ONE file for the section is still stored in your Windows file system. This behavior is "by design" so that you can disregard a section you're no longer using (say, notes for a class from a previous semester), but you can still keep the notes around so you can open them later if necessary.

As discussed in the "OneNote and the Windows File Structure" sidebar, these behaviors are consistent with the underlying Windows file structure in My Notebook. Just as in Windows, where many files can have the same name but no two files can share the same path in the directory structure, in OneNote many sections can have the same name, but no two sections with the same name can be in the same folder.

All names that are allowable for Windows files are allowable for OneNote section names.

 TIP Use common sense. Keep section names short, meaningful, and devoid of special characters.

Inserting New Folders

The Insert menu also offers an Insert New Folder command. This works like the New Section command, with the new folder appearing to the right of the insertion point. By default, new folders are empty and contain no sections, pages, or containers. For this reason, when you click a new folder, you see a warning message (see Figure 4-37). You must click anywhere in the square so that a new page (and section) will be created.

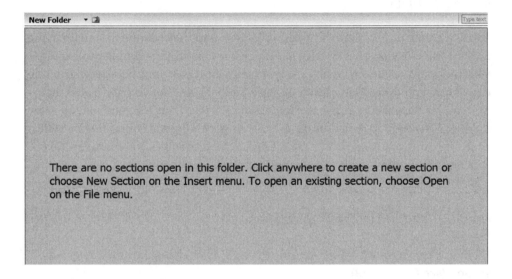

Figure 4-37. New folders begin empty.

The folder will now contain New Section 1, which has one empty and untitled page (see Figure 4-38).

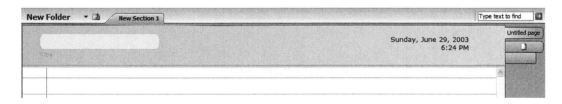

Figure 4-38. New folder, after the first click

Naming New Folders

Most of what's true for new section names is also true for new folder names. If you create *n* new folders within the same parent folder, they will be named *New Folder 1* through *New Folder n*. Any allowable Windows folder name is an allowable OneNote folder name. OneNote will not allow you to have two folders with the same name inside the same parent folder.

Nested Folders

You can create new folders within other folders, and they may be nested up to the limits of the Windows file system. But it's best to keep things simple by keeping your hierarchy as flat as possible. Set yourself a limit that your notebook structure can contain no more than *x* levels of nested folders, and set yourself a goal that each folder should contain up to *y* folders or sections. Four is a good default value for *x*, and 20 is a good default value for *y*. Twenty folders each containing 20 folders each containing 20 folders each containing 20 sections gives you room for 160,000 sections. That's more than you should ever need.

Moving and Deleting Sections

It's pretty easy to move a section using the right-click dialog box for a selected section (see Figure 4-39).

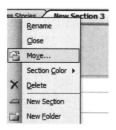

Figure 4-39. Right-click a selected section to move.

The Move Section To dialog comes up (see Figure 4-40). This is essentially the same thing as the Move Page To dialog box but without the options Create New Section and Copy (the section, because by definition you're already moving it.)

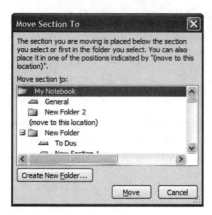

Figure 4-40. The Move Section To dialog box

While in this dialog box, you can, if you want, create a new destination folder.

You can delete sections via the right-click dialog box (see Figure 4-41) or by deleting the file within the Windows file system.

Figure 4-41. Deleting via right-click

TIP   Deleted sections go into the Windows Recycle Bin, from which you may be able to restore them. Just put the file back in the My Notebook file structure, and it'll be visible the next time you launch OneNote.

Moving Folders

You *can't* rearrange folders while within OneNote. But you *can* rearrange them within the Windows file system. Just go into My Notebook and move the folders where you want them. The next time you go into OneNote, the rearranged folder structure will be visible.

Using Special Folders and Sections

By default, OneNote creates some predefined sections and folders that are available from the first time you use the program. They're useful, and I recommend you leave them in place unless or until you have a good and specific reason to rename or delete them.

Using General and Meetings Sections

The first two sections created by default are General and Meetings. I use General for pages such as Daily To Do Lists, Music I Like, and Books to Check Out. The purpose of Meetings is pretty self-explanatory, but you may find that after a while you need to create a couple of additional Meetings folders, perhaps on a project-by-project or class-by-class basis. In Chapter 7, "Integrating with Other Microsoft Tools," I'll discuss how you can use OneNote stationery to make your to do and meeting notes more effective.

Using Notes Emailed to Me

I'll discuss this special topic in more detail in Chapter 6, "Customizing OneNote." For now, suffice it to say that this is only relevant if friends and colleagues are mailing OneNote sections *to* you.

Using Side Notes

As discussed in Chapter 3, "Taking Your First Notes," you can create a Side Note by clicking the OneNote icon in the system tray (see Figure 4-42).

Figure 4-42. The OneNote icon in the system tray

As you as you create your first Side Note, OneNote will create a section for it (see Figure 4-43).

Figure 4-43. The Side Notes section

Each time you create a new Side Note, a page will be added to the Side Notes section (see Figure 4-44).

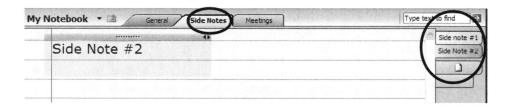

Figure 4-44. Each new Side Note is a new page.

Using Deleted Pages

The Deleted Pages section holds pages you've deleted during the current session. By default, OneNote empties this folder when you exit the program. I'll discuss how to customize this behavior in Chapter 7, "Integrating with Other Microsoft Tools." Unlike normal sections, you can't add new containers, audio links, or pages to the Deleted Pages section.

Other Locations for Notebook Folders

By default, all OneNote folders are located within the My Notebook folder. OneNote assumes you'll put all your notes for every project in that folder. However, this isn't a hard preset. You can, if you want, store and open folders and sections elsewhere. I'll discuss network and Internet scenarios in Chapter 5, "Sharing Your Joy." Here, let's look at the scenario where you may want to store sections or folders elsewhere on your local drives. For example, you may want to store your OneNote work on a project in the same location as other data files related to the project, perhaps for logic's sake or to facilitate backup or sharing. To store a OneNote section in another location on your local drive(s), all you need to do is navigate to File ➤ Save As. When you save the file in a remote location (not within My Notebook), a little "link" icon is added to the section tab (see Figure 4-45).

Figure 4-45. The link icon

The link icon is present for that section from now on, whenever you use OneNote. Everything is the same as if you had saved the section in My Notebook—you've just added a "virtual" file. The virtual file *is* included in backups carried out by OneNote.

Understanding Universal Navigation Tools

Now that you've seen a variety of techniques for creating and rearranging complex organizational structures made up of pages, subpages, page groups, sections, and folders, this is a good time to make sure you're aware of a couple of basic yet powerful navigation tools that are available in OneNote (see Figure 4-46).

Figure 4-46. The Back, Forward, and Up buttons

The Back and Forward buttons function exactly as you're accustomed to in your Web browser. If you just keep clicking Back, you'll return to any previous page you've visited in your session. If you're lost, Back is a good thing to click. Note the availability of the drop-down list, which lists pages visited in the current session (see Figure 4-47).

Figure 4-47. For visited pages, click the down triangle.

Forward is also useful, but my experience has been that in OneNote, as in the browser, I use Back quite a bit more than Forward.

The Up button (to navigate to the parent folder) is especially useful when you're within a nested folder structure.

Using Find

I've spent quite a bit of time in this chapter talking about powerful ways to organize OneNote content, but the reality is that even in information systems with powerful organizational tools, a lot of users find things by doing simple keyword searches. The blank search box has a strong allure! In OneNote, the search box is always available toward the top right of the page (see Figure 4-48). The words *Type text to find* inside the search box are there to clue you to type into the search box, not the help box.

Figure 4-48. The OneNote search box

You can enter terms in this box and hit the green go arrow, and OneNote will search your entire notebook and return a set of documents that match your search criteria.

Using the OneNote Search Syntax

OneNote designers have done what they can to make searching intuitive so that you can just type in the search box and go, but some users may appreciate some more detail about how the search syntax works.

OneNote search provides an implied NEAR connector for unquoted terms. So if you enter the search string *Tablet GPS*—no quotation marks—OneNote will interpret your search as *Tablet* near *GPS* and return a list of pages that contain the word *Tablet* near the word *GPS*.

A subtlety is that OneNote searches for variations of unquoted words. This means that it doesn't look for just the word *Tablet*, but for any word beginning with the string *tablet*. So a search for *Tablet GPS* would return any pages that contained *TabletPCtalk.com* or *Tabletiod* near *GPS*.

If you put the terms in quotation marks—"Tablet GPS"—OneNote looks for those two terms and requires they be adjacent and in that order.

The AND connector looks for any pages that include both search terms, regardless of whether the search terms may be quite far from each other on the page.

TIP   The AND connector must be in uppercase. If you enter *and* in the search box in lowercase, the search will find results that include the word and as well as Andrew.

The OR connector looks for any pages that include either of the search terms. Obviously, it's better to use specific keywords with the OR connector; otherwise, you'll wind up bringing back a list of too many pages.

TIP   The OR connector is also case sensitive. Searches that include the lowercase string *or* will find results including *or*, *ore*, and *ornithology*.

Using the Page List

Once you've carried out your search by clicking the green go arrow, the appearance of the OneNote page changes to reflect that your search results are now available. It becomes the Page List pane.

Getting the Zero-Matches Message

If you submit a search that finds no matches, you'll receive a warning error message that provides suggestions to tweak your search so that you're more likely to find results (see Figure 4-49):

- Check your spelling.

- Try a different keyword.

- Use fewer keywords.

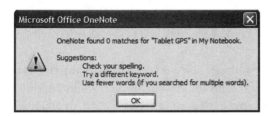

Figure 4-49. Zero-matches message

This error message is a nice amenity and usability feature, especially because zero-answer searches are quite common in search tasks involving digital content. For example, some premium online services make as much as a third of their revenue from zero-answer searches!

I'll add that if you submit your search from the page list, you should remember to make sure you're searching in your entire notebook using the drop-down control at the bottom of the page list.

Evaluating Performance

If you have a lot of OneNote pages, sections, and folders, a search "thermometer" may display before your search results are visible. Searches are pretty fast…in my test environment with 47 sections of 24.4MB and several hundred pages, searches were resolved in less than three seconds.

Using Term Mode Browse

OneNote offers what some people call *term mode browse*—a powerful way of displaying results that allows the user to flip through search results by hopping from one search term to another using the directional arrows in the yellow result box. In Figure 4-50, the term mode browse block is yellow.

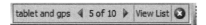

Figure 4-50. Term mode browse

As you flip through the terms via the Back and Forward buttons, OneNote automatically highlights search hits in yellow. This makes it easier to find them in a busy page of text.

One advantage of term mode browse is that before you even explore your results, the user interface immediately provides you with some valuable background information about your results…just by glancing at whether there are 1, 10, or 100 hits, you learn something about the nature of your search results.

TIP   If there are more than 999 hits, OneNote doesn't provide the exact number but merely displays you're looking at hit *n* of more than 999.

CAUTION   The number of hits is less useful if one of your search terms has a large number of occurrences.

Using Page List Controls

The page list displays in the task pane if the task pane is open (see if thFigure 4-51). You can navigate from here to other task pane activities such as Research or the Note Flags Summary pane.

Figure 4-51. The Page List pane

The Sort List By control allows you to choose whether you sort your search results by section name, page title, or date. Section name is the default. You can toggle between ascending and reverse alphabetical order.

The search results then display in a window that takes up the bulk of the pane. The search results are hyperlinked so that you can click and go directly to the occurrence of the search terms.

The Search scope control at the bottom of the Page List pane allows you to determine whether you're searching your entire notebook (the default) or just the current section, current folder, or current folder and its subfolders. The current scope selection is always visible.

Finally, the Search Tips link provides a less technical explanation of the OneNote search syntax than is provided in this book.

Saving Automatically

By default, OneNote automatically saves all your work every 30 seconds. (I'll discuss how to customize this figure in Chapter 7, "Integrating with Other Microsoft Tools.") You don't need to specify a filename! There's a Save As command but no Save (see Figure 4-52).

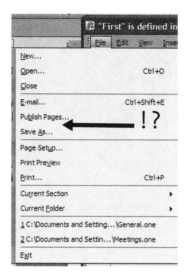

Figure 4-52. Save As..., but no Save

At first glance, this looks different from just about every other Windows application on the planet.

When you delve a little deeper, though, you realize that the change isn't quite as radical as it seems. The user interface hides the Save command from the user, but there's still a save going on in the Windows file system. To demonstrate this point to yourself, create a new section. For demonstration purposes, I created a section named *To Dos*. Now see what happens when I use Save As—there's a new file in my Windows folder called *To Dos* (see Figure 4-53).

You'll note from the Save As Type dialog box that by default the file is saved as the type OneNote Sections. (I'll talk about other file types in Chapter 5, "Sharing Your Joy.") So OneNote did an *implied* save behind the scenes, and named the Windows file on the basis of the OneNote section name.

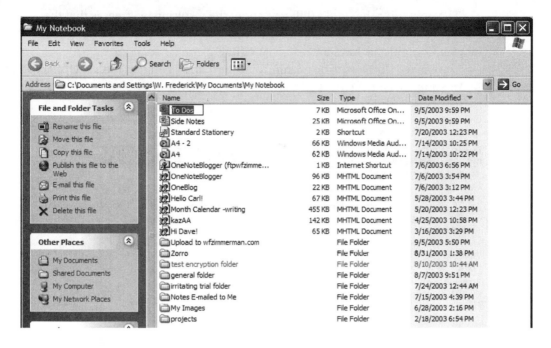

Figure 4-53. I didn't type Save As To Dos.

Performing Backups

By default, OneNote backs up all your Notebook files every day in a folder located at the following place in the Windows file system: Documents and Settings\ [Username]\Local Settings\Application Data\Microsoft\OneNote\Backup. (I'll discuss how to customize this location and how frequently backups arc carried out in Chapter 6, "Customizing OneNote.") When the backup is executed, OneNote simply copies all the folders and sections in My Notebook and puts them in the backup location.

NOTE   If you put files not created by OneNote inside your My Notebook file structure (for example, a Word or PowerPoint document), they will be backed up by OneNote.

The only thing that looks different about the resulting file trees is that the backup process adds an OneNote Table of Contents file for each directory. These Table of Contents file have extension .ONETOC.

You can tell OneNote to do an immediate backup by going to Tools ➤ Options ➤ Backup and clicking the Backup Now button (see Figure 4-54).

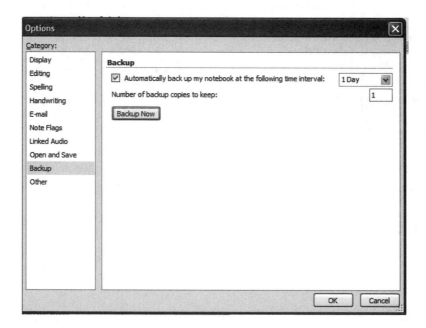

Figure 4-54. The Backup Now button

 CAUTION   As long as Number of Backup Copies to Keep is set to the default value, 1, any automatic or manual backups that are executed will *replace all previous backups*. For this reason, I recommend you change the default value. I'll discuss relevant considerations in more detail in Chapter 7, "Integrating with Other Microsoft Tools."

The backup features were added in response to user requests expressed during the beta period.

Using a Binary Editor to Fix a Corrupted File

If OneNote reports a corrupted file and your backups fail or have somehow been lost, you can follow Christopher Thompson's useful suggestion from Usenet news:microsoft.public.onenote:

Using a binary editor (you can find a free one at www.download.com*), I removed a small chunk of the data at the end of the file and resaved it. When I opened it again with OneNote, the program said it was corrupt and would need to be rebuilt and then did rebuild it. Most or all of the data appears to be there. I'm sure I lost a little data (I know I deleted a small amount at the end of the file).*

The first time I did this, it erased all the titles from each note. I tried it again, deleting a very small amount of data, and it simply didn't work. I tried it a third time, deleting a little more data, and it worked. I can't find the data that's missing except some of the titles although it'd be hard to notice it right away.

I'm not even a computer expert and was able to fix the problem within a matter of a couple hours of trial and error.[1]

If the alternative is irretrievable loss of data, this approach may be worth a shot. But proceed with caution!

Addressing Concerns About File Size

You may be concerned about file size. How much room will .ONE files take on your system? As with many multimedia applications, the short answer is a not terribly definitive "your mileage may vary."

 CAUTION Disregard anything you may have heard or read about file size from people who may be relying on their experience with the first and second OneNote betas. Those beta version software had known major bugs that caused file sizes to be vastly increased.

---

1. Microsoft.public.onenote, July 18, 2003; message-id 11ef01c34da7$6dcd3cb0$3501280a@phx.gbl

How big can your OneNote files become? One important to point to remember is that as you add sections, folders, audio recordings, and published pages, you're adding individual files to your Windows file structure under My Notebook. So you may wind up with a considerable number of files, some very small, some quite large.

Before feeling any angst about having a lot of files to track, remember that the alternative is winding up with one huge file! Experience with other applications (including certain members of the Microsoft Office family) suggests that having all application data in a single huge file makes life inconvenient when it comes time to back up or move crucial data. Breaking storage into multiple files was a good design decision by the OneNote team.

In my case, I've been using OneNote on a daily basis for about four months, and I now have 47 files in nine folders taking up 24.4MB. That works out to be less than 100MB per year, which strikes me as quite reasonable in this day of 40, 80, and 100GB hard disks.

Of more concern may be the question of maximum file size because even in the era of broadband, you may feel some concern about mailing or copying large files from one place to another.

Simple textual notes are modest in terms of file size per page. A test section that I created with no content is 7KB. Adding four additional blank pages increased the file size to 18KB, or about 2.4KB per additional page.

Pasting HTML into OneNote can be more or less efficient depending on how OneNote processes the pasted HTML. My test results varied significantly with some HTML pages using much more space in OneNote than in Internet Explorer and some others being quite a bit more efficient in OneNote. On the side of efficiency, remember that OneNote may not render HTML content such as JavaScript, Cascading Style Sheets (CSS), and complex nested tables. All this information, which can take up considerable space in an HTML page, isn't needed in a OneNote page.

On the other hand, pasting images increases the size of a particular OneNote page, just as it would in any other Windows application. OneNote is just as efficient as any other application in pasting images, with a very small increment associated with the metadata for URL flagging.

When saving ink, OneNote also appears to be slightly less efficient than the baseline ink application, Windows Journal. I experimented with saving several simple phrases scribbled in ink (see Figure 4-55) in both OneNote and Journal and found that OneNote file sizes were always slightly larger.

Figure 4-55. Zorro!

Bear in mind that if you paste ink into OneNote from another application, such as Journal, it's less efficient than if you wrote the ink into OneNote yourself because you're pasting an image.

When publishing files as .MHT files, my rule of thumb is 60 to 100KB/page. This does mean that you'll probably think twice before posting 20 pages of hand-written notes. The best advice I can give you is that if you know ahead of time that you're going to be mailing or publishing your notes, avoid creating huge page groups.

Summary

In this chapter, you learned the following:

- OneNote organizes your content in a hierarchical outline: My Notebook ➤ Folders ➤ Sections ➤ Page Groups Primary Page ➤ Subpages ➤ Containers (on pages).

- Apply note flags liberally to containers as you take notes. This is crucial because without lots of note flags that you've applied, you can't take advantage of the extremely cool Note Flags Summary pane.

- Page groups have only one primary page, and it must occur at the beginning of the page group. There may be any number of subpages.

- Folders may contain either sections or other folders.

- OneNote's folder and section hierarchy is basically a view in My Notebook of the Windows file structure.

- OneNote has a fast, powerful search tool. Don't worry about the search syntax unless you enjoy doing so.

- Don't worry about file space. You're not likely to run out of room soon.

- Know that OneNote always keeps at least one backup version for you.

Now that you have a pretty good handle on organizing materials in OneNote, it makes sense to move to a discussion of how to share them with colleagues and friends—"Sharing Your Joy" is the topic of Chapter 5.

Sharing Your Joy

EXPERIENCE SUGGESTS THAT at some point you're going to want to get some of your notes out of OneNote and into the bigger world. In this chapter, you'll explore the tools that OneNote gives you to print, e-mail, and publish notes.

The Perils of Being Just a Note "Collector"

The collector mentality has a strong appeal deep in the human psyche, not least when it comes to note taking. Stamps, coins, books, miniature soldiers, teapots, quilts, figurines, rocks (!), notes—sometimes it seems that everyone collects *something*. It doesn't matter if you never use the objects; it's the getting and having of them that gives pleasure.

Most of us have experienced a collector's frenzy for note taking at some point in our lives, dutifully taking tens or hundreds of pages of notes on a new subject or project. We often take notes intensively in challenging situations because the activity gives you a feeling of security, purpose, order, and (alas, often transitory) competence. We obsess over details such as which color highlighters to use in particular situations. As we glance down at our notes, we feel a sense of accomplishment and pride. In short, we're experiencing many of the same feelings as collectors.

Indeed, you can steam merrily along for days or weeks in OneNote, adding colorful new pages to your notebook like so many new friends for Thomas the Tank Engine (the children's video star who meets colorful new friends such as Harry the Helicopter every episode). Even for the most dedicated collector, though, there comes a time when the joy of acquisition must be supplemented by the thrill of action. You must actually use your notes, or share them with others, for your joy to be complete.

To be sure, you can act on notes by reviewing them on screen and without printing, e-mailing, or publishing them. As discussed in Chapter 4, "Organizing Your Notes," the Note Flags Summary pane makes it easy to find all the notes you've flagged with personal metadata, and you can certainly review and act upon those notes online. OneNote's powerful organizational, navigational, and search features make it easy to find particular items in even a large corpus of notes; it'd be counterproductive to print or publish your whole notebook to find a single item. If you have a Tablet PC, you can hold the device at the most comfortable distance from your eyes, adjust the viewing angle, and scribble on the OneNote page with your electronic pen—experiencing better ergonomics and greater functionality than you'd have with a desktop PC. In short, OneNote is a wonderful tool for collecting notes if that's your only goal. But the point of this chapter is that for OneNote to be truly effective, you must synthesize and share the value embodied in your notes.

Printing Your Notes

I'll begin with printing because it's such a fundamental activity. The 50,000-foot view is that printing works pretty much like any other Microsoft application. There are a few wrinkles, created primarily by OneNote's unique user interface, and I'll discuss them throughout the chapter.

Because printing, despite the advent of various new printing technologies over the years, is still all about printing pages, you need to understand what a page is in OneNote, what a *printable* page is, and whether they're different.

For this discussion, I'll return for a moment to the "blank sheet of paper" that greets the new OneNote user the first time she opens the program. She will see a page that looks something like Figure 5-1.

By default, pages begin with no ruled lines, except when OneNote is running on a Tablet PC, in which case rule lines are on by default.

CAUTION Although the OneNote page surface looks like a standard piece of paper, resist the temptation to expect that it'll behave in every respect like a piece of paper. It's an electronic metaphor for paper that behaves differently. In particular, the right and bottom margins can extend far beyond the normal page margin, and page sizes can vary dramatically.

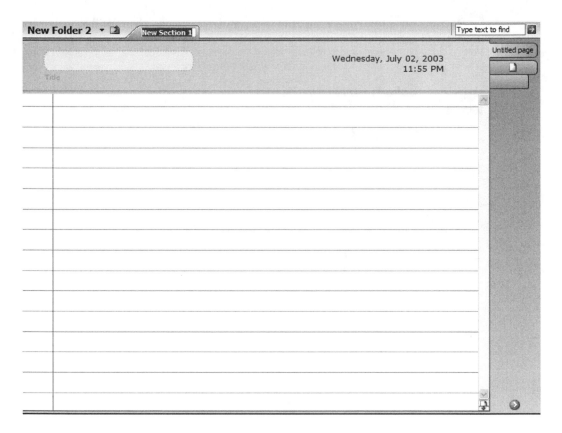

Figure 5-1. A blank page in OneNote on Tablet PC, with ruled lines by default

Setting Up Your Page

The command for opening the Page Setup dialog box is on the File menu
(see Figure 5-2).

Figure 5-2. Selecting Page Setup

When you select Page Setup, the task pane of the same name will appear (see Figure 5-3).

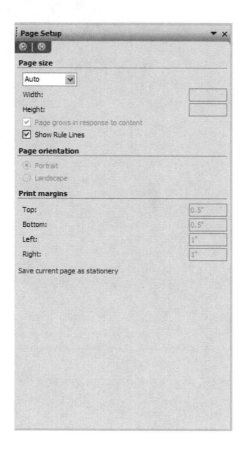

Figure 5-3. The Page Setup pane

Page Grows in Response to Content

Note that in Figure 5-3, the Page Size setting is Auto, and the Page Grows in Response to Content checkbox is grayed out in the on state. When the Page Size setting is Auto, the page *must* grow automatically to the size of the content. This is a powerful feature that takes advantage of the flexibility afforded by OneNote's electronic page surface. But it does require some mental adjustment if you're accustomed to the page layout behavior in Microsoft Word, where a page is usually the same size within a section of a document.

NOTE The page doesn't *shrink* if the content on it is small.

It's necessary to offer a few words of explanation about *how* the page grows. The page only grows automatically to the right and to the bottom. It *never* grows automatically to the left (extending the space that's available to the left of the red margin line), but you can add space to the left using the Insert Space tool. The page never grows automatically to the top, but you can insert space underneath the page header information using the Insert Space tool. (You can never have additional space above the page header.)

The page will grow automatically to fit the size of the window available to OneNote. If you have a huge monitor, you can draw ink all the way across the screen—far more than a standard page width. Basically, where you can see, you can draw.

As a convenience, OneNote will perform a word wrap at the place where letter-sized paper would terminate so that you won't inadvertently generate content that can't print onto letter-sized paper (see Figure 5-4).

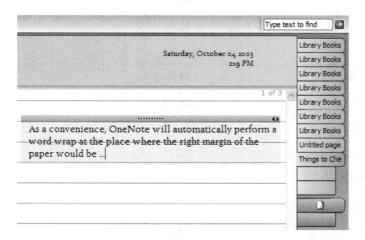

Figure 5-4. The text inside the container wraps at the right margin.

The page will grow indefinitely to the bottom. You can verify this for yourself by selecting an image or handwriting object and dragging its vertical resize handle down or by typing a bunch of lines of text (*asdf* followed by a Return is a fast way to generate a lot of test lines of text!) Note that there are no visual page break symbols as in Microsoft Word. As far as OneNote is concerned, it's a single page of huge height.

Page Size Measurements

OneNote offers a number of fixed page size options. For all these options, the "autogrow" just described is off by default. Table 5-1 provides the dimensions of each format measured in inches. In international versions of OneNote, dimensions are in metric units. See the "ISO Paper Sizes" sidebar for more information about metric paper sizes.

 TIP   OneNote will accept measurements in inches, centimeters (cm), and points (pt). You can set the preferred units of measurement in Tools ➤ Options ➤ Other. If measurements are entered in different units, the values will be converted to the preferred units after a brief delay.

Table 5-1. Page Size Options in the Page Setup Pane

Page Size Option	Width in Inches	Height in Inches
Auto	Grows toward the right depending on size of content	Grows toward bottom depending on size of content
Statement	5.5	8.5
Letter	8.5	11
Tabloid	11	17
Legal	8.5	14
A3	11.69	16.54
A4	8.27	11.69
A5	5.83	8.27
A6	4.13	5.83
B4	10.12	14.33
B5	6.93	9.85
B6	5.04	7.17
Postcard	3.94	5.83
Index Card	3	5
Billfold	3.75	6.75
Custom	Minimum 3, maximum 22	Minimum 1.25, maximum 22

CAUTION   You'll also see quite a few page size options available on the Print Preview and Settings dialog box. Those options relate to the size of the paper that might be in the printer. The Page Size parameter on the Page Setup pane just discussed controls the size of the *onscreen* page display. The page size values in the Print Preview and Settings menu control the size of the paper onto which the onscreen pages are printed.

Note that the Auto and Custom page size options aren't truly indefinite; the page can grow up to 22 inches wide × 22 inches high.

 TIP   Unless you have a strong, specific reason to change the paper size, it's best to stick to Auto. As I'll discuss in subsequent sections, OneNote is pretty smart about printing even variable-sized pages.

Bear in mind that you can use large paper sizes to do interesting things such as draw maps, floor plans, or flowcharts.

Other Parameters

The other parameters on the Page Setup pane are fairly straightforward.

There's a checkbox that allows the user to turn on or off ruled lines. This is independent of the control on the View menu that allows you to specify the type and width of rule lines. Regardless of what type rule lines you set on the View menu, you can turn them off on the Page Setup pane.

Additionally, you can switch page orientation from the Portrait to Landscape setting. These radio button choices are only available when the page size is set to a value other than Auto. With Auto, you can, in effect, force landscape mode by dragging content to the right past the default right margin.

You can also set the top, bottom, left, and right print margins. By default, the top and bottom margins are set at 1/2 inch, and the left and right margins are at 1 inch.

 CAUTION   Left and right margins are still at 1 inch even if you set the Page Size option to Index Card, which is 3 × 5. When selecting smaller page sizes, you may want to reset the left and right margins.

Finally, the Save Current Page As Stationery option sets the current page as stationery, which you can use to "jump start" new pages with predefined content from the current page. I'll discuss stationery in Chapter 6, "Customizing OneNote."

ISO Paper Sizes

If you acquire OneNote through an international distribution channel, OneNote will most likely be preset to print using A4 paper, in which case you can disregard the following discussion. Otherwise, this sidebar is relevant to you.

OneNote makes it look easy to use international paper sizes: Have you ever wondered whether there might be any practical advantages to using them?

If you're a typical American knowledge worker like me, you may have sailed blithely along noting, but not really understanding or questioning, the ubiquity of international paper sizes such as A4. Because one of the objectives of this book is to leave you with a deeper understanding of everything related to OneNote and note taking (both electronic and paper), the following is a brief detour to explain the inside story behind A4 and all those paper sizes that are a standard everywhere outside the United States, Canada, and a few Latin American and Caribbean nations.

The German standards organization DIN adopted the A, B, and C series paper formats in 1922, followed by many other nations over the years. The International Organization for Standardization (known everywhere by its language-independent faux acronym, ISO) adopted these formats as ISO 216 standard in 1975, and in the same year they were approved as the official United Nations document format.

Markus Kuhn's excellent Web site on international standard paper sizes[1] synopsizes the ISO 216 standard in the following lucid manner:

ISO 216 defines the A series of paper sizes as follows:

The height divided by the width of all formats is the square root of two (1.4142).

Format A0 has an area of one square meter.

Format A1 is A0 cut into two equal pieces, i.e. A1 is as high as A0 is wide, and A1 is half as wide as A0 is high.

All smaller A series formats [through A10] are defined in the same way by cutting the next larger format in the series parallel to its shorter side into two equal pieces.

---

1. http://www.cl.cam.ac.uk/~mgk25/iso-paper.html

He added the following in personal correspondence: "The B format has been chosen carefully such that you have the same scaling factor (sqrt(sqrt(2))) when you magnify from an A size to the next larger B size as you have when you magnify from a B size to the next larger A size. Similarly, the C sizes are halfway between the A sizes and their next larger B counterparts and used mostly for envelopes for A paper."

The crucial advantage of the ISO format is that because the aspect ratio is always based on the square root of 2, duplication and magnification are always easy because every size paper divides evenly into the next one. The same isn't true of North American standards, which use varying aspect ratios.

To make a long story short, the ISO 216 paper standard is infinitely more logical than the North American standard and is accepted in every major market except the United States and Canada. If your concern is personal productivity and efficiency—shouldn't you switch?

I must note as a negative that in most North American offices, you'd need to change the paper tray to print A4 paper. This is a huge disadvantage, unless you're in charge of your own printing equipment and paper. To outweigh this disadvantage, the advantages of ISO must be significant.

In the practical world of note taking, if you take notes on a piece of A4 paper, you can cut them in half and make them into A5 flash cards. That is somewhat useful if you're a student.

Another advantage is that A4 paper has about 3 percent more area than the U.S. letter standard. Using A4 rather than letter-sized paper, you have that much more room to prepare information for review at a glance. On the other hand, ISO's aspect ratio of 1.4142 may not be the best for diagramming and sketching; a paper shape closer to square might be better for those purposes. You may want, therefore, to consider whether your notes are primarily textual and list-like or are impressionistic and visual.

So far, the advantages identified don't seem significant enough to justify asking your boss to switch the company to A4 paper. Are there any scenarios where using ISO paper is a must?

If you're collaborating with colleagues overseas who will need to print information that you will share with them via e-mailed .ONE files, and the North American contingent is in the minority, it's clearly more considerate to use a paper format that's consistent with the majority's printer paper.

You'll find a brief discussion of customizing stationeries with ISO paper sizes in Chapter 7, "Integrating with Other Microsoft Tools."

Using the Print Preview and Settings

The command to open the Print Preview and Settings pane is located in the familiar location on the File menu (see Figure 5-5). You can use Alt+F+V as a keyboard shortcut.

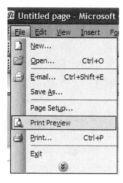

Figure 5-5. File ➤ Print Preview opens the Print Preview and Settings dialog box

Although the File menu only mentions Print Preview, the dialog box itself is Print Preview and Settings (see Figure 5-6). I saw only Print Preview and didn't notice for quite a while that there are some significant settings included.

NOTE   Note that the File menu is the only place where the Print Preview command is available. Preview *isn't* available as a "second thoughts" shortcut from the Print dialog box, as it is in some other applications.

Note that the Print Preview and Settings dialog box does a pretty fair job of rendering multimedia content, including ink, pasted Hypertext Markup Language (HTML), and images. Even if you've used the Zoom control on the Standard toolbar to shrink or enlarge the display view, the Print Preview and Settings dialog box will ignore those values as it prepares its display view, which is normally shrunk about 40–45 percent from actual size. There's no way to zoom in or out from inside the Print Preview and Settings window, but when you expand the Print Preview and Settings dialog box itself by dragging from the lower-right corner, the zoom level changes in sync.

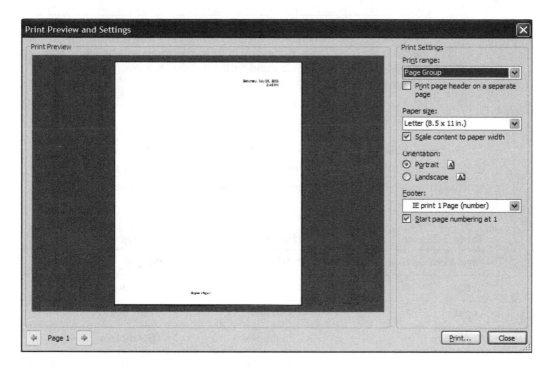

Figure 5-6. The Print Preview and Settings dialog box

The Print Range drop-down list lets you choose from three printing options: Page Group, Current Page, and Current Section. The order in which the options are presented is somewhat interesting in that it goes from broad to narrowest to broadest. Page Group, of course, includes the primary page and any number of subpages. Current Page is only one "logical" page, whether it's a primary or subpage. And the Current Section option could include any number of pages and page groups.

A checkbox, unchecked by default, allows you to specify that the page header should be printed on a separate page. Presumably, this feature is most relevant in situations when the header is large.

Even More Page Sizes

The Paper Sizes drop-down list on the Print Preview and Settings dialog box has even more options than the Page Setup pane. What's going on? You're pouring content *from* a set of pitchers *into* a set of cups. Generally speaking, the pitchers are bigger than the cups.

TIP   There are two kinds of page sizes. The Page Sizes control on the Page Setup pane controls the size of the *onscreen* page. The Page Sizes control in the Print Preview and Settings dialog box controls the size of the *printed* page.

Note in Table 5-2 that the drop-down list in the Print Preview and Settings dialog box describes a wider variety of types and sizes of output media. In other words, you have more cups to choose from than you have pitchers.

Table 5-2. Page Size Options in Print Preview and Settings Dialog Box

Page Size Option	Width	Height
Letter	8.5 inches	11 inches
Legal	8.5 inches	14 inches
Executive	7.25 inches	10.5 inches
A4	210 millimeters (mm)	297 mm
A5	148 mm	210 mm
B5	182 mm	257 mm
Index Card	3 inches	5 inches
Index Card	4 inches	6 inches
Index Card	5 inches	8 inches
Photo 4 x 6	4 inches	6 inches
A6 Card	105 mm	148.5 mm
No. 10 Envelope	4.12 inches	9.5 inches
A2 Envelope	4.37 inches	5.75 inches
C6 Envelope	114 mm	162 mm
DL Envelope	110 mm	220 mm
Banner [Letter]	8.5 inches	11 inches
Banner [A4]	210 mm	297 mm

Table 5-2. Page Size Options in Print Preview and Settings Dialog Box (Continued)

Page Size Option	Width	Height
Hagaki Card	100 mm	148 mm
Borderless Photo [with tab]	4 inches	6 inches
Borderless Photo	4 inches	6 inches
Borderless Hagaki Card	100 mm	148 mm
Borderless A6 Card	105	148.5 mm
User Defined Paper Size		

Hagaki Cards

For inquiring minds, a *Hagaki card* is a common Japanese postcard format. The Bank of Japan has a useful Web site that explains the interesting origin of the meaning of the word *Hagaki:*[2]

In Japan, the first paper money in recorded use was Yamada Hagaki, notes issued in the lse Yamada region circa 1600, somewhat predating the use of paper money in England. These notes were issued by the Yamada Oshi, who were priests at the famous lse Shinto Shrine. (An oshi *was a sort of intermediary who officiated in the addressing of people's prayers to deities and also acted as a merchant.)*

The note stated that it was exchangeable for silver coins. The word hagaki *is composed of the characters for* wing *and for* writing; *one theory holds that* wing writing *replaced the homophonous combination of characters used initially (*fraction writing, *meaning a slip of paper denoting a small amount) to emphasize the convenience with which paper money could be distributed, as if paper money had wings.*

The exchange of Hagaki cards with pictures printed on is a popular New Year's custom in Japan, similar to Christmas cards in the United States. OneNote's multimedia tools, direct layout control, and support for handwriting should make it a useful tool for homegrown desktop publishing of Hagaki cards.

---

2. http://www.imes.boj.or.jp/cm/english_htmls/feature_gra2-1.htm

Scale Content to Paper Width

The Scale Content to Paper Width setting is on by default. You want to leave it that way because in the Page Setup pane, the paper size is Auto by default, which means that it's fairly easy for you to create an onscreen page that's wider than your printer paper. So scaling the content means that no matter how big your onscreen page, the printout will be fitted onto one page.

 CAUTION   If the content onscreen is too big, you may have difficulty reading the scaled-down printout.

If you turn content scaling off on a page where the content on the display page is wider than the printed page, OneNote will break the display page into one or more rows of printed pages. Most people find this inconvenient because it means that sentences may be broken across two pages horizontally.

By default, the Portrait or Landscape setting on the Print Preview and Settings dialog box follows the value set in the Page Setup pane. Landscape display will print in landscape.

 TIP   You can sometimes fit overly wide content into a single printable page by switching from Portrait to Landscape mode. Of course, this decreases the vertical height of the printed page and may result in more pages being printed.

Smart Footer

You're automatically presented with four footer options:

- Print both section name and page number (the default)

- Print section name but not page number

- Print page number but not section name

- Print no footer

If you're printing for your own personal reference, I recommend you print the section name. Even though OneNote has good search tools (see Chapter 4, "Organizing Your Notes"), it's usually a nicer feeling to know where something is than to have to search for it. You may want to consider omitting the section name in situations where you're printing materials for others and don't want to confuse them with unnecessary detail.

Finally, you can select whether you want to restart page numbering at 1. This can be a useful option if the pages you're printing begin in the middle of a section and thus have numbers greater than 1.

 TIP   You can check the current page number by using View ➤ Show Titles in Page Tabs to turn off titles. They'll be replaced by page numbers. Alternatively, you can go to Page Setup, turn off the Restart Page Numbering option, select Print, and toggle the Page Range radio button to Selected Pages. The page number box on the Print dialog box will be populated with the page numbers of the current pages.

Now that I've covered all the options on the Print Preview and Settings page, it's time to get down to business and print!

No "OneNote Writer" in Version 1.0

One question that arose frequently during the OneNote beta was whether a "print-writing utility" would be available for OneNote version 1.0. The short answer is "no."

The reason why the concept kept coming up was that many users have had good experiences with print-writing utilities available for the Tablet PC for Windows Journal and for other applications such as Franklin Covey's TabletPlanner software. For those who haven't come across these utilities before, it's pretty simple to understand if you look at a sample Print dialog box on the Tablet PC that shows the Journal Note Writer.

You can select the print writer just as you would select any other printer. Of course, you must be within an application that can print. Instead of sending content to the printer, you are sending it to a file. In the case of Journal Note Writer, you're sending the content to a file in Journal's special file format (.JNT). You can open the file using Windows Journal.

The reason why this concept is so appealing for OneNote users is that it'd offer a convenient shortcut for getting content into OneNote in a high-fidelity mode. Reading an e-mail or Web page that you want to file away in your research notebook? Print to OneNote Writer. Using a specialized scientific application that's generating experimental data? Instead of printing to paper or a special file format, print to OneNote.

Microsoft heard a number of requests for this feature on news:microsoft.public.onenote (which the OneNote program managers monitored carefully during the beta) and is considering it for future versions of OneNote. No promises, but they heard you.

Using the Print Dialog Box

You can open the Print dialog box using the File menu or via Ctrl+P (see Figure 5-7).

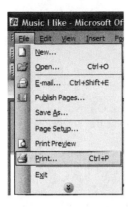

Figure 5-7. Selecting File ➤ Print

Most of the features in the Print dialog box are generic Windows printer features that don't have functionality specific to OneNote, so I'll touch on them rather lightly (see Figure 5-8).

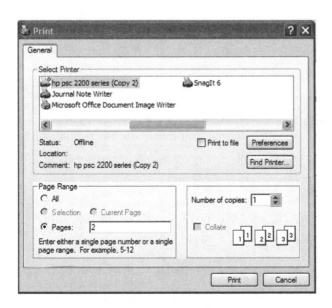

Figure 5-8. The Print dialog box

For more information about particular features, see your Windows Help Center or any good book about Windows.

Available printers are listed in the Select Printers area.

 TIP   If you're a Tablet PC user, you can print Microsoft OneNote content to Journal Note Writer. This way you can access the larger set of inking features available in Journal.

The printer status may be either Online or Offline. Since version 1.0 of OneNote doesn't allow you to embed "live" Office objects via Object Linking and Embedding (OLE) linking, being offline doesn't hurt your printing much. Whatever you print, whether you're online or offline, will be the latest version. If you've saved OneNote sections as remote links, they'll print as long as they're available in your local environment (see Figure 5-9).

Figure 5-9. A remote link

 CAUTION   Print to file prints in PostScript printer format, not .ONE. If you want to print to the .ONE format, you should use File ➤ Publish Pages.

The Preferences link takes you to a set of controls for the selected printer. These are printer specific and not directly related to OneNote.

 TIP   If you have a choice, a color printer will certainly enhance your experience with OneNote, especially considering its strengths in capturing HTML, images, and ink. Would you choose to use a black-and-white monitor?

The Page Range controls allow you to select some or all pages in the current section only. Unfortunately, you can't print more than one section at a time, and you can't issue a print command on a page list that results from a search (see Figure 5-10).

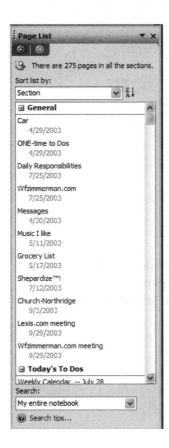

Figure 5-10. You can't print this directly.

Of course, there are a variety of ways you can print a portion of the screen, including the Alt+PrintScreen combination or an image capture utility such as Snag-It, described in Chapter 9, "Using OneNote with Other Applications."

 TIP You can bring together search results from multiple sections for printing by using the Create Summary Page option in the Note Flags Summary pane. (Figure 5-11 shows an example of something that might be useful to print.) This is all the more reason to add a lot of note flags as you take notes!

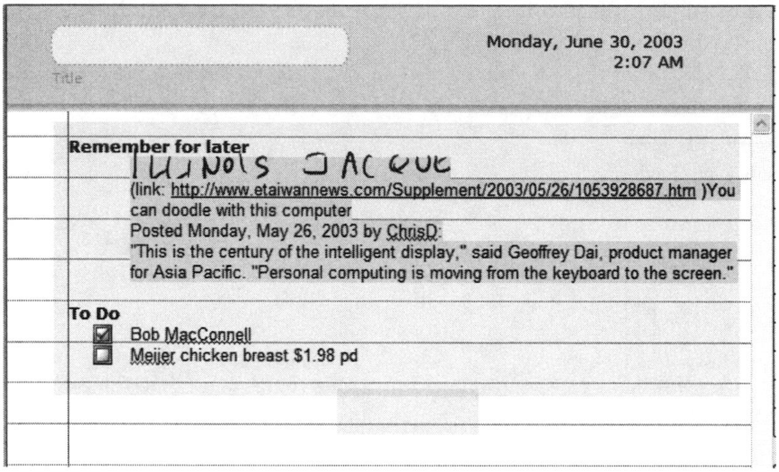

Figure 5-11. You can print this.

Finally, you can control the number of copies and whether they're collated. These features work exactly as they do in other applications.

During the beta, some users asked for various print features available in other Office applications:

- Thumbnail prints

- Printing styles

- Right-click printing of pages

- Printing multiple items without intervening page breaks

These features aren't available in the first version of OneNote.

E-Mailing .ONE Files

If you have Outlook 2003 installed on your PC, you can e-mail any selected page or pages in OneNote by clicking the e-mail button in the Standard toolbar, going to File ➤ E-Mail (see Figure 5-12), or using the keyboard shortcut Ctrl+Shift+E.

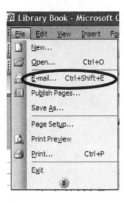

Figure 5-12. Sending e-mail

TIP   You can select more than one page before sending e-mail.

CAUTION   If you don't have Outlook 2003, you won't be able to send e-mail from OneNote.

An Outlook message header will appear above the selected page (see Figure 5-13).

The Outlook toolbar at the top of the message header is automatically set to Send a Copy—no other value is selectable, which tells you that you're sending a copy of the current page to the message recipients. Via other toolbar buttons, you can choose accounts, attach additional files, use the address book, set message importance, and select various other message options.

You then will see the blank To and Cc fields. The Subject field will be prepopulated with the title of the page, regardless whether View ➤ Titles in Page Tabs is turned on. The Attachment field will be prepopulated with a .ONE file that has the same name as the page title. You can attach additional files if you want. Note that by default linked audio files *aren't* attached, but you can change this default in Tools ➤ Options, as I'll discuss in Chapter 7, "Integrating with Other Microsoft Tools."

Figure 5-13. Outlook message header for mailed page

 NOTE The .ONE file attachment to be mailed is a newly created temporary file. Unless all the pages in the current section are selected, this .ONE file will be smaller than the .ONE file for the current section (which is normally stored in My Notebook). The .ONE file attachment to be mailed will *not* be found in My Notebook.

Finally, there's an Introduction field in which you can type a brief introductory message that will be inserted at the beginning of the e-mail when you send it.

TIP   *Always* put a quick comment here—such as *HTML e-mail below; let me know if you can't read it!*—unless you know for sure that your recipient(s) has HTML-capable e-mail clients *and* they have set HTML as their preferred view.

The body of the e-mail message contains an HTML representation of the selected OneNote page(s). The cool part is that multimedia content of the OneNote page—ink, pasted HTML, images, text—will display in the HTML e-mail message just as it appears in OneNote.

CAUTION   Obviously, the HTML e-mail will be difficult to read unless the recipient has an e-mail client that's capable of reading HTML *and* he has his client set to view HTML e-mail. Microsoft tends to gloss over the reality, which is that a vocal portion of the population simply doesn't like HTML e-mail and deliberately avoids it. Your only recourse is to know your audience. For example, you may want to be careful about using HTML e-mail when participating in mailing lists.

A text signature is appended to the end of the message:

Created with Microsoft Office OneNote 2003

One place for all your notes

You can modify this signature in Tools ➤ Options, and I'll discuss all the details in Chapter 7, "Integrating with Other Microsoft Tools."

Just to recap, you're sending two versions of the same content—both a OneNote .ONE attachment *and* the HTML body text. Unless you know that the recipient has OneNote, it might be worth explaining in the Introduction field that the content of the attachment is the same as the content of the message. Otherwise, your recipient may waste time clicking an attachment he can't open.

CAUTION   Also bear in mind when you send .ONE file attachments via e-mail that some virus-blocking programs will flag or sequester messages that contain attachments with unfamiliar extensions such as .ONE. (This is another one of those unfortunate realities that Microsoft tends to gloss over.) This may prevent your recipient from getting your message at all unless you first delete the attachment. Again, know your audience.

Once you've e-mailed your message, OneNote retains no visible record that you have e-mailed the page(s), and they look just the same as they did before you selected the File ➤ E-Mail option. The only way you can go back and verify what you mailed is to go into the Sent Items folder in Outlook.

TIP   If you want to send a complete OneNote folder or even an entire Notebook, there's nothing to stop you from compressing the files in your Windows directory and sending the Zip file as an attachment. The recipient would then uncompress the files and either move them into his My Notebook structure or use File ➤ Open to set up a remote link to the directory where he unzipped your files.

Troubleshooting

If you have trouble with using Outlook e-mail in OneNote, the first order of business is to determine whether you have a general problem with Office e-mail. You can test this by going into another Office application, such as Microsoft Word, selecting Send to Mail Recipient, and picking a recipient. If this doesn't work, then you have a problem with how your Office e-mail is configured.

If when you select File ➤ E-mail or hit the E-Mail button on the toolbar, you see this error message:

> *OneNote could not load the e-mail envelope. This could be caused by a network connection problem or a problem with your Office installation.*

The reason is that OneNote doesn't have enough information to create the e-mail envelope. This can occur in two situations: if you run OneNote before you've ever run Outlook (admittedly, a rare scenario) and if you have Outlook configured to run in cached mode.

In either case, there's a two-step workaround provided by Microsoft's Tom Oliver:

> *Run Outlook before OneNote and verify you have correctly connected to the server. If this does correct the problem, you may need to use the e-mail features in another Microsoft Office application before they work in OneNote.*

In other words, Outlook needs to "check in" with the e-mail server at least once before you launch e-mail from OneNote.

Receiving OneNote E-Mails

You'll be able to tell when you receive an e-mail from a OneNote user because the e-mail will probably have a .ONE attachment and a *Created with OneNote* signature at the bottom. Simply double-click the attachment to add the OneNote file to your Notebook. It'll be inserted in a special folder called *Notes E-Mailed to Me*. If you want to move it somewhere else, go right ahead! The section name (and filename) will be the same as the sender provided unless you change it, which you're free to do.

Exchanging OneNote Sections via E-Mail

Consider the following scenario: Your friend Al sends you a OneNote section (a .ONE file) called *Proposal_Ideas* (Proposal_Ideas.ONE) that he wants you to annotate and return.

You double-click the attachment and add it to your Notes E-Mailed to Me folder. The section name will be *Proposal_Ideas,* and the filename in the Notes E-Mailed to Me folder is Proposal_Ideas.ONE.

If you go ahead and make changes in Proposal_Ideas and send it back without changing the file name, when Al clicks the attachment it'll be added to *his* Notes E-mailed to Me folder.

NOTE   There are no version tracking or file merger features in version 1.0 of OneNote.

He'll have two sections, each called Proposal_Ideas, in different folders of his Notebook.

TIP   To avoid this possibly confusing scenario, I suggest you make a habit of updating filenames when you return modified sections—perhaps add your initials, so the section you send back is Proposal_Ideas_wfz.

Replying to OneNote HTML E-Mails

When you receive a OneNote page or pages with an HTML message body in an e-mail, you can simply reply to it as with any other e-mail.

There are a couple of points to remember. First, remember that you're answering e-mail using the e-mail editor, not using OneNote! E-mail editors have familiar limitations. Specifically, you won't be able to just drop onto the page surface and start typing or put the cursor anywhere you want to add an inline, or embedded, comment. Those are features of OneNote's unique writing surface and accordingly aren't available in the e-mail editor. OneNote constructs HTML e-mail when it sends by pasting together a mosaic of text, ink, images, and HTML (see Figure 5-14).

Easy to insert text here. ◀——————————

From: WFZ [mailto:wfz@wfzimmerman.com]
Sent: Monday, July 07, 2003 10:50 PM
To: 'wfz@wfzimmerman.com'
Subject: Music I like

  Music I like
Sunday, May 11, 2003
  12:51PM

Happy Go Lucky (a.k.a Night Train)
Oscar Peterson Trio
Night Train EASY TO INSERT TEXT HERE ◀——————————
Ellington

Pasted from http://www.accuradio.com/radioplayers/radioplayerie_Channel9_SubPrimary.asp??format=Channel9

Jump The Joint — *Eugene*
      Can't insert " *Hi cleaner* "

Figure 5-14. Replying to an HTML e-mail

It's easy to add comments at the top of the return e-mail. It's also easy to add inline comments in a reply where the original OneNote page had a text container. It's impossible to add inline comments in a reply (in HTML e-mail clients) by typing over the ink or images where the original OneNote page had containerized ink or images. Of course, the same is true if you put an image in a normal e-mail.

TIP If you're a Tablet PC user, you can print the e-mail message to Journal Note Writer and then scribble ink over the whole message with Olympian impartiality.

Sharing OneNote via the File System

Users who share local area or wide area network access to the same files can share—or, more precisely, rotate—access to OneNote .ONE files, which will be represented as remote links if the files aren't in the user's local My Notebook directory. This means it's quite feasible for a team to make a series of edits to documents in OneNote. One likely scenario would be a team editing or commenting upon multimedia notes taken by one member of the team.

 CAUTION There's no revision control or change tracking in version 1.0 of OneNote.

How OneNote Files Behave via the File System

OneNote files obey the same rules as most other application files in Windows; namely, only one person can have them open for write access at a given time. If you have the OneNote file open on a network, anyone else trying to open it will get a "file locked" message. Because this could be a pretty big inconvenience if someone leaves a file open overnight, OneNote intelligently releases the lock after five minutes (the default value, which can be customized; see Chapter 6, "Customizing OneNote").

Using Web Site Storage

Chris Pratley of Microsoft told beta users on news:microsoft.public.onenote about a nice trick: You can store OneNote files on third-party Web sites. The advantage is that you can always access the documents as long as you are connected to the Internet. This will work on MSN, on Web sites that support the Web-based Distributed Authoring and Versioning standard (WebDAV), and on your Web sites if you have file write privileges.

Go to File ➤ Save As and navigate to My Network Places in the bottom-left corner (see Figure 5-15).

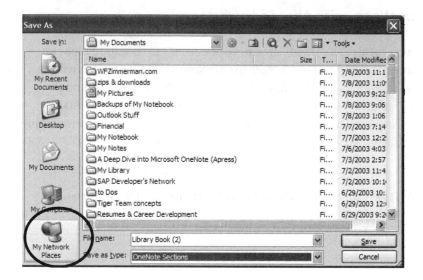

Figure 5-15. My Network Places

To save on MSN, choose My Web Sites on MSN (see Figure 5-16). Don't worry that you don't have one yet—actually, you do. You may be asked for a Microsoft Passport. Go ahead and provide your ID and password.

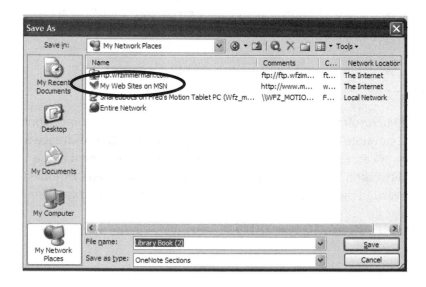

Figure 5-16. My Web Sites on MSN

Did you know that all Office users get some *free* storage on MSN? Well, you do. Open My Web Documents and save your OneNote section inside that folder (see Figure 5-17).

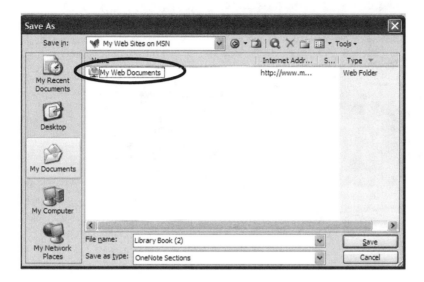

Figure 5-17. My Web Documents

The save will create a remote link from your notebook to the file stored on MSN.

From another machine (such as your home machine, if the first one was at work), you can now open the same file via My Network Places (don't navigate to the page in your browser and open that way—OneNote won't properly know about the file in that case). The beauty is that as long as you make all your changes to the file stored on the network, you can make the changes from anywhere and see them anywhere.

 TIP On MSN you can give other users rights to access documents in your free storage if you create a *group*. Be sure to add them as assistant managers or higher. This works best with small groups that are aware of each other's schedules. If two people open the same document on MSN (or any other simple Web storage service that doesn't offer file-locking features), the last one to save will overwrite the other one.

For those who may not be familiar with MSN (I wasn't!), you can also navigate to My Web Documents by going to http://www.msnusers.com/ (see Figure 5-18).

As long as you provide your Microsoft Passport information, you should be able to go seamlessly to this site from anywhere on the Web.

Figure 5-18. My Web Documents on `http://www.msnusers.com/`

Publishing OneNote Pages

You can publish selected OneNote pages to a local or wide area network location via File ➤ Publish Pages (see Figure 5-19). Remember, you can select one or more pages before invoking the Publish Pages command.

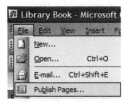

Figure 5-19. Selecting Publish Pages

There are two options under Publish Pages: Save As Single File Web Page and Save As OneNote Section.

Clearly, the most important decision you must make is whether to save as a single-file Web page or to save as OneNote section. I've already talked about saving files as OneNote sections. What does Microsoft mean by saving files as single-file Web pages? It turns out that it's talking about saving files in a particular format called MHTML (.MHT).

Introducing MHTML

MHTML (or .MHT) stands for *MIME-embedded Hypertext Markup Language.* (MIME stands for *Multipurpose Internet Mail Extensions,* and it's the leading standard that defines how e-mail programs should deal with multimedia objects such as images.) MHTML is a *proposed* standard, defined by a Request for Comment (RFC) organized by the Internet Engineering Task Force (IETF). RFC 2557, "MIME Encapsulation of Aggregate Documents, such as HTML (MHTML)," is the authoritative definition of MHTML.[3] One of the standard's authors, Jacob Palme, maintains a comprehensive Web site at http://www.dsv.su.se/jpalme/ietf/mhtml.html. According to Palme, RFC 2557 is still in predraft stage because although most vendors support MHTML as a standard for reading mail, only one vendor (Microsoft) fully supports sending mail in MHTML.[4] MHTML is basically a method for encapsulating all sorts of HTML objects within a simple nested structure inside a single Web page that's itself contained within a MIME e-mail.

---

3. ftp://ftp.ietf.org/rfc/rfc2557.txt

4. http://segate.sunet.se/cgi-bin/wa?A2=ind0211&L=mhtml&F=&S=&P=66

This usually works quite nicely in Internet Explorer; see, for example, the document in Figure 5-20 mostly composed of ink, which has been saved in the .MHT file as images.

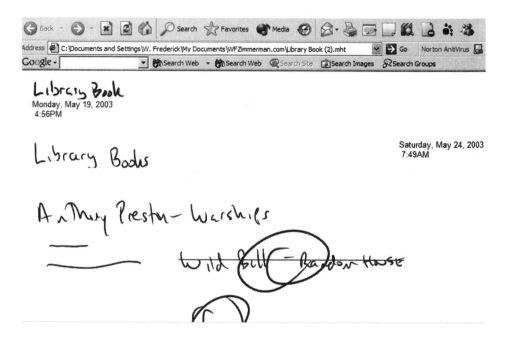

Figure 5-20. An .MHT document viewed in Internet Explorer

If you select View Source from within Internet Explorer, you'll see that the .MHT document looks just like an HTML document (see Listing 5-1).

Listing 5-1. Viewing the Source of an .MHT Document in Internet Explorer

```
<html xmlns:o="urn:schemas-microsoft-com:office:office"
xmlns:dt="uuid:C2F41010-65B3-11d1-A29F-00AA00C14882"
xmlns="http://www.w3.org/TR/REC-html40">

<head>
<meta http-equiv=Content-Type content="text/html; charset=utf-8">
<meta name=ProgId content=OneNote.File>
<meta name=Generator content="Microsoft OneNote 11">
<link id=Main-File rel=Main-File href="LibraryBook(2).htm">
<link rel=File-List href="LibraryBook(2)_files/filelist.xml">
</head>
```

```
<body lang=EN-US>

<div>

<p style='margin:0in;font-family:Arial;font-size:14.0pt;color:blue'><img
src="LibraryBook(2)_files/image001.gif" width=230 height=32></p>

<p style='margin:0in;font-family:Arial;font-size:10.0pt'><span
style='position:relative;left:.125in'>Monday, May 19, 2003</span></p>
...
```

 CAUTION Neither Opera nor Netscape can view .MHT documents properly. Although the text is readable, it's surrounded by technical mumbo-jumbo, and images and page layout are no longer visible. Users report inconsistent experiences with the America Online (AOL) browser (even though it's supposedly based on Internet Explorer)!

If you open the same document in Opera or Netscape, you'll see some quite different stuff at the beginning (see Listing 5-2).

Listing 5-2. Opening a .MHT Document in Opera

```
MIME-Version: 1.0 Content-Type: multipart/related; boundary="----
=_NextPart_000_0001_01C343D8.1B1DA370"; type="text/html" X-MimeOLE:
Produced By Microsoft MimeOLE V6.00.2800.1165 This is a multi-part
message in MIME format. ------
=_NextPart_000_0001_01C343D8.1B1DA370 Content-Type: text/html;
charset="iso-8859-1" Content-Transfer-Encoding: quoted-printable
=
=
= Page 1 of 20
=00 ------=_NextPart_000_0001_01C343D8.1B1DA370 Content-Type: image/jpeg Content-
Transfer-Encoding: base64 Content-ID: <000001c343f9$a2230e70$2415fea9@dns>
/9j/4AAQSkZJRgABAQEAYABgAAD/2wBDAAgGBgcGBQgHBwcJCQg
KDBQNDAsLDBkSEw8UHRofHh0a
HBwgJC4nICIsIxwcKDcpLDAxNDQ0Hyc5PTgyPC4zNDL/2wBDAQk
JCQwLDBgNDRgyIRwhMjIyMjIy
MjIyMjIyMjIyMjIyMjIyMjIyMjIyMjIyMjIyMjIyMjIyMjIyMjIyMjIyMjIyMj
L/wAARCAONAukDASIA
AhEBAxEB/8QAHwAAAQUBAQEBAQEAAAAAAAAAAECAwQFBgcI
CQoL/8QAtRAAAgEDAwIEAwUFBAQA ...
```

Whoops! As you can see, the MHTML contains all the image content in binary format. Internet Explorer is smart enough to parse it out into individual images. Opera isn't.

Understanding Issues Regarding Publishing via MHTML

As the preceding discussion suggests, the principal problem with MHTML is that not everyone supports it. That's unfortunate because it does quite a nice job. Although Microsoft does seem to be the leading believer in MHTML, it would be unfair to characterize it as a proprietary format. As far as I can tell, there are no "hooks" built in that would cause MHTML to lock customers into Microsoft products. Microsoft simply has had more vision than other vendors in understanding that the need for a "high production value" data format that allows users to save complex multimedia HTML objects in a clean, readable way.

No Direct Import or Export of Files in Version 1.0

Bad news! This first version of OneNote doesn't provide any mechanisms for exporting files in any formats other than MHTML and .ONE. And it doesn't provide any mechanism for importing files in other formats. The only way you can get data into OneNote is by the "manual" mechanisms discussed in Chapters 4 and 5—drag and drop, paste, and so on.

The good news is that Word, Excel, and PowerPoint can open .MHT documents.

Introducing OneNoteBlogger

As an example of the power of MHTML, take a look at OneNoteBlogger at `http://www.wfzimmerman.com/onenoteblog/OneNoteBlogger.mht`; this is a simple demonstration of using MHTML to publish OneNote pages as a *blog* (see Figure 5-21).

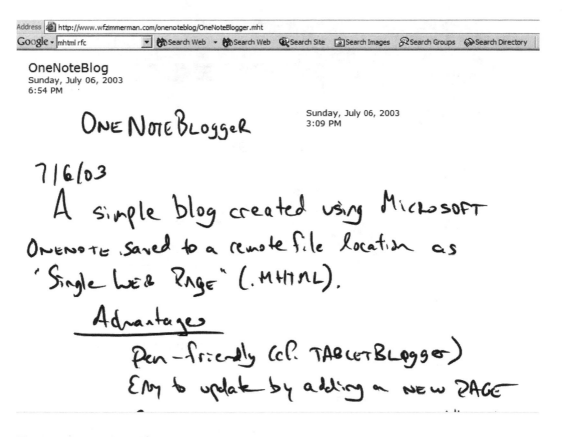

Figure 5-21. OneNoteBlogger

I simply saved this file to the File Transfer Protocol (FTP) server on my Web site via the File Name box in the Save As dialog box (see Figure 5-22).

If you have a password-protected network file storage location, you can do the same.

 CAUTION If you use remote locations to store OneNote files in your OneNote Notebook, be aware that OneNote will try to connect to those files when starting up or doing operations (such as search) that span the entire Notebook. This can be annoying if you're working offline. The workaround is to store these files somewhere outside of your Notebook.

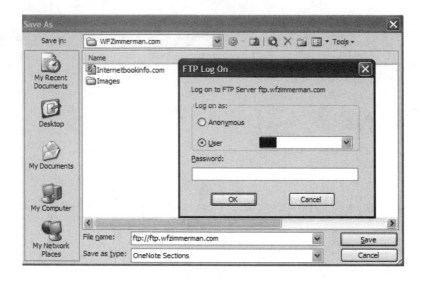

Figure 5-22. Saving to FTP

I won't pretend that OneNote is in any way a mature blogging tool, but there are some interesting advantages:

- For Tablet PC users, it's pen-friendly.

- It provides a multimedia blogging tool that takes advantage of OneNote's direct layout on the page surface.

- It's easy to update—just add a new page.

On the negative side, as I already noted, not all browsers read MHTML. Another minor nit from experience is that the near-standard Apache Web server requires that the administrator add a special directive (DirectoryIndex) before Apache will serve up an .MHT file as the index to a directory. That is necessary if you want to use a page exported from OneNote as an index page to your Web site (as I did with OneNoteInfoCenter.com)!

Summary

This chapter covered the following:

- Stick with the print defaults unless you have reason to disturb them.

- Notice that the Print Preview command opens the Print Preview and Settings dialog box.

- When you e-mail .ONE files, remember that the recipient must have OneNote to be able to use the attachment.

- You can save OneNote sections to network locations and edit them there.

- You can't import or export files directly in version 1.0, but Word, Excel, and PowerPoint can read MHTML exports.

- The Save As Single File Web Page command refers to saving the data in the MHTML format.

- You need Internet Explorer to view .MHT files.

As promised, the next chapter shows how to customize OneNote to your satisfaction.

Customizing OneNote

Now that you've familiarized yourself with the basic operation of OneNote, it's time to customize it to suit your needs more exactly.

Working with Options

The primary way you can accomplish customization in OneNote is through the Tools ➤ Options command (see Figure 6-1).

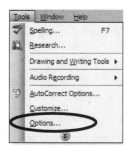

Figure 6-1. Selecting Tools ➤ Options

When you select Tools ➤ Options, the Options dialog box opens and presents a categorized list of options you can set (see Figure 6-2).

If you click a category in the left pane, you'll be taken to a page of controls corresponding to that category.

NOTE   Some of the controls displayed for particular categories will depend upon your current hardware configuration. Generally speaking, if you don't have it, you can't see it, and you can't change it.

In the following sections, I'll explore each set of controls, explain their purpose, and provide the rationale for recommended settings.

Figure 6-2. Navigating to Display and other categories in the Options window

Setting the Display Options

OneNote provides good support for left-handed users by allowing them to put the vertical scroll bar and the page tab bar on the left. I should note that you don't need to be left-handed to prefer the page tab bar on the left; I put it there for a while because I thought the right side of the page was too crowded with the task pane. Figure 6-3 shows the options to accomplish this.

TIP   If you have a Tablet PC, its handedness controls (see Figure 6-4) *don't* override or affect the OneNote settings in Tools ➤ Options.

If you have a Tablet PC, I suggest you leave Create All New Pages with Rule Lines in the Display options set to the default, which is on. During the beta test, some users expressed that they had difficulty writing between the ruled lines of the page. If it's difficult to write a straight line *with* rules, it's going to be even harder without them! Also, as I'll discuss later in this chapter in the "Setting the Handwriting Options" section, writing on the baseline makes handwriting recognition work much better.

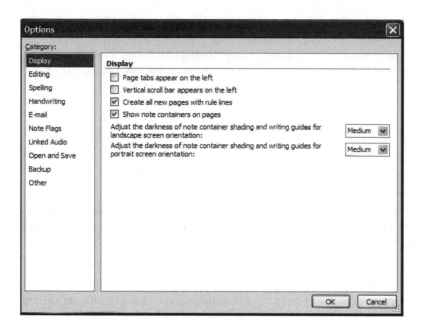

Figure 6-3. The Display window

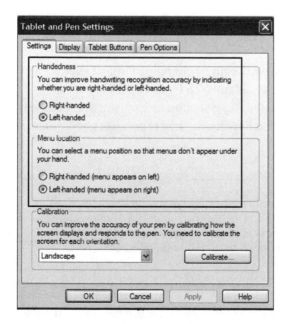

Figure 6-4. Selecting Control Panel ➤ Tablet and Pen Settings

CAUTION The Create All New Pages with Rule Lines doesn't apply to pages created with stationery, except for the Blank Page stationery. Otherwise, the "ruledness" of stationery overrides this setting.

I recommend you leave Show Note Containers on Pages set to on, at least during the early stages of your experience with OneNote. During the beta test, one of the most common roadblocks encountered was a failure to understand the nature of containers, which are fundamental to OneNote. You're likely to be better off with the relatively unobtrusive container boxes on so that you can see what OneNote is actually doing. I suggest turning off Show Note Containers on Pages if you really like a clean page *and* you understand what OneNote is doing "behind the scenes" with containers or if you're a flexible soul who doesn't mind a few moments where you're not quite sure why the program is doing what it's doing.

The question of how dark your note containers and writing guides should be follows a similar logic. If you want them more visible, set the drop-down lists to Dark or Darkest. If you want them to be unobtrusive, set the drop-down lists to Lighter or Lightest.

Setting the Editing Options

In the Editing window, I recommend you begin by changing Empty Deleted Pages Folder on OneNote Exit to off; it's on by default (see Figure 6-5). The reason is simple. If you leave pages in your Deleted Pages section on exit, you may be able to retrieve them later. If you empty the section on exit, they're gone for good—at least as far as OneNote is concerned.

TIP You may be able to restore otherwise permanently deleted pages by consulting either your OneNote backup folder (I'll discuss later in this chapter) or your backups of your Windows file system (if you're prudent and scrupulous enough to maintain regular backups).

When Empty Deleted Pages Folder on OneNote Exit is unchecked, you have the option to check the box that allows you to permanently delete pages after *n* days. The default value, 365, may be a bit excessive. Ninety days, or even 30, is probably long enough to realize that you made a mistake by deleting a particular page. Remember that this value only applies to restoring intentionally deleted pages; there's nothing to stop you from saving regular OneNote pages and sections forever.

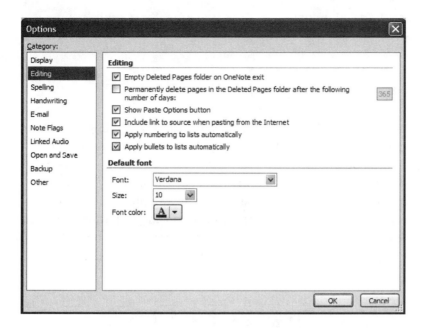

Figure 6-5. The Editing window

The Show Paste Options Button option is a necessity, at least in this version of OneNote with its rather limited capabilities for What You See Is What You Get (WYSIWYG) pasting of Hypertext Markup Language (HTML). You need to be able to select Paste As Picture as you paste in that information from a Web page. Leave this option checked unless you have an unusual work setting where you paste only a single type of content and always want it to be formatted in the same way.

The Include Link to Source When Pasting from the Internet option should be left on, unless you're engaged in a substantial cut and paste project where you don't want the links to show up. (Remember, you can always delete the links manually.)

You should leave the Apply Numbering to Lists Automatically and Apply Bullets to Lists Automatically on unless you find the features annoying.

You should leave the default font in 10-point Verdana unless you have strong stylistic or usability preferences otherwise. Remember that usability testing consistently shows that sans serif fonts are more readable and that 10–11 point fonts are the most readable.

TIP   Two lines of 10-point Verdana match one line of college-ruled paper on the OneNote screen, without text printing over lines.

The use of color fonts should depend mostly on your readability and printing concerns.

Setting the Spelling Options

The spelling controls in OneNote function much the same as spelling controls in other applications (see Figure 6-6). The only OneNote-specific issue raised by these controls—as opposed to general issues about spell checking—is whether you want to have your on-screen display made that much busier by showing squiggly red underlines beneath questioned words. If your preference is to take your notes down "fast and dirty" and you're not worried about sharing them, you can change the Hide Spelling Errors from the default off to the less obnoxious on. If you don't mind a few extra squiggles in the service of increased quality, leave it off.

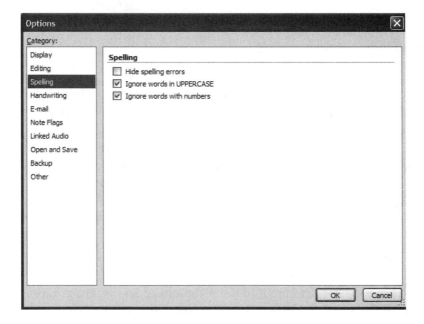

Figure 6-6. The Spelling window

Given the note-taking focus of this program, the default setting to turn off spell checking in words in uppercase is probably correct. Many people use uppercase for emphasis when taking notes. You're not likely to spell words such as *IMPORTANT* and *ON EXAM* wrong! The other classic reason to turn off spell checking for words in uppercase is that too many acronyms appear as questioned words. If you're working in an ACronym-Rich ENvironment (ACREN), such as corporations, the military, or the government, leave the Ignore Words in Uppercase option on.

The spell checker does seem to do pretty well in recognizing appropriate capitalization for common proper nouns such as PowerPoint and JavaScript. Naturally, it tends to do better with Microsoft terms and a little less well with newly coined terminology.

> **TIP** Turn the Ignore Words in Uppercase option off if you're working in an acronym-deprived environment *and* you frequently share your notes with others.

The same logic applies to turning off spell checking for words with numbers. The spell checker will have a tough time with words that contain numbers. If you don't have a compelling reason to examine them with this imperfect tool, leave them alone!

Setting the Handwriting Options

The handwriting controls are of the most relevance to Tablet PC users (see Figure 6-7). Pen pressure sensitivity is essentially a good thing; it's a feature of the Tablet PC platform that distinguishes it from other types of pen-enabled devices.

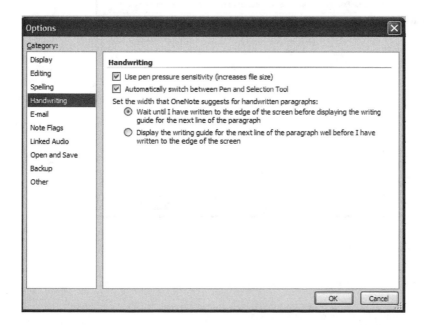

Figure 6-7. The Handwriting window

The Automatically Switch Between Pen and Selection Tool option is a user convenience, as Tom Oliver of Microsoft explained in the beta newsgroup:

> *It means that when you switch to a new device it should automatically switch into the "natural" mode for that device. So if you've been using a pen in Pen Mode, then move the mouse, we'll switch you into mouse mode.*[1]

If your note-taking style causes you to write a lot of short lines, you may find that OneNote isn't ready to start a new line as soon as you are. If you want the writing guide to appear more quickly, switch the option value to Display the Writing Guide...Well Before I Have Written to the End of the Screen.

Setting the E-Mail Options

You can customize certain settings related to how OneNote handles e-mail (see Figure 6-8).

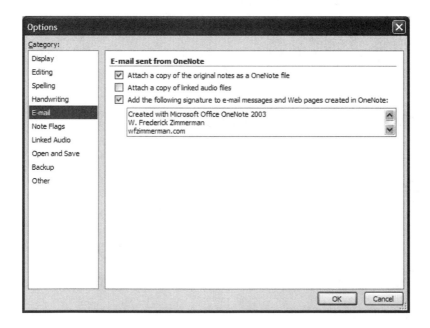

Figure 6-8. The E-Mail window

---

1. News:microsoft.beta.o11ep.onenote, message
    news:<#Os7RcxSDHA.1128@CPMSBNEWSW01.betanews.com>

As discussed in Chapter 5, "Sharing Your Joy," the default setting to attach a .ONE file with every e-mail may be a little premature. The reality with version 1.0 of any product that introduces a new file format is that unless you already know that many of your recipients have the correct program to read it, you might save some bandwidth by setting this switch to off and mailing only MIME-embedded Hypertext Markup Language (MHTML) in the message body. You should leave the switch on if you know that you'll be mailing notes to others in an enterprise who also have OneNote installed or if you know that you'll be mailing notes mostly to other electronic note-taking enthusiasts who have OneNote.

CAUTION   Another reason to turn this off is that both enterprises and individuals react with suspicion to files that have unfamiliar extensions, such as .ONE. When I first started sending .ONE files to friends who didn't have OneNote, some of them asked if I was sending a virus! Similarly, many corporate firewalls automatically screen or segregate messages with unfamiliar attachments.

TIP   You can verify for yourself whether security concerns are necessary in the case of OneNote. You can search the various databases maintained by the CERT Coordination Center for references to OneNote. None were mentioned during the beta, but it was available to the public for several months.[2] You can also check the Microsoft HotFix & Security Bulletin Service and search by product.[3] Remember to search for both OneNote and Office 2003.

The option to add linked audio files to e-mail by default is an interesting one that calls for some consideration of your user scenario. First, consider bandwidth. Audio recordings generated in OneNote (or any other program) can take up considerable space, and most recipient e-mail systems have some sort of limit somewhere between 1MB and 5MB. Some people start getting annoyed if you send attachments larger than 500KB.

---

2. http://www.cert.org

3. http://www.microsoft.com/technet/treeview/default.asp?url=/technet/security/current.asp

TIP Always look at the file sizes before you hit Send on a message with automatically added attachments. If the attachments are too big, you can easily delete them.

If you're a student who routinely shares lecture notes, and your lecture room audio recordings are of acceptable quality, why not share the audio with your friends? The same applies for users who take notes during professional meetings. Sharing audio files can be invaluable if it allows understanding of nuance and "who said what."

CAUTION Just remember, everything said in your vicinity is going out as part of the audio file!

Although I sometimes take a dim view of Microsoft "boosterism," the signature block at the bottom of the E-Mail window is actually pretty useful because many recipients won't recognize this odd-looking message body. I recommend you leave the signature block on until OneNote is more widely known.

Unfortunately, there are a couple of gotchas. This is the only signature block you're going to get in your OneNote e-mail. Your own default e-mail signatures established in Microsoft Outlook aren't available when you e-mail from OneNote. (Of course, you can always e-mail from OneNote to yourself, then add your own signature before you forward to the ultimate recipient.) So you'll want to make sure that your OneNote signature block contains a concise version of your usual signature. I say *concise* because you're limited to five lines and you can't apply formatting to the signature.

CAUTION Signature text *isn't* hyperlinked when the recipient views it in e-mail, even if the text is an `http://` expression (see Figure 6-9).

Figure 6-9. Signature text isn't hyperlinked in OneNote e-mail.

You can't paste images or ink into your signature (nice try!), but if you try pasting ink into the signature box, you'll notice an interesting wrinkle. OneNote will automatically insert the equivalent text, based on its application of Tablet PC's handwriting recognition algorithms. OneNote just inserts its highest-confidence translation of your handwriting; it doesn't allow you to use Tablet PC's correction procedures.

Setting the Note Flags Options

As discussed in Chapter 4, "Organizing Your Notes," note flags are small symbols that you can attach to note containers to help you keep yourself organized. You can sort notes flags in the Note Flags Summary pane. The Note Flags window allows you to control some aspects of how note flags behave (see Figure 6-10).

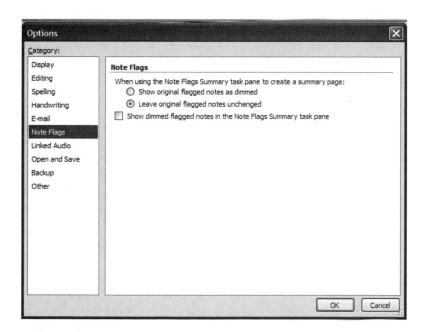

Figure 6-10. The Note Flags window

The note flag options are available to deal with a classic problem in recursive logic. Imagine the following scenario: In section A of your Notebook, you have three pages, A1, A2, and A3. Page A1 has a note with the To Do flag. Page A2 has a note with the Definition flag. Page A3 has two notes with the To Do flag. You use the Note Flags Summary pane to find all the note flags in the current section. A total of four notes are displayed in the Note Flags Summary pane (see Figure 6-11).

Figure 6-11. Section A has four note flags.

Now you use Create Summary Page in the Note Flags Summary pane to create a new page, A4, in that same section. Page A4 has four flags on it now (see Figure 6-12).

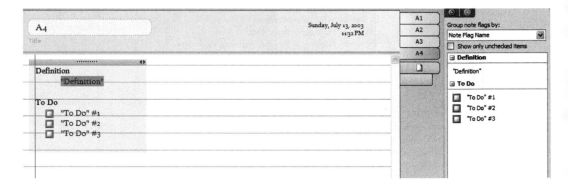

Figure 6-12. A summary page with four note flags

Does section A have a total of eight flags or four? Justify your response, citing relevant authorities (in the words of your favorite teacher in high school…). When the program displays eight flags for Section A, the result looks, frankly, stupid (see Figure 6-13).

If you keep creating summary pages in a section, you wind up with a recursive absurdity where successive summary pages must include flags that exist only in other summary pages (see Figure 6-14).

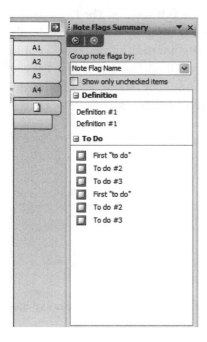

Figure 6-13. Redundant flags listed

Figure 6-14. A recursive absurdity

Note in Figure 6-14 that the original flags, the source of the flags listed in the summary, are dimmed out so that you know you should now use the summary page as the main place to interact with note flags in this section. The Options ➤ Note Flags window allows you to control whether the original flagged notes should be dimmed (I recommend turning this on) and whether the dimmed notes should be displayed in the Note Flags Summary pane (avoid this). Having original flagged notes dimmed makes it easier to realize that you should be paying attention to the notes on your new summary pages. Displaying dimmed notes in the Note Flags Summary pane simply adds unnecessary clutter.

TIP   Try to keep to one summary page per section.

Setting the Linked Audio Options

The Linked Audio window is available to control the behavior of particular aspects of OneNote's audio recording features (see Figure 6-15).

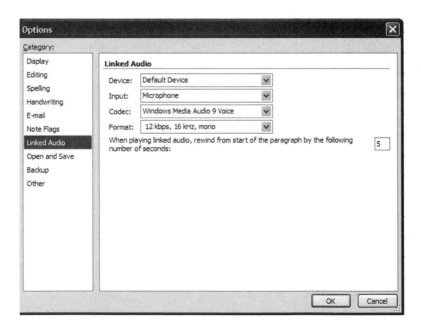

Figure 6-15. The Linked Audio window

The first drop-down list, Device, in the Linked Audio window is hardware driven. If you have additional sound recording hardware attached to your system, you'll see it listed in the drop-down menu. If you have an external microphone, make sure to select it here. Otherwise, you can simply ignore this drop-down list and stick with Default Device.

The second drop-down list, Input, lists all the possible ways sound could come into OneNote. With modern computers, there are quite a few sound input possibilities, as shown in Figure 6-16.

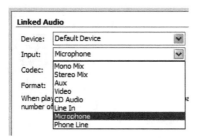

Figure 6-16. The Input drop-down list

Microphones aren't the only way you can get sound into OneNote. If you have a PC that can play streaming audio or CD sound via its monoaural or stereo speakers, you can also pipe that sound into OneNote and link it to your notes. Figure 6-17 shows the streaming of audio from a CD of the Kettering Children's Choir into OneNote.

This opens all sorts of silly opportunities for enhancing your notes. When you're taking notes on a particularly bombastic speaker, why not link his comments with an audio clip from the "Ride of the Valkyries" song?

TIP   If you listen to music while you take notes or review them online, you can link your background music to your notes. The association with favorite music may help you remember the material.

Note also that you can set the Input Device option to Phone Line. This can be handy, especially if you have a handset splitter so you can run the phone line to the handset as well as your PC's phone input jack.

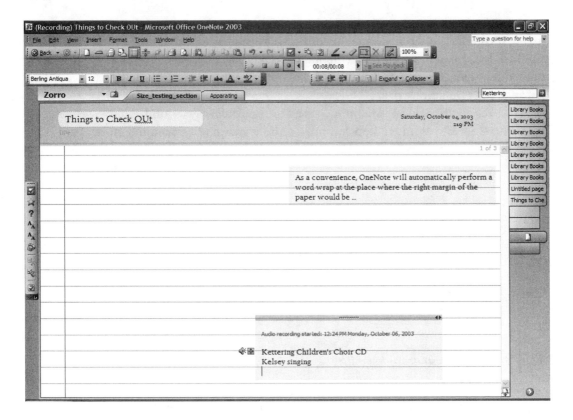

Figure 6-17. Sound from a CD linked to notes

It's quite conceivable that a user might want to use more than one audio input option in a single OneNote session. For example, you might want to use the external microphone to record one of your own comments and then go back to recording streaming audio as you take Web research notes. In such a scenario, the Input drop-down list really ought to be visible on a main menu as well as in the Linked Audio window. Maybe in a future release of OneNote!

A *codec* is simply a recipe or program instructing the computer how to play a media clip. OneNote supports whatever codecs you have installed. My machine, for example, supports four Windows Media Audio codecs, plus an industry standard, Acelp.net, which is well regarded for its sound quality at low bandwidth and, significantly, is supported by both Windows Media Player and the RealPlayer from RealNetworks.

OneNote also supports a variety of audio formats, defined in terms of kilobits per second (kbps) and sampling rate expressed in frequency in kilohertz (kHz). As a rough rule of thumb, the higher the rate in kilobits, the better the sound quality and the larger the file size required. The same is true of sampling rate. The values supported on my system (without an external microphone) range from 4kpbs at

8kHz to 20kbps at 22kHz. As a point of reference, these aren't CD quality because that isn't necessary for voice recordings. If you choose Windows Media Audio Professional for your machine, you'll have additional CD-quality choices.

You should leave the option for rewinding a few seconds before playback set to a nonzero number. Five seconds is a reasonable value, but you can tweak it if you want. Microsoft's Chris Pratley explains, "It's adjustable because different people have different reaction times before they start to write or type a new item."

Setting the Open and Save Options

Reviewing and saving notes is, of course, a critical activity for the OneNote user, and there are several options you can set (see Figure 6-18).

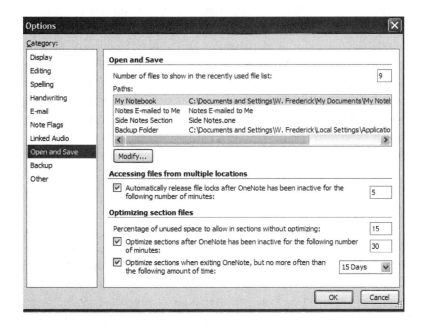

Figure 6-18. The Open and Save window

I like to have the number of files in the recently saved files list set to 9. My attitude is "the more, the better." Why test your memory?

The paths listed in the Open and Save window are all set to reasonable defaults. You should make sure you know where your backups are being stored and that they're in an area of your PC that you're backing up. I've always had a terrible time finding files in that Application Data directory, but it's not a bad thing that your backup files are in a different location than your main working files.

TIP Microsoft's Chris Pratley says, "If you have a second hard drive, or a second machine [available over a local area network], it's a good idea to point the backup there in case your hard drive goes south."

If you accidentally "scrunge" the files in My Documents, the backup files in Application Data will be safe.

You should leave the option for the delayed release of file locks when OneNote is inactive checked if you plan to use OneNote in multiple locations or to share a file with others on your network. If file lock release is unchecked, you run the risk of being unable to access your OneNote file at all if someone else has left it open.

The Optimizing Section Files for OneNote are all preset to on by Microsoft; you should leave them as is, unless for some reason you like having suboptimal, larger than usual files. You should leave the percentage of unused space at 15. If you change the delay before optimizing option to, say, 5 minutes, you run the risk of optimizing a page to which you were about to add a bunch of content.

The only reason to worry about optimizing when exiting OneNote is that it may slow down the exit process, especially in periods when you accumulate lots of new notes. This may seem like a trivial concern, but if you're exiting OneNote so you can shut down your laptop and hurry to your next class or meeting, you don't want to have to wait even a few additional seconds during exit. This is actually a nice example of Microsoft's tight focus on the note-taking user scenario. Well done!

Setting the Backup Options

Every computer user and note taker should have some investment in controlling the way his system does backups because it's, as Windows likes to say, a "fatal error" to trust the system to do everything for you. The Backup window allows you to control some aspects of how OneNote does backups (see Figure 6-19).

You should certainly leave the automatic backup setting checked—but how often should you back up, and how many copies should you keep? The answer to the first question is that you should back up every time you take enough notes so that it would be painful to lose them. If you have meetings or classes every day, do a backup every day. If you have important meetings all the time or you really can't afford to lose any notes, you can back up as frequently as every minute. If you only use OneNote once a week for a particular class, you might be able to get by with weekly backups. But I really wouldn't recommend it. As soon as you start backing up once a week, you're going to have a crash and lose six days of notes!

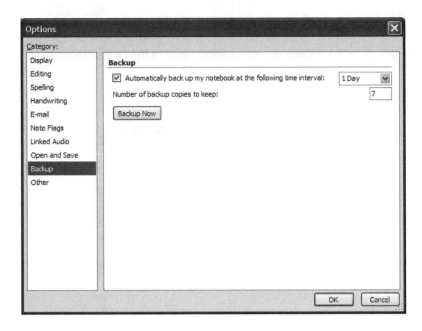

Figure 6-19. The Backup window

So the question really is, How many sets of backups should you keep? The answer to this question requires a bit of "back-of-the-envelope" calculation. Every time OneNote does a backup, it makes a copy of the entire My Notebook folder and all its contents. If you have extensive notes or considerable multimedia content, this can be a pretty large folder. Let's say you have 100MB of notes and you save 99 days of backups. That's 9.9GB, which, even with today's large hard disks, is a fair amount of storage. As the late Sen. Everett Dirksen of Illinois was famous for saying, "A billion here, a billion there…pretty soon you're talking real money."

I suggest using a combination of automatic and human action. Set the Number of Backup Copies to Keep to something reasonable—5, 10, or 30, depending on the size of your Notebook folder and your available hard disk space. But supplement the automatic backup with a human backup. Every so often, make a manual copy of your My Notebook folder and stash it somewhere safe—ideally, on a CD.

If you're comfortable backing up less frequently than once a day, the numbers work better. If you back up once a week and save 13 copies, all of a sudden you've got backups that cover your work over a period of three months. The downside, of course, is that the gaps are bigger, and if you have a problem, you're going to lose more of your interim work.

Setting the Other Options

Options that don't quite fit into any other category reside in the Other window (see Figure 6-20).

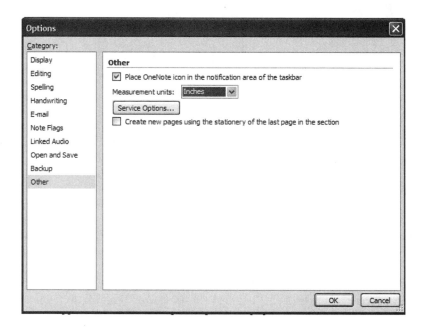

Figure 6-20. The Other window

You should leave the OneNote icon visible in the notification area of the task bar so that you can right-click it to quickly launch Side Notes *or* start recording audio (see Figure 6-21).

Figure 6-21. Right-click OneNote in the notification area

The downside is that the notification area can get pretty crowded. But if you don't use OneNote spontaneously, you're undercutting one of its chief benefits.

In typical Microsoft style, you can choose from a profusion of measurement units—inches, centimeters, millimeters, points, and picas. As an FYI, points and picas are often used in publishing and may be a good choice if you see OneNote as a desktop publishing tool.

The Service Options button is a poorly designed bit of User Interface (UI) because underneath that cryptic label there are in fact three completely unrelated options, none of which are really guessable based on the label *Service Options* (see Figure 6-22).

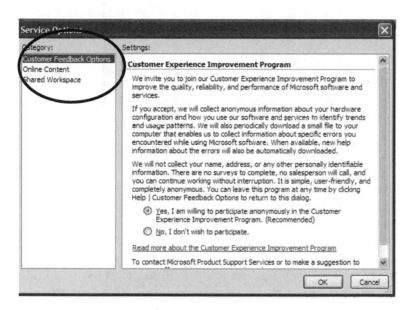

Figure 6-22. Underneath the Service Options button

Your decision whether to participate in the Customer Experience Improvement Program depends on how much you trust Microsoft and want to help it make better software. There's no known technical downside.

The Online Content Settings options give you the chance to opt out of Microsoft Office Online services, which is checked by default (see Figure 6-23).

I recommend you leave these checked because Microsoft Office 2003 has an increasingly significant proportion of its help and other resources available online at Microsoft. If you turn these services off, you may not get as much help as you're expecting!

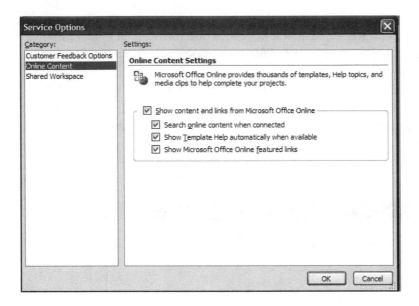

Figure 6-23. The Online Content Settings options

I'll discuss the Shared Workspace options in greater detail in Chapter 7, "Integrating with Other Microsoft Tools," when I discuss SharePoint services (see Figure 6-24).

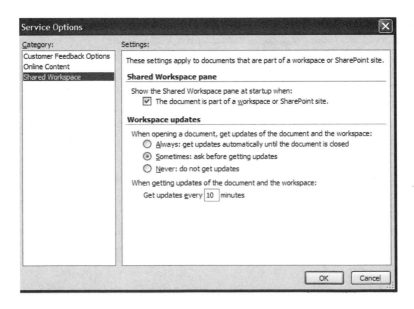

Figure 6-24. The Shared Workspace options

For now, I'll simply point out that the default value Sometimes: Ask Before Getting Updates gives the worst of both worlds: Your workflow is interrupted, and you don't get an automatic update. I recommend switching it to either an automatic update or no update.

Returning to the top level of the Other window, the last item on the page is a gem (see Figure 6-25).

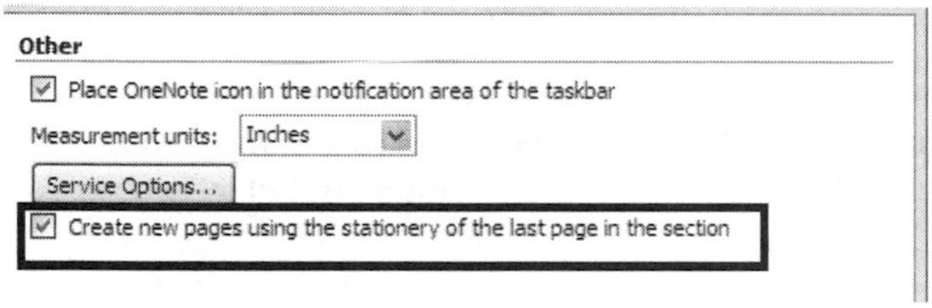

Figure 6-25. Turn this switch on!

By all means, override the default and check the Create New Pages Using the Stationery of the Last Page in the Section box. That's almost always what I want to do when I create new pages.

Now that I've discussed the Tools ➤ Options settings, this is probably a good time to remind you that you can always change them back to the defaults.

Restoring Your Defaults, the Easy Way

In the event you need to restore your option settings to their default values, you can follow two procedures. This method is very simple and low-tech. It involves going into the Options dialog box and resetting the boxes to the appropriate values. The figures in the preceding section provide you with the default values. All you need to do is check or uncheck the appropriate boxes.

Restoring Your Defaults, the Hard Way

The other method for restoring your option settings is high-tech and very risky because it involves modifying a value in your system registry. The consequences of improperly modifying your system registry can be anything up to complete system failure.

CAUTION   The consequences of improperly modifying your system registry can be anything up to complete system failure.

Before you even look at your system registry, you should do the following:

- Establish a new System Restore point by navigating to Start ➤ All Programs ➤ Accessories ➤ System Tools ➤ System Restore.

- Back up crucial data using the Windows Backup Utility or another backup tool. At a minimum, back up all users' personal files and settings. (Your colleagues won't love you if you back up your own data but fail to back up theirs.)

When you look at your registry, I recommend you use the Registry Editor, which you can invoke by entering *REGEDIT.EXE* at the Start ➤ Run prompt.

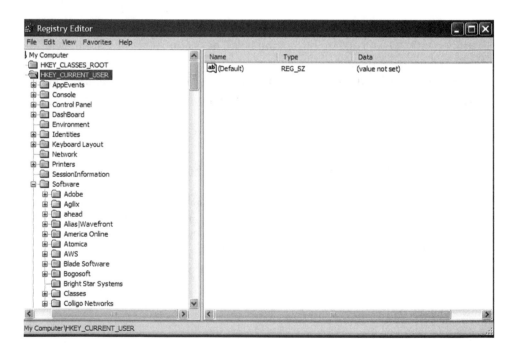

CAUTION   The Registry Editor writes changes immediately. In other words, *there's no Undo command.*

The registry is a database that's organized around five *root keys*, which have many subordinate subkeys and values. All the subkeys and values associated with a single root key are called a *hive*. (I'm not making this up.) The root key you care about for this purpose is officially called *HKey_Current_User* but is often called *HKCU* for short. (You're going to change a single subkey underneath the HKCU root key.)

Before you make any changes, back up the HKCU root key and its associated hive. To do this, select the HKCU root key and then open the menu File ➤ Export. In the Save As dialog box, choose Registry Hive Files. This is your backup. If you need to restore it, you can go to File ➤ Import and select the backup file.

Now you need navigate down the hierarchy to the key HKEY_CURRENT_USER ➤ Software ➤ Microsoft ➤ Office ➤ 11.0 ➤ OneNote, which appears as a folder in the Registry Editor display. Underneath this folder you'll see three other folders that correspond to settings you can change in the OneNote Tools ➤ Options dialog box. This is where OneNote looks to find your latest option settings. If there's nothing there, it'll use the default settings. So what you need to do now is rename the OneNote folder to something else—say, *OneNote_old*.

Okay, you've done it! Now take a deep breath and exit the Registry Editor. Don't go there again unless you really, really know what you're doing.

Now you have some simple things to do in the regular Windows file system.

Do you want to keep your old Notebook folders, sections, and pages handy? If you do, skip to the next paragraph. If you don't, you need to rename the My Notebook folder to something else (*My Old Notebook Files* will do). OneNote, finding My Notebook missing, will create a new folder.

 TIP Your old Notebook files aren't really gone. From within OneNote, you can open them in the renamed folder.

Now go to My Computer ➤ Local Disk ➤ Documents and Settings ➤ *[your user name]* ➤ Application Data ➤ Microsoft ➤ OneNote. In this folder there will be two files named *Preferences.dat* and *toolbars.dat*. Make backup copies of them (just in case), and then delete them.

When you start OneNote again, the system will run through a brief reinstallation process. If you did a complete install and saved the installation files (as recommended in Chapter 4, "Organizing Your Notes"), you won't need your CD. (If you did anything else, you may need your installation CD and, of course, the infamous product key.) When the OneNote screen comes up, your options will be back to their original, default values.

Customizing Your Toolbars and Menus

OneNote enjoys the same high degree of customizability as the rest of Office 2003. Besides customizing the default settings, you can customize the toolbars and menus in OneNote. Under Tools ➤ Customize, you can customize the appearance of toolbars and menus (see Figure 6-26).

Figure 6-26. Selecting Tools ➤ Customize

Although in Word you can customize keyboard shortcuts via Tools ➤ Customize, that isn't the case in OneNote; you can't customize keyboard shortcuts in this first release.

Using the Toolbars Tab to Customize

There are three tabs in the Customize dialog box: Toolbars, Commands, and Options (see Figure 6-27).

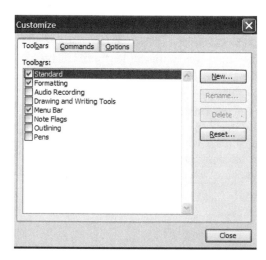

Figure 6-27. Three tabs in the Customize dialog box

Buttons on a OneNote toolbar can be shown or hidden by clicking the downward-pointing triangle on the far right (or bottom) of the toolbar (see Figure 6-28) and then selecting Add or Remove Buttons (see Figure 6-29).

Figure 6-28. Controls to move or customize toolbars

Figure 6-29. The Add or Remove Buttons command

You can also select whether you want the toolbar to take up one line or two lines of the OneNote screen. I recommend using the Show Buttons on One Row setting unless you're operating on a portrait mode screen for a Tablet PC. Over time, buttons that you don't use will migrate toward the right so that they'll be the first to drop out of sight if you have a constrained screen size.

Display of each toolbar in OneNote can be turned on and off by navigating to View ➤ Toolbars and checking or unchecking the appropriate controls (see Figure 6-30).

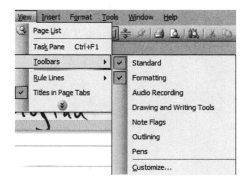

Figure 6-30. Selecting View ➤ Toolbars

Selecting View ➤ Toolbars ➤ Customize takes you to the Customize dialog box that you can reach via the first tab on Tools ➤ Customize (refer to Figure 6-27). By default, the Standard and Formatting toolbars are on. In some Microsoft applications, such as Word, there are so many toolbars that you should keep most of them off; otherwise they'd chew up all the real estate at the top of your screen. In OneNote, there are only eight: Standard, Formatting, Audio Recording, Drawing and Writing Tools, Menu Bar, Note Flags, Outlining, and Pens. For this reason, I recommend you turn on Note Flags and Outlining. You don't necessarily need to turn on the Audio Recording toolbar because the Start/Stop Recording button is in the Standard toolbar, and clicking that button opens the Audio Recording toolbar. And if you're not going to do any recording, why bother? However, I like to keep the Audio Recording toolbar on to give my eyes a bigger target to remind me of this useful functionality. If you're a Tablet PC user or have another pen input device, you should also turn on the Drawing and Writing Tools and Pens toolbar.

TIP   If you're going to turn on any one toolbar, make it Note Flags. The Note Flags Summary pane is only useful if you get in the regular habit of adding note flags to your notes as you go along, and the toolbar can only help with that.

Using the Commands Tab to Customize

If you're not happy with the predefined toolbars, you can customize them on the Commands tab in Tools ➤ Customize. You can also reach this tab by navigating from the downward triangle on the far right of each toolbar to Add or Remove Buttons and onto the submenu where Customize is listed as the last option (see Figure 6-31).

Figure 6-31. Customizing a toolbar

TIP If you're a visually oriented, twiddling type of person, you can bypass many of the customization menu commands by simply pressing the Alt key, pointing at the control you want to move (for example, the Research icon), and dragging it to the menu or toolbar where you think it belongs.

The Commands tab contains a hierarchical listing of most (but not all) of OneNote's commands (see Figure 6-32).

Figure 6-32. The Commands tab

In the left pane are categories corresponding to the major menu commands (File, Edit, View...) in the same order as those commands appear on the top menu bar.

The content of the right pane depends on the category selected in the left pane. You can rearrange the contents of the menu using the Rearrange Commands button. This is the place to go if you've decided that you don't like the order in which commands are presented on a particular menu, for example, if you think it makes more sense for Insert New Folder to appear above Insert New Section (the default is the reverse). To accomplish the switch, simply click Rearrange Commands and then select Insert for the Menu Bar option (see Figure 6-33).

Figure 6-33. Rearranging the Insert menu item

Then click New Folder and then Move Up, and—*voilà!*—your Insert menu is customized in the manner that you prefer (see Figure 6-34).

Figure 6-34. A customized Insert menu

The Modify Selection button gives you great—indeed, perhaps rather excessive—control over the objects on the menus and toolbars (see Figure 6-35). Presumably, this is available as a shared feature in Office 2003. This degree of control is, frankly, not essential for OneNote users who are using their version 1.0 product—but you've got it anyway, so you might as well know what's there.

Figure 6-35. Underneath the Modify Selection command

After clicking Modify Selection, you can perform a variety of operations on the selected menu item. You can delete it or reset it to its default value. You can rename it, which may be useful to help you remember important distinctions. For example, I renamed my E-Mail command to Send MHTML E-Mail to remind myself of the format in which my outgoing mail will be delivered.

If I'm not enamored with the button image next to the menu command (see Figure 6-36), I can copy a different image and use it instead (see Figure 6-37).

Figure 6-36. Default button image

Figure 6-37. Replacing the button image

As you can see, I chose to replace the rather boring e-mail icon with a more dynamic running figure. I even used the Button Editor to add a halo over the runner's head and to change the color of the "speed lines" to the rear (see Figure 6-38).

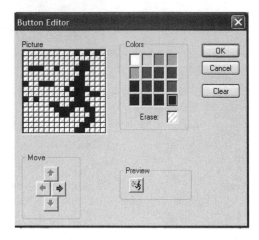

Figure 6-38. The superpowerful Button Editor

The next group of commands on the Modify Selection submenu allows you to determine whether the menu command should display in text only, in image only, in text and image or simply accept OneNote's default. Personally, I always like to display both text and image because the visual cue helps me navigate more quickly.

You can also determine whether this command should begin a group—in other words, you can determine whether there should there be a horizontal rule immediately before this menu item to provide spacing from other menu items.

The last command on the Modify Selection submenu is the Assign Hyperlink command, which allows you to assign an arbitrary hyperlink, or Uniform Resource Locator (URL), that *replaces* the command on the menu (see Figure 6-39).

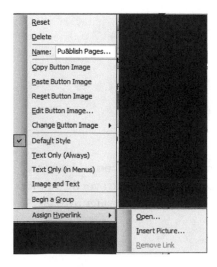

Figure 6-39. The Assign Hyperlink command

Don't use this unless you know what you're doing. This is a power user or enterprise customization feature that requires you to have significant programming skill and control over a Web server.

Using the Options Tab to Customize

The Options tab in the Customize dialog box allows you to set your preferences for certain global behaviors of menus and toolbars (see Figure 6-40).

Figure 6-40. The Options tab

I recommend you accept the default and show the Standard and Formatting toolbars on one row, unless you're viewing in portrait mode where it may be difficult.

I recommend you check the box for Always Show Full Menus, unless you like hitting the little button to expand what may seem like arbitrarily shortened menus. A Microsoft spokesman pointed out that the menus are shortened to reflect commands that users commonly use "hardly arbitrarily." Unfortunately, if a user's profile diverges from the norm and a command that she needs isn't readily visible, it's likely to seem arbitrary *to her*.

You should use the Reset Menu and Toolbar Usage Data button judiciously because when you reset this, you lose the system's accumulated knowledge about which commands you use most frequently.

The Large Icons checkbox makes the icons really large (see Figure 6-41). I recommend against turning this on, unless necessary for visual reasons.

Figure 6-41. Large icons take up a lot of screen space.

I recommend keeping the rest of the default settings on the Options tab. Why wouldn't you want to see fonts as they'll appear? Why would you want to hide ScreenTips and shortcut keys? My advice is to give yourself every advantage.

Using Stationery

OneNote allows you to create *stationery* so that you can create new pages that come pre-equipped with images and text. The concept of "stationery" is familiar in other Office applications such as Word and Outlook, but in those settings stationery is primarily concerned with the "look and feel" of the page. Stationery is more powerful in OneNote. Templates in other Office applications also prepopulate structure and initial content so that you can carry out common tasks, such as constructing a contemporary memo or a résumé. You can do the same thing with stationery in OneNote, as I'll demonstrate in this section.

I had a difficult time when I first tried to create stationery because I couldn't find the link. I was looking for the word *Stationery*, and I should have been looking for *New*. You navigate to File ➤ New, and the New panel appears in the task pane (by default, on the right side of the screen).

TIP   If you create stationery only infrequently, you may want to customize your menu using Tools ➤ Customize ➤ Commands ➤ Rearrange ➤ Modify Selection (as discussed earlier in this chapter). I added a duplicate New command to my File menu and then renamed the second New command to *Stationery* (see Figure 6-42).

Once you've made your way to the New pane, you'll see that about half the pane is taken up by a window containing stationery options. Note that my window shows the following categories: My Stationery, Tablet PC Portrait, Tablet PC Landscape, Planners, Decorative, Business, Blank, and Academic (see Figure 6-43).

Figure 6-42. Adding a custom Stationery command to your File menu

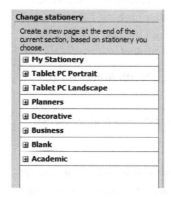

Figure 6-43. Available categories of stationery

It would be a nice amenity if a future version of OneNote included the number of stationeries in the category in parentheses, as in Planner (3), so that you could quickly assess the categories that are the most promising. For now, though, in version 1.0 of OneNote, you need to click the plus signs to see the stationery choices that are available by default. So that you won't need to click through every item, Table 6-1 summarizes them.

Table 6-1. Summary of Stationery Categories

Category	Items	Comments
My Stationery	0	Empty by default.
Tablet PC Portrait	4	For Tablet PC users in portrait mode. Two meeting and two lecture stationeries.
Tablet PC Landscape	4	For Tablet PC users in landscape mode. Two meeting and two lecture stationeries.
Planners	3	Simple, Prioritized, and Project To Do lists. Note that there's no integration with Microsoft Project in this first release of OneNote.
Decorative	32	A rather excessive profusion of designs characterized by soft, semitransparent, pastel shapes. Where are the duck hunting and sailing ship stationeries from the Cards from Guys to Guys section of the Hallmark store?
Business	8	The design is a little more sober. Some of the meeting outlines actually add some useful structure. I liked the thoroughness of the Project Overview section, which encourages discussion about a number of important issues that are easily overlooked by busy teams, for example, the ultimate goal of project.
Blank	13	Includes all the most common North American and metric paper sizes.
Academic	6	Four kinds of lecture stationeries plus Math/Science and History. The History Notes stationery takes a refreshing counter-Reformation approach to historiography by providing an Important Dates field. Hasn't anyone told Microsoft that history isn't about memorizing dates anymore? The general concern about these stationeries for academic users is whether the target audience is organized enough to use them. Studies of student computer use in classrooms have found that when possible, e-mail and Web surfing are popular applications. What I want to know is where to find the stationery called *Writing a Letter to Your Girlfriend While Pretending to Pay Attention in Class?*

Once you select a stationery and click the link, the page to the left is immediately populated with the design you've chosen. Note that you can rapidly cycle through possible designs by clicking stationery links, but each time you do so, you create a new page. There's no way to apply a different stationery to the current page once one has been applied.

Saving the Current Page As Stationery

This is the most powerful stationery feature in OneNote. If you find yourself repeatedly taking notes on a certain type of meeting or activity, why not create a custom stationery that will speed up and standardize your future efforts? As discussed in Chapter 5, "Sharing Your Joy," decades of research on putting quality into processes suggests that it's far more cost-efficient to build quality in at the beginning of a process than to add it at the end. Once you've got a good page design, navigate to File ➤ New and then select Save Current Page As Stationery at the bottom of the pane. The resulting stationery will be added to the list under My Stationery.

A few wrinkles to note:

- Stationeries *aren't* read-only. You can type over, move, change, or delete the container content in any stationery.

- You can save audio links as part of a stationery. The links will go to the original audio file. This means you can save that useful Klaxon sound as part of a template. "Study! Study! Study!"

- New stationeries are displayed in the order they're created, not in alphabetical order or anything else.

- If you create a stationery with the same name as one of your previous ones, OneNote will ask you if you want to overwrite.

- Microsoft-provided stationeries are stored in a set of .ONE files in Program Files\Microsoft Office\Templates\1033\ONENOTE\Stationery.

- Your own stationeries are stored in your user profile under Documents and Settings ➤ Username ➤Application Data ➤ Microsoft ➤ Templates as a file called *My Stationeries.ONE*. If you try to open this file where it sits, you'll get an error message that My Stationeries is already open. If you copy the file and move it outside of the Templates folder, you can edit it directly in OneNote and then move it back to replace My Stationeries.ONE.

In the next section, you'll look at a sample OneNote stationery, inspired by Bill Gates himself.

Using the BillG OneNote Stationery

Microsoft employee Rob Howard used his blog to narrate an interesting account of a meeting with Bill Gates (BillG). Among a number of interesting details, Howard provided a glimpse at BillG's note-taking strategy.[4] The blog is quoted in some detail here because there's a fair chance that anyone who buys a book about Microsoft OneNote is interested enough in how meetings work to enjoy reading a first-person account of a BillG meeting:

> *Last Wednesday at 9:30 a.m. we had our caching task force BillG review. I came into work at my normal time that morning, about 7:30 a.m., and did the usual e-mail/spec. update/bug review/forum work. At 9:00 a.m. I decided that although I'm not presenting, it probably wouldn't be a bad idea to print out copies of my caching-related specs. I didn't think I'd need them, but you never know. At 9:10 I headed out to the meeting....*

> *At 9:35, a few more people show up. A few seconds later, BillG walks in the room; minutes later, Jim Alchin and Paul Flessner join us, too. I watch a couple other folks from the caching task force somewhat nervously introduce themselves—and notice that BillG kind of smiles/smirks with a couple of the more nervous exchanges, the kind of smirk you give someone when you can tell they are nervous, but there isn't a reason to be. Either way, it's both intimidating and exhilarating to sit in the room with BillG.*

> *The first thing I notice as the meeting starts is that BillG is left-handed. He also didn't bring a computer in with him but instead is taking notes on a yellow pad of paper. I had heard this before—BillG takes amazingly detailed notes during meetings. I imagine he has to, given all the information directed at him. The other thing I noticed during the course of the meeting is how he takes his notes. He doesn't take notes from top to bottom, but rather logically divides the page into quadrants, each reserved for a different thought. For example, it appeared that all his questions were placed at the bottom of the page.*

> *...The BillG review was like a feature team meeting: filled with debate, ideas, changes, etc. but at a slightly higher level!*

The following are comments posted to Rob Howard's blog:

> *Wow. Mr. Gates takes notes like I do. I use three sections (notes on what was said, notes on what I think about what was said, and questions).*
> *—posted at 10:18 a.m. April 28, 2003*

---

4. http://dotnetweblogs.com/rhoward/posts/6128.aspx#comment

So much for Microsoft OneNote, ehh?! —posted at 6:43 a.m. May 11, 2003

Inspired by this example, I created the BillG OneNote stationery, shown in Figure 6-44.

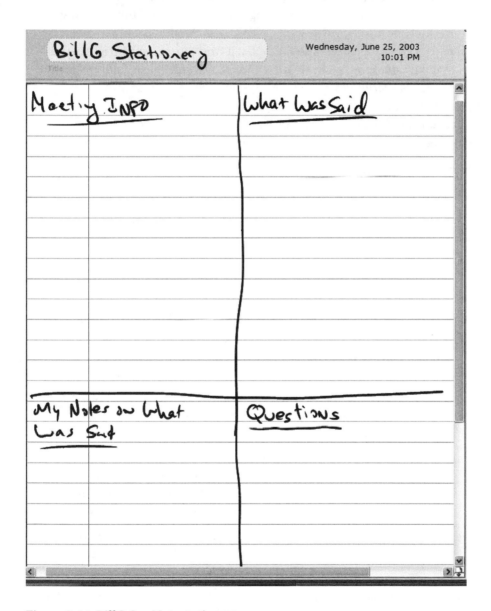

Figure 6-44. BillG OneNote stationery

An electronic version of this and other stationeries I've created are available at http://www.wfzimmerman.com/index.php?topic=OneNoteInfoCenter.

Entering Run Switches

The final mode of customization I'll discuss in this chapter is entering startup *switches* via the Run command on the Windows Start menu.

As discussed in Chapter 4, "Organizing Your Notes," one of the many ways you can start OneNote is to type the word *ONENOTE* at the Run prompt. You can add switches to this startup command that will tell OneNote to start up in a certain mode or condition. You type the word *ONENOTE*, then a space, followed by the switch, which is a *forward* slash (/), followed immediately by a word or string. For example, to open a new Side Note, you'd enter *ONENOTE /sidenote* at the Run prompt. Table 6-2 describes the switches available in OneNote.

Table 6-2. Switches Available in OneNote

Command with Switch	Function	Comments
ONENOTE /side	Opens a Side Note window	You can use this switch to create a shortcut that launches a Side Note from the Desktop. Or you can launch a Side Note from the system tray with a click.
ONENOTE /new *filename*	Opens a new section	Puts the new section in the currently active folder of My Notebook and calls it *New Section 1* (*not* the filename). You can omit the *filename* parameter.
ONENOTE / newfromexisting filename folder	Copies the file specified by filename into a new folder and opens the file there	Set up a "clean" version of a file in a new folder.
ONENOTE /openro	Opens the file in read-only mode	Perhaps most useful as a shortcut alias (see the following Tip) if you need to ensure that notes borrowed from a colleague, say, are treated as read-only.
ONENOTE /print *filename*	Prints the OneNote section named	Use judiciously because *all* pages in the section, however numerous or lengthy, will be sent to the printer.
ONENOTE /audio	Starts recording on the page you most recently accessed	Not a bad way to surreptitiously start recording a conversation.

Table 6-2. Switches Available in OneNote (Continued)

Command with Switch	Function	Comments
ONENOTE /newtaskpane	Opens the New task pane	Useful if you're frequently creating new sections that you share with colleagues or if you need to select a different stationery every time you open the program.
ONENOTE /paste	Pastes the content of the Clipboard	*Doesn't* provide access to the 24 entries on the Office Clipboard. May be worth a try if you're having difficulty pasting unusual or large material. Also useful if you're in the midst of using another program and want to transfer some data into a new OneNote session.
ONENOTE / launchtraininghelp	Launches a training program on the Microsoft Office Web site	You must be connected to the Internet for this to work.
ONENOTE /forcerepair *filename*	Forces OneNote to run repair routine on fully qualified filename	You can achieve the same effect by trying to open a damaged file from within OneNote. This switch is worth a shot if that doesn't work.

TIP   You can create a Desktop shortcut to any of these commands with switches by right-clicking anywhere on the Desktop, selecting New ➤ Shortcut, and entering the *full* path to OneNote in the Browse box. Whereas the abbreviated path (ONENOTE) will work from the Run box, it *won't* work in a shortcut. The default path to OneNote is C:\Program Files\Microsoft Office\OFFICE11\OneNote.exe or C:\Program Files\Microsoft Office\Office 2003\OneNote.exe, where C: is the hard drive where Office 2003 is stored.

Summary

This chapter covered the following:

- Keep the figures in this chapter handy so you can restore your OneNote defaults without using the Registry Editor.

- Turn *off* the e-mail option that automatically sends .ONE files as an attachment when you send e-mail unless you know that most of your recipients will be running OneNote. Otherwise, you may run into problems with corporate antiviral software and firewalls.

- Remember that you can use Linked Audio window to pipe audio from your system speaker(s) or a CD into OneNote. The opportunities for musical commentary are endless.

- Use Tools ➤ Customize ➤ Commands ➤ Rearrange Commands ➤ Modify Selection to change the name of any menu commands you find difficult to remember and locate.

- Check out `http://www.wfzimmerman.com/index.php?topic=OneNoteInfoCenter` for an archive of user-created stationeries.

- Create desktop shortcuts to the executable with a command line switch (for example, *ONENOTE\Full\Path /switch*) to "hard-wire" behaviors that you want to require every time.

In Chapter 7, "Integrating with Other Microsoft Tools," I'll discuss integration between OneNote and the rest of Microsoft Office 2003.

Integration with Other Microsoft Tools

AS DISCUSSED PREVIOUSLY, OneNote is part of the Microsoft Office 2003 family, which itself is part of a much broader constellation of Microsoft software tools. The integration of OneNote with programs that reside outside the "four corners" of the OneNote user interface will be of great interest to many OneNote users, since most people who use OneNote rely heavily on Office 2003 and other Microsoft applications.

I must warn you, though, to set your expectations on the cautious side. The reality is that, as for the first version of any software product, top priority is usually accorded to core OneNote functionality. By the same token, other product teams usually don't regard support for new products as *their* top priority. So while a lot of integration works in the first version of OneNote, there are also quite a few holes to be filled in later!

In this chapter, I'll discuss several modes of integration. First, I'll talk about hyperlinking to and from OneNote within Windows. Then I'll show you how OneNote interacts with shared services in Microsoft Office such as Object Linking and Embedding (OLE), the Research pane, and SharePoint. Having cleared away the shared services,I'll then cover some details about getting information from OneNote into other Office 2003 programs, such as Outlook. Finally, you'll see how to work with Microsoft software that has no explicit connections to OneNote, but that nevertheless may be of interest to OneNote users, such as the Pocket PC operating system (now officially known as Windows Mobile 2003).

Linking from OneNote to Documents in the Windows File System

The easiest way to bring documents residing in your local Windows file system into OneNote is to drag them into the current OneNote window. A copy of the file will be created in the same directory as your OneNote section and a "file:" hyperlink will be added for you. This technique works for any type of document. See for example Figure 7-1, where I create an external link to both a Microsoft Word document (.DOC) and an Adobe Reader document (.PDF).

CAUTION   When you click a link, the file type must be registered with Windows in Control Panel ➤ Folder Options ➤ File Types, or else you'll get an error message. This problem, which I encounter only occasionally, is a function of the Windows file system, not OneNote.

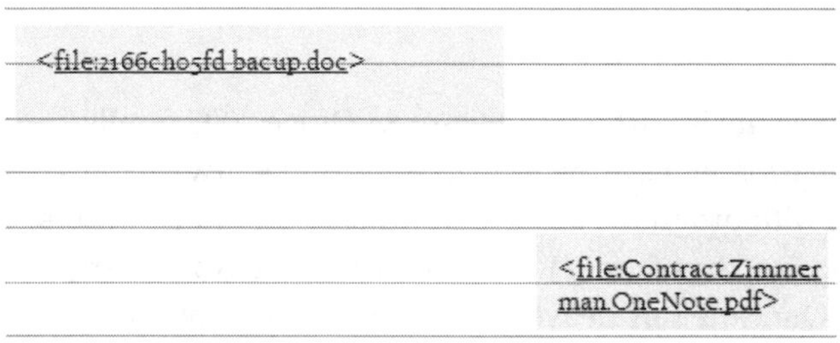

<file:2166cho5fd bacup.doc>

<file:Contract Zimmer
man OneNote.pdf>

Figure 7-1. External links

You can create an external file: link to a .MHT file that originated in OneNote's Publish Pages or Save As commands, but the .MHT file will no longer be readable by OneNote. Instead it will be opened in Internet Explorer. On the other hand, if you create an external link to a .ONE file, and then open it by clicking the link, it will appear as part of your Notebook in OneNote.

These behaviors are normal in Windows—the files are being opened by the application registered to the extension. What is mildly inconvenient in this first release is that OneNote can export files, but then is unable to import those same files.

Warning Messages

When you click a file: link, such as the one shown in Figure 7-2, to a document in your Windows file system whose file type isn't registered, a warning message like the one in Figure 7-3 will appear.

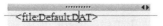

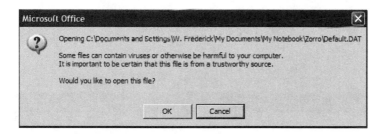

Figure 7-2. File: links are Uniform Resource Locators (URLs) that go to documents in your Windows file system.

Figure 7-3. Unregistered file type

This warning message is issued by design—it isn't a bug. The concern is to prevent end users from inadvertently triggering viruses or other harmful software. Unfortunately, it doesn't make much sense to issue this particular warning only when going to file: documents of unregistered type. It would make more sense to issue this warning whenever a hyperlink (whether of type http://, type outlook:, or type file:) goes to a URL that ends in a suspect executable extension.

"Apparating" Inside OneNote

OneNote provides instantaneous shortcuts that bring to mind the world of Harry Potter, in which wizards can appear instantaneously in a new location by *apparating*.

You *can* create a file: type link from within OneNote to another OneNote section through at least two methods.

First, you can simply type **file:sectionname.one** on the current OneNote page. A hyperlink to that section will be created in the OneNote page, and you can click it to go straight to the location you mentioned. This is very useful as a quick reference tool. For example, I might write "play back exact words in file:interviews.one" as a reminder to myself to go to the Interviews folder and play back an audio interview.

Second, you can go to the My Notebook directory and drag a OneNote .ONE file into the open target page in OneNote. It will create a link of the form file:sectionname.one as shown in the example in Figure 7-4.

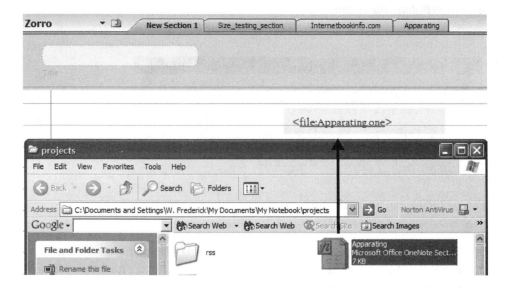

Figure 7-4. File link

Click that link, and you're *instantly* transported to the destination section as demonstrated in Figure 7-5.

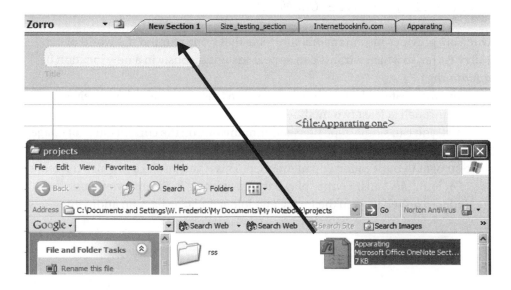

Figure 7-5. A new section apparates when a link is clicked.

It's very, very fast, presumably because everything is happening within random access memory. If you find the hierarchy navigation occasionally tiresome, this is a pretty good shortcut. Click the link as many times as you like, but no more sections will be added to the current folder. Put the link on as many pages as you want, and you can instantly hop to the apparated section.

TIP　You can right-click+drag a .ONE file onto a Word document to create a hyperlink. A Windows menu will appear with four choices, including the move here, copy here, create a hyperlink, and cancel options. If you choose the create a hyperlink option, the resulting link in Word will look like this: C:\Documents and Settings\W. Frederick\My Documents\My Notebook\projects\Apparating.one.

OLE

Object Linking and Embedding is a mature Microsoft technology that has been part of Microsoft Office for many years. In a nutshell, this is what enables you to put a spreadsheet document inside a Word document, or a Word table inside a PowerPoint document, and so on, and to keep those documents dynamically updated and refreshed by linking back to the original. Many types of OLE objects exist, as you can verify by navigating to Insert ➤ Object ➤ Create New Object in any Office application.

OneNote doesn't import or export OLE objects. This first version of OneNote can't accept OLE objects—you can't insert OLE objects like Word or Excel documents into the OneNote page—and none of the other Office 2003 applications can accept OneNote native format (.ONE) documents. Hopefully this will change in the future. Nevertheless, OLE is still important because (as I'll discuss in a moment) OneNote *can* generate two types of files that can be imported into Office as OLE objects.

Using OLE from Within Office Applications

OneNote routinely can generate two file types that *are* OLE objects—Windows Media Audio (.WMA) and MHTML (.MHT) files.

NOTE　Note that OneNote's native file format, .ONE, is *not* an OLE object. Other Office applications *cannot* open .ONE files.

Listening to OneNote Audio from Within Office Applications

From within Office applications, you can insert *audio files* that you recorded and stored in the OneNote folder structure, because Office does provide OLE support for audio files.

Let's say I want to insert an audio recording I made in OneNote of a conversation about the author Gwin Dye. From *within an Office application such as Excel 2003,* I would select Insert ➤ Object ➤ Create from File, and use Browse as shown in Figure 7-6 to navigate to the place in My Notebook where the desired Windows Media Audio file is stored.

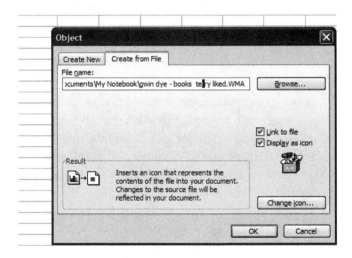

Figure 7-6. From within Excel 2003

The .WMA file will be stored in the spreadsheet (see Figure 7-7).

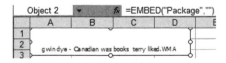

Figure 7-7. Audio file stored in Excel 2003

When you click the icon, a message will pop up warning you that "You are about to open an OLE object that may contain viruses." You can disregard the warning, since you inserted the file yourself and know its content. Next, you'll see a File Download message—you're downloading the audio file from a location in My Notebook. Click Open. Windows Media Player will launch, *and will play the audio file that you originally recorded in OneNote*.

CAUTION   For access to the synchronization information that OneNote stores about audio recordings, you must play the recordings back from within OneNote.

You can also link to an audio file using the same technique, with the exception that on the Create from File tab of the Insert Object window you would click the checkbox for the link to file option. While linking is often the best technique when inserting editable Word or Excel documents in another Office document, it may not be necessary in the case of OneNote audio files. The only reason to link to an audio file as opposed to inserting one is if you want to keep the file size of the recipient document down. On the other hand, if you're going to share the document that contains the OneNote audio, you probably want to insert the file rather than link to it, so that the inserted data is available when the document is read on another user's PC.

Extracting "Sound Bites" from OneNote

If your goal is to extract a "sound bite" from an audio recording that you created and play it back within another Office application (say, PowerPoint), you'll need to use a Windows sound editor.

CAUTION   Unfortunately, you can't play a portion of synchronized sound from one instance of OneNote and record it in another one!

Inserting .MHT Files in Other Office Applications

You can also insert .MHT files created by OneNote into other Office applications. Recall that you can always use the File ➤ Save As or Publish Pages commands to save selected OneNote pages as .MHT files, which OneNote (and Office) calls "Single File Web Page." You can then insert these files into other Office applications. Unfortunately, the results can look odd, especially if the .MHT file contains ink or images, which is probably the case (otherwise, you could simply copy and paste text into the target document).

For example, let's say I used OneNote to hastily scribble down the names of two library books that I want to check out. In OneNote's native display format, .ONE, it looks reasonable, although my handwriting is pretty bad (see Figure 7-8).

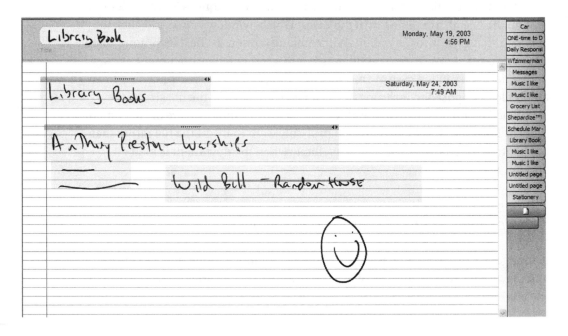

Figure 7-8. Library books in OneNote's native display format (.ONE)

This page also looks pretty reasonable when you save it as MHTML and view the file in Internet Explorer (see Figure 7-9).

Figure 7-9. MHTML viewed in Internet Explorer

Results are also pretty good when you copy the MHTML page from Internet Explorer and paste it into Word.

Things break down a bit if you use Insert ➤ File to place it in a blank Word document (see Figure 7-10).

It appears that the program is taking each ink object and putting it on a separate line, and making some inferences about font size based on the size of the handwriting. Nice try, but it doesn't look so hot, does it? On the plus side, each element that originally came from OneNote is now editable in Word.

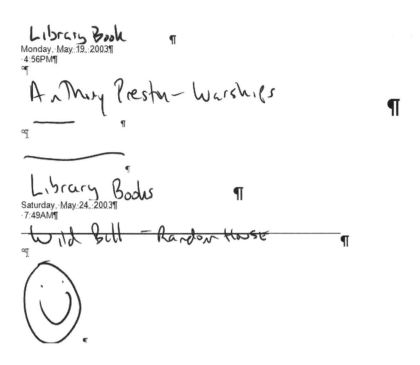

Figure 7-10. MHTML inserted into Word

Links to the Microsoft Research Service

The Research service is available within all Office 2003 applications and provides the ability to search external information services such as LexisNexis, Factiva, and Encarta. The Research pane may be viewed by navigating to View ➤ Task Pane (or using the Ctrl+F1 shortcut) and then selecting the Research drop-down list shown in Figure 7-11.

As you can see, the service lets you submit searches to a variety of research tools, including dictionaries, translators, news, and financial sites. I'll just touch lightly on a few of these to give you a flavor for what the Research service can do.

WARNING   If you aren't connected to the Internet, the Research pane can't pass requests to and results from remote services. But local services such as bilingual dictionaries and thesauri are searchable when offline.

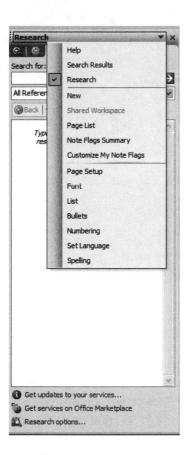

Figure 7-11. The Research drop-down list

The translation tool renders "note taking is important" in French as "la prise de note est importante," as you can see in Figure 7-12, and tries to upsell you to a full-service translation shop called WorldLingo (other translation services will be available in the future that will offer a different experience). Microsoft's Chris Pratley gives an example:

This tool is handy if you have been collecting articles or fragments of Web pages from IE or other courses in different languages, and want to see what they mean (such as if you are planning a trip, or buying a special product that is best described by its foreign manufacturer's Web page, as was the case for me when I was researching some Italian lamps).

Figure 7-12. OneNote en français

A few of the external research services listed are Factiva, LexisNexis, and Gale. While some portions of these services are free (for example, the LexisOne case law service), these services may require you either to provide a credit card number or an ID/password for access to premium content. The Research panes are available from within Office applications such as Word and OneNote and may involve some drop-downs to structure your query (see Figure 7-13).

When you select an item from the result list by clicking it, your default browser will open and the resulting document will appear in the top browser window. If Internet Explorer is selected as your default browser, the Research pane will also appear in the left-hand side of Internet Explorer.

TIP If Netscape is selected as your default browser, the Research pane does *not* display in the Netscape browser. This is a minor problem, as the Research pane is still visible in the Office window, and the document itself is still visible in Netscape.

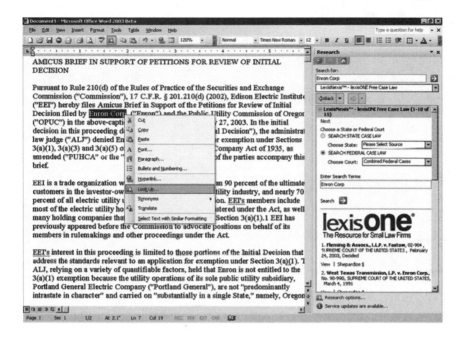

Figure 7-13. A structured query using LexisOne

Under All Business and Financial Sites, Gale Company Profiles offers introductory information about companies for free, but cordons off other information as registration and premium content. The MSN Money Stock Quote service is free and lets you enter current stock prices in OneNote. Let's enter a ticker symbol or company name in the Search box and select the MSN Money Stock Quote service. A window comes back with a 20-minute delayed price for the latest price of the company submitted (see Figure 7-14).

Figure 7-14. MSN Money Stock Quote service

Check out the Insert Price button. You can use this to insert the stock price directly into a OneNote text container (see Figure 7-15).

US:RUK 33.20

Figure 7-15. Inserted stock price

While this may seem like a fairly ho-hum feature, it's actually pretty useful, because of limitations of Office and OneNote. You can't copy entire answer sets from the display window of the Research service (although you can copy individual items). You have to follow the link to MSN Money for a Detailed Quote, which is of course a Web page that may take a moment to bring up if you have a slow connection. And as discussed in Chapter 3, OneNote doesn't necessarily behave quite the way you want when you paste HTML from Web pages. For example, Figure 7-16 shows how the Detailed Quote page looks when pasted into OneNote.

Quotes delayed 20 minutes
Quick Quote
fyi
Last **33.20**
Open 32.85
Change +0.19
Previous Close 33.01
% Change +0.58%
Bid NA
Volume 15,100
Ask NA

Figure 7-16. Detailed Quote page in OneNote

It may be easier to click Insert Price!

Unfortunately, the *refreshable* stock quotes add-in, which is available for the 2003 versions of Word and Excel, is *not* available for this version of OneNote, since that add-in uses the new XML functionality of Word 2003 and Excel 2003 Professional versions.

You can and should click the link that invites you to get updates to your Research services. You'll be presented with a checkbox list that shows the services that you currently have plus others that are now available.

TIP The update link will disappear when no updates are available—for example, right after you've just added some updated services! It will reappear when new services are advertised by Microsoft. Given that only about 30 services were available during the beta, it may be an interval of weeks or months before new services are added.

The Get Services on Office Marketplace link takes you to a Web page where you can purchase subscriptions to Factiva, Gale, eLibrary, and other premium services.

The Research Options link at the bottom of the Research task pane brings up a corresponding window. In addition to the checklist of services, there are three buttons at the bottom: Add Services, Update/Remove, and Parental Controls.

Add Services allows you (and requires you) to enter the URL address for a Research service (see Figure 7-17).

Figure 7-17. You must know an address to enter.

If you don't know the address you're being asked to enter here, you should go to the Office Marketplace or consult your corporation's IT administrators. Don't bother trying to guess or make up a URL—you're out of luck. There is no mechanism for you to discover additional Research services from within OneNote.

You might know this address if it's being provided to you by an organization, or if you're developing your own service. For the latter group, I'll point you to online documentation at MSDN—there you can find a good article by Jan Fransen called "Customizing the Microsoft Office 2003 Research Task Pane."[1] The gist of it is that you need to create a .NET registration service running on a Web server and a .NET query service that takes the user query, passes it to a database, parses the results, and returns them to the Research pane. In other words, this is a fairly substantial programming project. I should also tell you that Chris Kunicki did a piece for MSDN called "Build Your Own Research Library with Office 2003 and the Google Web Service API."[2] It's several hours' work for a developer to add a Research service that points to Google.

1. `http://msdn.microsoft.com/library/default.asp?url=/library/en-us/odc_wd2003_ta/html/odc_customizingtheresearchpane.asp`

2. `http://msdn.microsoft.com/library/default.asp?url=/library/en-us/dnofftalk/html/office03062003.asp`

Update/Remove lists services, grouped by provider, and allows you to update or remove them.

Parental Control allows you to turn on filters that limit objectionable material and, optionally, to display only services that can be filtered. You can enter a password so that only you can adjust these settings.

A Comment on the Research Pane

A personal comment on the Research pane: great idea, but too inconvenient for individuals and integrators to use. A year from now, I believe there will be more or less the same narrow selection of premium publishers offering thin slices of their offerings. Microsoft talks about having 40 or so publishers within a year. That's nice, but the Research pane would be so much more exciting if it was really exponential in numbers...why not a thousand services, or ten thousand? After all, the Office audience is 300 million end users. A properly implemented Research pane ought to be able to support a thriving ecosystem.

Everyone—Microsoft, publishers, and end users—would have been much better served with a simpler and more open Research pane. Amazon.com has set the gold standard in "build it yourself" tools for its third-party community. Wouldn't it be great if there was a Microsoft Web site called "Register your Web site with Office Research"?

SharePoint

SharePoint Portal Server 2003 and its companion product, Windows SharePoint Services, are Microsoft's portal tools and collaboration servers, used to organize teams and information around a common Web site, often an employee intranet or access-controlled customer Web site (extranet). OneNote works with SharePoint Portal Server 2003 and Windows SharePoint Services. Windows SharePoint Services is a free add-on to Windows Server 2003, and SharePoint Services is built on top of the Windows Server 2003 technology.

You have a couple of ways to interact with SharePoint via OneNote. The simplest mechanism is to use File ➤ Save As to put a OneNote document into a SharePoint document library. This requires that you be able to navigate to the Windows file location of the document library. As an end user in your enterprise, you may or may not have this information at your fingertips. One typical usage scenario is to use SharePoint's My Site link (in the upper right of the portal home page) to create a site just for yourself on the portal. You'll be asked if you want to register My Site with your local machine, and, if you agree, My Site will show up as an option in OneNote's File Open and Save As dialog boxes. If you don't know where the SharePoint document libraries of interest are located, ask a system administrator or a knowledgeable friend.

TIP   System administrators can enable SharePoint portal to search .ONE files located on the server simply by installing OneNote on the server, since it includes an *iFilter* for the .ONE files, which allows the SharePoint indexer to read text out of the OneNote files. Microsoft says a stand-alone iFilter will be available in the future so that a OneNote installation on the server won't be necessary.

The Shared Workspace task pane is available via navigating to View ➤ Task Pane and the drop-down menu. This is a shared service that is available in all Office 2003 applications if your organization is running SharePoint Team Services.

CAUTION   The link to Shared Workspace on the task pane drop-down menu is grayed out if the document you're opening isn't part of a shared workspace.

In the Shared Workspace pane, you can issue a variety of collaboration commands regarding OneNote documents that are stored in a SharePoint document library and regarding the team members that are collaborating with you. Note, however, that you can't *create* a shared workspace from within OneNote as you can in Word, Excel, and PowerPoint. You must first create the workspace from one of those applications. Of course, the workspace can contain many different types of documents, including (but not limited to) OneNote documents.

With regard to the OneNote file itself:

- You can check to see whether the OneNote file has been updated.

- You can view file properties.

- You can request to receive an e-mail alert whenever this OneNote file changes.

You can control how frequently OneNote checks to update the Shared Workspace pane using Tools ➤ Options ➤ Other ➤ Service Options (see Figure 7-18).

OneNote always works off the OneNote file that is stored on the server. Since OneNote autosaves, that version is always the latest version.

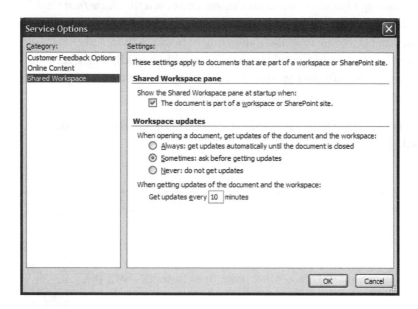

Figure 7-18. Change frequency of update checks here.

If you don't seem to be getting notification of updates (in other words, if the program is *not at all* annoying), check to make sure that you have the Document Update Utility installed.

You can also control whether you want opening the document to trigger opening the Shared Workspace pane. Although this feature is on by default, you might want to turn it off (see Figure 7-18) if you know you'll never or rarely use the Shared Workspace pane.

With regard to the team, you can check to see if any of your fellow team members are online. This enables you to do some near-real-time collaboration on a shared OneNote page or pages. No more than one person can be writing to the OneNote file at the same time, but you can make a quick change in a shared document (say, a meeting report), then fire off a message to your colleague: "Take a look at this, and make any changes needed." Your colleague can make the changes, and then (knowing that you're still online) tell you to take a look at the latest version.

In short, if you've selected OneNote as the preferred format for a document maintained by a team, SharePoint provides a good set of tools. It's worth emphasizing that SharePoint is sort of a special case of a more general proposition, which is that this first release of OneNote offers a pretty handy set of "rough and ready" tools for collaboration via shared files. Microsoft's Chris Pratley points out:

> *It is as easy as doing File/Save As and putting a section on a file share (not only SharePoint), then having other people open that section. Dial down the setting in Tools/Options/Open and Save about releasing file locks to its lowest (1 min), and then you have a sort of shared logbook (sort of like a wiki), where each person in a group can edit the same section of notes that appears in everyone's notebook.*

That's a pretty cool perspective...maybe a future version of OneNote will be Microsoft's wiki tool (see Figure 7-19).

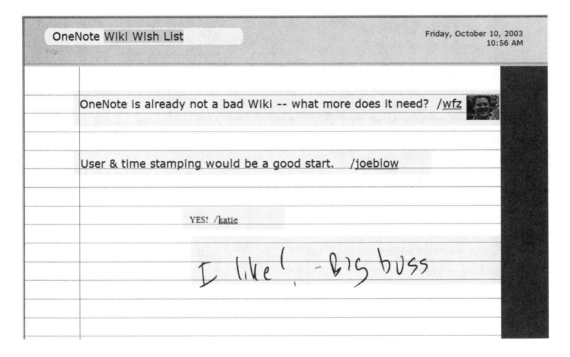

Figure 7-19. A simple demo of a group using OneNote as a shared logbook

Microsoft Office Document Imaging (MODI)

This helper program comes standard with Office XP and Office 2003, and it can be a big help with OneNote. It's available under Microsoft Office ➤ Office Tools (see Figure 7-20).

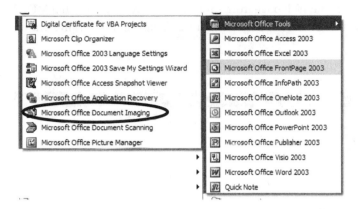

Figure 7-20. Finding Microsoft Office Document Imaging

There's a lot to the MODI program, including optical character recognition and image manipulation capabilities, but all you really need to know is that the Microsoft Office Document Image Writer, which comes with MODI, provides an easy way of turning any Microsoft Office or Internet Explorer document into an image. From there, you can paste the image into OneNote.

The print driver is visible in the Printers window once you have installed Office, as you can see in Figure 7-21.

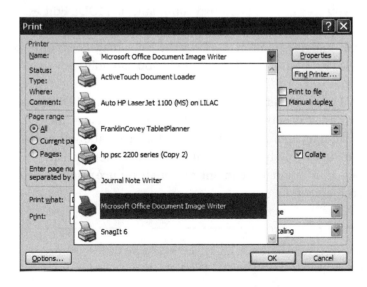

Figure 7-21. Microsoft Office Document Image Writer

When you print a sample Web page from Internet Explorer, you see that MODI presents printed results as a series of pages with thumbnails in a left-hand pane (see Figure 7-22).

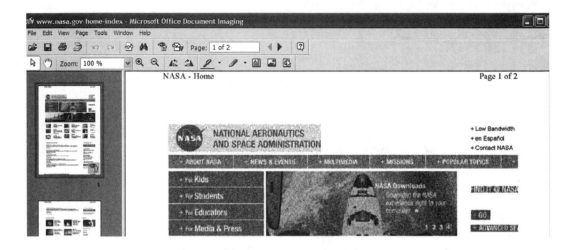

Figure 7-22. Page thumbnails in the left pane

You'll note that MODI works in black and white, not color.

As a OneNote user, you only need to know two commands in MODI: Edit ➤ Select All and Edit ➤ Copy Image. Be sure to use Copy Image rather than Copy, as Copy will extract a rather random jumble of text from the page image. Be aware that Select All means Select Current Page. Unfortunately, you can only copy one page image at a time.

The MODI pages that you paste into OneNote are in TIFF format. MODI allows you to adjust various parameters of the TIFF format, including dots per inch resolution and compression techniques. You probably don't care about those capabilities for OneNote unless you have a special need to take notes on an unusually accurate image of an original document, or want to reduce resolution so as to reduce storage requirements.

TIP If you need to crop or resize, check out Microsoft Office Picture Manager, also available under Office Tools.

Office 2003 shared services including OLE, the Research pane, SharePoint, and Microsoft Office Document Imaging add a lot of flexibility and power to OneNote. But that just scratches the surface...most of Office 2003 is based on a powerful new XML plumbing, which the first version of OneNote doesn't use at all. You'll see interesting things in this arena in future releases of OneNote.

Getting Information from OneNote into Other Office Applications

In Chapter 3, I spent quite a bit of time discussing how to get information from other programs *into OneNote*. In this section, I'll discuss getting information from OneNote *into other programs*.

Most people spend a substantial percentage of their day in e-mail, and Outlook 2003 is Microsoft's preferred e-mail solution.

Sending E-Mail via Outlook

As you've already learned in Chapter 6, you can send OneNote documents via Outlook, either in their native format (.ONE) as an attachment, saved as a single Web page (.MHT attachment), or in the body of the message as MHTML.

TIP   There is nothing to stop you from using other e-mail programs such as Outlook Express, Eudora, or even Netscape mail to mail .ONE or .MHT attachments. All you need to do is save the files using Save As (into your Windows file structure), and then use the standard attachment functionality of your e-mail client to select and attach the .ONE or .MHT files.

Outlook Tasks

You can create an Outlook 2003 Task in OneNote using the Create Outlook Task icon on the Standard toolbar (see Figure 7-23). The Standard toolbar is the one that normally appears at the top of the page and begins with the Back button. The Create Outlook Task icon is about three-quarters of the way to the right of the toolbar. The keyboard shortcut is Ctrl+Shift+K.

Figure 7-23. Create Outlook Task icon

NOTE The Add Task command is *not* listed on the default version of the drop-down menus. This can be a nuisance if you're one of those people who finds the toolbar icons too tiny and looks at the menu first. You can, however, use Tools ➤ Customize to add the command to a drop-down menu of your choice. Go to Tools ➤ Customize ➤ Commands ➤ Rearrange Commands. You'll see the Rearrange Commands window. Choose the menu bar to which you want to add the task command (I chose Tools). Select Add. You'll see the Add Commands window. In the left-hand Categories scroll box select All Commands. The right-hand scroll box will be populated with a list of most (but not all) of the commands. Scroll down to Create Outlook Task, select it, and click OK. The command will be added to your menu at the insertion point. You can use the Move Up and Move Down buttons to relocate it if necessary.

When the Outlook Task window shown in Figure 7-24 comes up, you're actually in Outlook 2003.

You can paste selected text, ink, and image content from OneNote into the task description window.

CAUTION The info in the task description window will look pretty close to what it looks like in OneNote, but won't include the paper background (ruled lines, etc.) from OneNote. *Nor will outline structure be passed along.*

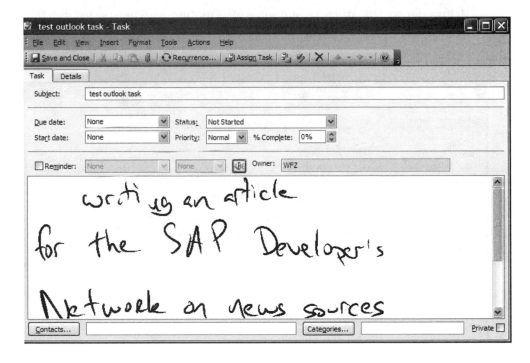

Figure 7-24. You can insert OneNote content into the Outlook Task.

These are fairly serious limitations. See for example the OneNote outline in Figure 7-25.

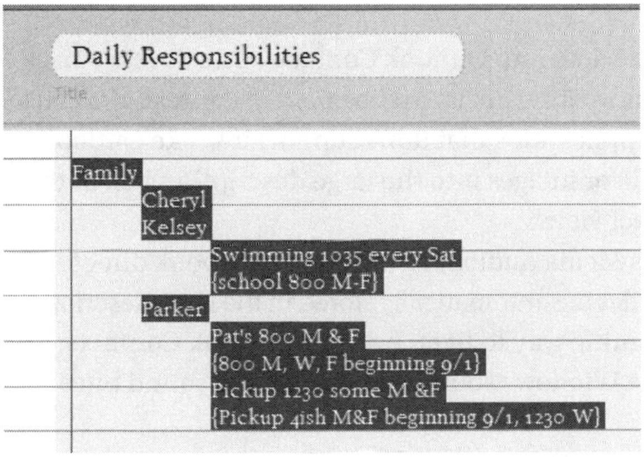

Figure 7-25. Nicely structured outline in OneNote

It loses most of its structure, and some of its usefulness, when pasted into the Outlook Task (see Figure 7-26).

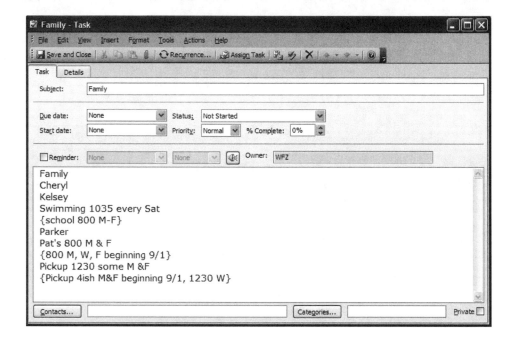

Figure 7-26. OneNote structure gone in Outlook Task

Copying from OneNote into Outlook Contacts

You can copy and paste from OneNote into Outlook Contacts. OneNote is smart enough that when you paste handwriting ink into a text field in context, it will use an alternate textual format for applications that don't support ink, like Outlook Contacts fields. You can paste ink or images into the large description box in the right-hand side of the full Contact view.

You can also paste Windows Media Audio files from the Notebook directory into the Outlook Contact. These files are automatically stored in the large description area. This can be a very entertaining way to liven up your Outlook Contacts, especially if you have access to a Windows sound editor to create sound bites.

From OneNote into Word

All OneNote types of content stored within containers (text, images, ink, and pasted HTML) can be pasted into modern versions of Word. Also, Word can read .MHT files published from OneNote. Text and images from OneNote will be rendered with high fidelity in Word. Outline format will be maintained with accuracy. Ink and pasted HTML or MHTML won't look quite the same—you'll lose some of the fine detail.

You'll also encounter some issues because of the fundamentally different page metaphors in OneNote and Word. Whereas in OneNote content is organized in containers that can be located anywhere on the page surface (including on top of each other!), in Word content is organized in terms of lines and characters, and although it's possible to superimpose objects upon each other, it requires special construction of the objects. Thus, when you transfer content from OneNote into Word, you may see that Word has difficulty maintaining layout relationships precisely as you created them in OneNote.

TIP   if you're planning to copy material from OneNote to Word, remember that Word doesn't support two-dimensional image positioning, and ink in particular is often hard to place correctly after a copy operation.

OneNote into Excel

Numerical calculation is an integral aspect of many types of note taking. For example, a substantial proportion of academic disciplines include numerical analysis, such as science, math, and social science. It's difficult to take class notes in such disciplines without occasional recourse to numeric calculations. Similarly, many aspects of business revolve around the intelligent analytical use of numbers in meetings and informal discussion. It's often useful to carry out quick numerical analysis in such settings. For these reasons, let's take a look at the integration between Microsoft's numerical analysis tool, Excel, and OneNote.

As with Word, there is no special integration between Excel 2003 and OneNote. To the extent that there is interoperability, it's a function of the normal operation of the programs themselves, the Microsoft Office family, and the Windows operating system.

Text, of course, pastes cleanly into Excel. OneNote pastes its recognition results into the clipboard as text (see Figure 7-27).

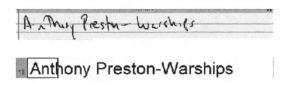

Figure 7-27. Ink in OneNote becomes recognized text in Excel.

Mixed handwriting and drawing ink doesn't paste so cleanly, but note that Excel 2003 is smart enough to put ink in one of its cells.

You can paste a doodled drawing from OneNote into Excel, as demonstrated in Figure 7-28.

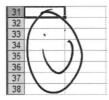

Figure 7-28. Doodle pasted into Excel

Note that just like any other image in Excel, the drawing doesn't occupy just one cell, but is pasted on top of several cells, which now can't be occupied by numeric values.

Image content in OneNote can be pasted into an Excel spreadsheet, just like image content from any other application.

If you paste content that has associated OneNote audio links into Excel, the links don't follow along because that is a OneNote feature.

Moving from OneNote into PowerPoint

If you're moving textual content from OneNote into PowerPoint, beware of PowerPoint's auto-formatting features. Text that looked small and inoffensive on a OneNote page, nicely laid out with extra white space, may suddenly look awkward in PowerPoint, which formats text to fit the available space in the design template, ignores outlining information in OneNote, and adds bullets to every line, including blank lines that were carriage returns in OneNote.

TIP   If you apply bullets or numbering in OneNote before you paste, all is well in PowerPoint on arrival.

Ink is recognized as text, and spatial relationships among containers in OneNote are lost on pasting into PowerPoint. (For an example, see Figure 7-29, which depicts OneNote objects before pasting, and Figure 7-30, which shows those same objects after pasting them into Excel.)

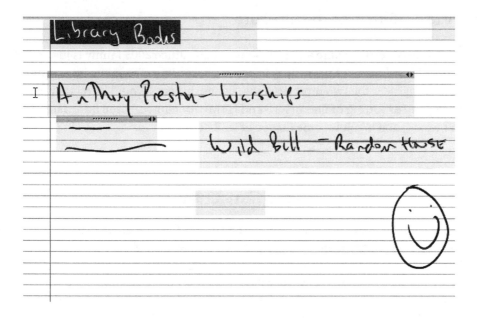

Figure 7-29. Spatial relationships among OneNote objects before pasting

Saturday, May 24, 2003
AM 7:49

Library Books

Anthony Preston-Warships

in

Wild Bill -Random tlouSE

Figure 7-30. Spatial relationships lost after pasting into PowerPoint

Overview of Office ↔ OneNote

Integration between OneNote and its siblings in the Office 2003 family is just beginning. It's to be hoped that future releases will see improvements in sharing content. In my view, the two most desirable enhancements would be to allow importing and exporting of files in RTF and HTML (of course, some information would be lost), and to allow some degree of OLE behavior.

Troubleshooting with Other Tools

If you experience unforeseen difficulties when using OneNote in conjunction with tools from Microsoft or third-party tools, there are some familiar, common-sense steps you can take to troubleshoot.

Begin by isolating the problem. Does the problem occur in the functioning of OneNote, or the functioning of the other tool? Does the problem occur whenever you run OneNote (regardless of whether other software is involved), or whenever you run the other tool (regardless of whether OneNote is involved)? If the problem truly appears to be a result of the interaction of OneNote and the other software, do you have the latest version of the other software? Do you have the latest version of OneNote? You can use Tools ➤ Help ➤ Check for Updates to be sure.

Another good place to check is Tools ➤ Help ➤ About Microsoft Office OneNote ➤ Disabled Items, which produces a list of software that has been disabled by OneNote to allow OneNote to run.

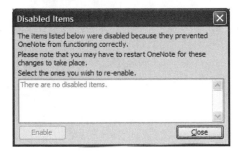

Exploring a Few Other Microsoft Tools of Interest

Now that you've explored integration between OneNote and Office, I want to turn your attention to a few other Microsoft tools and platforms of interest, including FrontPage, Pocket PC, and the Windows Journal utility in Tablet PC.

Going from FrontPage to OneNote

FrontPage and OneNote both determine page layout, but each uses a manner that is almost the inverse of the other. OneNote provides direct page layout with absolutely no visibility into the underlying Microsoft proprietary code that controls the appearance and location of containers on the page. FrontPage also provides direct page layout but offers complete visibility into the open standard HTML code that controls the appearance and location of objects on the page.

FrontPage can't export files in OneNote format. That's no surprise, since OneNote is the only application that "speaks" .ONE in this first release.

It's a bit more distressing that FrontPage can't save files as Single Web Page or MHTML format, considering that since November 2002 Microsoft has been offering Tablet PC applications that write in MHTML format.

Since the first version of OneNote has no file import capabilities, the only way to get HTML content from FrontPage into OneNote is to copy and paste.

FrontPage 2003 has several modes of displaying content: Design, Split, Code, and Preview. Copying from the Design mode (shown in Figure 7-31) into OneNote is interesting, because the paste drops out comments and subtle cues such as dashed underlines that are shown in Design mode (see Figure 7-32).

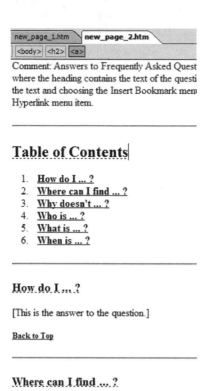

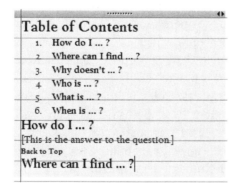

Figure 7-31. FrontPage Design mode

Figure 7-32. Pasted into OneNote without design cues

HTML copied from the Split or Code modes is simply pasted into OneNote as text. Content pasted from the Preview mode (shown in Figure 7-33) is pasted into OneNote without HTML page layout elements supported by HTML—the pasted content looks exactly like the results of Design mode (shown in Figure 7-32).

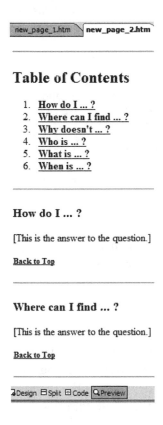

Figure 7-33. FrontPage Design mode

OneNote into FrontPage

FrontPage can't open .ONE or .MHT files. If you try to open an .MHT file in FrontPage, the file will be opened in a separate Internet Explorer window.

Let's say you try a workaround and invoke View Source on an .MHT file in Internet Explorer. What happens? Well, you see something that looks like HTML, but when you paste it into FrontPage's HTML editor (Code or Split mode), it doesn't retain the encapsulated image and ink information. When you display the pasted MHTML in Design or Preview mode, FrontPage fails miserably.

Pocket PC

One of the most frequent user requests during the OneNote beta was for a version of OneNote that runs on Pocket PC. *No such functionality was available with version 1.0 of OneNote*, but Microsoft definitely heard the requests, and the item is on the development team's radar screen for future releases. In the meantime, what workarounds are possible?

 CAUTION   If you're looking for a convenient way to get OneNote content onto a Pocket PC, wait for Microsoft. The following discussion describes some fairly awkward things that you can do now—only for those who absolutely must get some OneNote content into the Pocket PC.

Reading MHTML Files on Pocket PC

Unfortunately, Pocket Internet Explorer reads .MHT files as plain text. If you try to open an .MHT file with Pocket IE, you'll see the HTML source code.

Converting MHTML to HTML for Viewing on a Pocket PC

You can use Internet Explorer to open an .MHT file and save it as HTML. If you open an .MHT file in desktop Internet Explorer, you'll be able to view it. If you then save it using the Web Page, single page only option, ink and images will be stripped out—but it's now an HTML file, not an .MHT file, and you can therefore view it in Pocket IE.

If you must be able to use a Pocket PC to view images that originally resided in OneNote, you have some other options.

If you're viewing an .MHT file in desktop IE and save it using the Web Page, complete option, Internet Explorer will create a home HTML page *plus* a folder that contains each image as a single file. *Each* ink or image object from the OneNote page will wind up in this folder, which you can then sync to the Pocket PC.

This is by no means a foolproof approach. Obviously, the results will become cumbersome with a OneNote page that contains many ink or image objects. Also, OneNote ink and image objects saved in this manner become files with the extension .TMP. That means you have to change the .TMP extension to an extension that is readable by Pocket Internet Explorer, or associate the .TMP extension (on the Pocket PC) with Pocket IE. The former is probably the wiser course, since other types of files may use the .TMP extension.

Converting OneNote Pages to Images

Another option for viewing OneNote pages on the Pocket PC is to save the visible portion of your OneNote page as a single image in a standard format like JPEG or GIF, using either the Windows Alt+PrintScreen command or a screen capture program like TechSmith's Snag-It, which I'll discuss in detail in Chapter 12. You can then view the image via Pocket IE.

In practice, this can be difficult, because Pocket PC screen size is normally 320×240 pixels, and the actual usable dimensions in Pocket IE are much less (245×240).[3] You'll be trying to view a big image through a small window.

If you know you're going to be capturing image versions of OneNote pages for later viewing on a Pocket PC, you can make things easier on yourself by going to OneNote File ➤ Page Setup and creating a Custom page size. Unfortunately, Pocket PC screen size is measured in pixels, which isn't a measurement that OneNote recognizes. This means that you'll probably have to measure your Pocket PC screen in inches. Many models have a diagonal measurement of 3.5 inches with width and height approximately 2 inches by 3 inches.

Adjusting Pocket PC Display Resolution to View Larger Images

For hackers only: You *may* be able to change the Pocket PC display resolution to match the resolution of your original PC using a tool called dotPocket that is available from a small third-party software company.[4] dotPocket allows you to change the resolution of your Pocket PC from the default 320×240 to another resolution such as 640×480 or 800×640. Of course, the image will look smaller! It should go without saying that this approach is pretty risky in terms of potentially irritating consequences and should only be attempted if you're thoroughly familiar with your Pocket PC and prepared to restore it to its initial state by a hard reboot, with any custom applications and data fully backed up on secure media.

---

3. http://msdn.microsoft.com/library/default.asp?url=/library/en-us/guide_ppc/htm/
designing_web_sites_for_internet_explorer_for_pocket_pc_vtfo.asp

4. http://www.dotpocket.com/pocket-pc-screen-resolution.html

Capturing Ink on PPC, Moving to OneNote

Pocket PC has built-in support for a form of digital ink, which it captures in the Notes application and saves with the extension .INK. You can sync such files to the desktop. OneNote can't import those files, but you can open an .INK file with other applications such as Internet Explorer and then paste it into OneNote.

Working with Windows Journal on Tablet PC

Windows Journal is a notepad utility that comes standard with every Tablet PC. Quite a bit of the functionality of Windows Journal is similar to functionality in OneNote. In particular, both applications use a notebook metaphor and accept images and (on the Tablet PC) digital ink. So it isn't surprising that Tablet PC users have been asking for better integration between Journal and OneNote and that OneNote users have been eyeing certain Windows Journal features with envy. Again, there is no direct integration. This first version of OneNote can't import the Journal Note format (.JNT), nor can Journal (which was developed first) import .ONE files.

For that matter, the current OneNote can't import any Windows file types, including such common formats as HTML (.HTM), Word document (.DOC), and Rich Text Format (.RTF). Obviously, it's to be hoped that importing capabilities are added in future releases. Copy/paste accomplishes almost the same thing, but many requests were made for direct import features during the beta process, presumably because if you do a lot of importing data from one format to another, speed matters.

Why Can't OneNote Import Windows Journal files?

Unfortunately, the first release of Microsoft OneNote has no mechanism for directly importing Journal format files (.JNT) and Journal template files (.JNP) into OneNote.

This may seem odd to some Tablet PC users, since OneNote and Journal both manage text, ink, and images. The fundamental reason why OneNote doesn't support Journal import in its first release was that in 2003 there were considerably fewer than a million Tablet PCs available, whereas OneNote was intended as a product for the broad Office market, which had an installed base of more than 300 million users. While the OneNote team gave Tablet PC users some great features in terms of ink support, they just didn't have the bandwidth to do everything.

The OneNote team also found during field testing that Tablet PC users who had both Journal and OneNote available tended to gravitate to OneNote and leave Journal behind. They might occasionally refer to their old Journal files, but after a few weeks most of them moved over to OneNote for keeps. While Journal does have a few features that OneNote doesn't (for example, greater pen configurability), OneNote can do most of what Journal can, and provides a more organized framework for it.

As a workaround, you can copy pages from Windows Journal and paste them into OneNote. Unfortunately, you can only select pages in Journal one at a time.

 TIP   A speedier alternative is to use Journal's File ➤ Export As command and save your data using Tagged Image File Format (TIFF). Then navigate to the file storage location in the Windows file system and click the files to open them with Microsoft Office Document Imaging, which is part of the standard Office 2003 installation. You can select several TIFF pages in MODI, and then copy and paste them into OneNote. When you paste the TIFF pages into OneNote, they will be pasted as a series of pictures.

Summary

Here are the high points of what you learned in this chapter:

- Copy and paste is the single most reliable way to get information from OneNote to other Office applications, but results aren't always what you expect if content contains tables and other rich formatting, and speed can be an issue if you need to transfer many chunks of content from one place to another.

- You probably didn't even know you had Microsoft Office Document Imaging, but its print driver can be a great help to you!

- This first version of OneNote doesn't have the ability to import files, but remember you can always open them in the originating application and copy/paste instead.

- OneNote can export files as .ONE and .MHT files.

- No other Microsoft applications can read .ONE files yet.

- Internet Explorer is a free, high-quality viewer for .MHT files, and you can copy and paste from IE into other Microsoft applications. Internet Explorer is Microsoft's preferred path for viewing and copying .MHT files.

- No support exists yet for Pocket PC ↔ OneNote.

- Microsoft expects that OneNote will replace Windows Journal for Tablet PC users, but hasn't yet provided backward compatibility.

CHAPTER 8

Using OneNote
in Your Profession

THIS CHAPTER IS INTENDED to get you thinking about how OneNote might help you in your profession.

Some software books follow a rule of only talking with actual users of the program about features actually in the current release of the program. I've chosen to follow a different set of rules in this book, so not everyone you'll meet in the chapter is already a user of OneNote. I consider this a beneficial approach for several reasons:

- I believe it's most useful to talk about a new piece of software like OneNote from a range of perspectives.

- As this book coincides with the first release of the software, I thought it helpful to provide viewpoints that fall across the full spectrum between "never seen it" and "already addicted."

- As you consider using OneNote in your profession, it's helpful for you to see how people with deep domain expertise think about applying new software to their daily lives.

- The reality is that, as a person interested in using OneNote in your profession, you're going to hear about OneNote from people with all sorts of perspectives, ranging from complete zealots for other programs to total OneNote converts. Even the people coming from very anti-Microsoft perspectives may make some important points; the trick is sifting out the gold.

In the rest of this chapter, I'll show you the note-taking needs of a variety of professionals. I'll also expose you to the thinking of Lou Rosenfeld, coauthor of the standard work on information architecture, *Information Architecture for the World Wide Web*, to help you start thinking about your *personal* information architecture. The point of the material in this chapter isn't to provide full proofs of Microsoft's OneNote value proposition in every conceivable profession, but rather to stimulate thought about your own needs and what OneNote might do to help you.

Students

Students seem to respond readily to OneNote, which is understandable considering that student life is often characterized by extensive note taking and multiple concurrent research projects.

Kye Lewis in Melbourne, Australia, commented:

[For] taking notes during classes, OneNote is great—I've even managed to make my typing fast enough to complete mathematical work on there—complete with powers and bases (using subscript and superscript, of course).

Multitasking during class is a reality for all save the most conscientious (or intimidated?) students in today's world.

I also tend to use it for work during class as well—it's basically the most used application on my computer...

Whereas the Windows directory structure tends to present one's activities as a collection of individual, atomic projects, not really useful unless they are completed, OneNote's user interface presents the student's activities as an integrated whole.

...I just love being able to organize everything into folders, sections, pages, and subpages.

I also use it to keep track of computer/network stuff here and to keep track of any of the stuff I'm responsible for at school—I can just click a button to...[attach a To Do note flag to a container] and it's great how I can list those so easily.

Mathematical Equations and OneNote

Except for the subscript and superscripting features Kye Lewis mentioned, OneNote doesn't provide direct support for equations. But you may have a few worthwhile options.

Within OneNote, don't forget about the availability of the Insert ➤ Symbol command and the special Symbol font, which each contain a wealth of useful special characters.

If you're using Microsoft Office and in particular Microsoft Word, you should know about Microsoft Equation, which is available *in Word* via Insert ➤ Object ➤ Microsoft Equation. You can use Microsoft Equation to create simple equations in Word and paste them into OneNote.

Words of caution:

- Caution #1 about pasting Microsoft Equation objects into OneNote: Don't use "text only," which will make the object disappear.

- Caution #2 about pasting from Microsoft Equation: Don't resize the picture, or it'll get blurry fast.

If you frequently include equations in your Microsoft Word documents, Microsoft recommends that you upgrade to MathType by Design Science, a full-featured math editor (http://www.mathtype.com/msee). Dennis Silverman at the University of California, Irvine has a Web page with a very useful summary of shortcuts for Microsoft Equation.[1]

If you're a Tablet PC user, you can enter your equations into OneNote by hand. If you think you may want to export these equations elsewhere, go to Tools ➤ Pen Mode and set Pen Mode to Create Drawings. The reason is that if you have Pen Mode set to Create Both Handwriting and Drawings, OneNote will apply background text recognition to the alphanumeric portion of your entry. See for example the following equation, the square root of 4x + 3y.

If Pen Mode is set to Create Both Handwriting and Drawings, here's what happens when you paste that equation into Microsoft Word.

44*34

OneNote automatically passes the recognized version of the "handwriting" portion along to the Clipboard.

If Pen Mode is set to Create Drawings, the results of the paste look much better, because the entire equation is treated as an image.

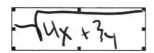

If you're a Tablet PC user, you may also wish to keep an eye out for special-purpose math software, coming from the University of Waterloo in Canada and xThink in Germany, that will allow users to enter equations and solve them algorithmically. The results, of course, could be pasted into OneNote at any juncture.

---

1. http://www.physics.uci.edu/~silverma/eqnedt.html

Law Students and Legal Professionals

In this section, you'll get a look at how OneNote seems to work for law students and legal professionals. Law students are a good case study of how OneNote works in a "texty" educational environment, minimally influenced by images and highly influenced by demanding writing and reading requirements.

OneNote for Law Students

OneNote might almost have been designed explicitly for law students, who may take hundreds of pages of highly detailed notes in each class every semester. The organizational structure of folders, sections, page groups, and subpages fits the organizational structure of a law school curriculum very well (see Table 8-1).

Table 8-1. The Law School Curriculum and OneNote

OneNote Navigational Element	Law School Curriculum
Folders	Semesters
Sections	Courses
Page groups	Weekly assignments or major topics
Pages	Daily class notes
Subpages	Cases briefed for each class

OneNote's URL flagging when pasting from Web pages is a useful tool for people who are being trained to attribute authority for every claim. It's not a complete solution, because when students prepare final work product, they'll need to take such citations and translate them into what's called *Bluebook style,* a standard citation format for law students. But it's certainly a help, especially if combined with Copy w/ Cite features that attach case citations to the Clipboard when copying legal content from the browser in the LexisNexis and Westlaw research systems.

Students and educators can do some easy things to enhance their experience with OneNote. Strategic use of hyperlinks can make for powerful stationeries. For example, I built a "case briefing" stationery that includes a hyperlink to the LexisNexis Get and Print page so that students can easily paste case law summaries into their OneNote pages (see Figure 8-1).

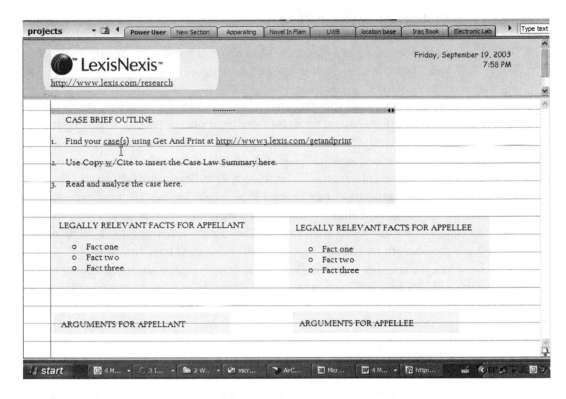

Figure 8-1. Case briefing stationery available at OneNoteInfoCenter.com

Case Study: the Life Cycle of Legal Professionals

I happen to know quite a bit about the information needs of legal professionals, so I'll use them as a case study to illustrate an important point: Even people with the same credentials and the same job title may have very different needs for note taking as they go through their professional life cycle.

The first two items on the post–law-school agenda in the United States are 1) find a job and 2) pass the bar exam. You can do these things in either order. Both studying for the bar and finding a job are intense note-taking applications in that they require tracking a great deal of information, most of which doesn't wind up in the final work product.

- Bar prep courses are multiweek marathons that involve several hours a day of highly focused note taking. The key point is that unlike regular school, where figuring out what is important can be something of a guessing game, in a bar prep course, *everything* you write down will be on the exam. In this case, a laptop with OneNote would be a godsend!

- Finding a job involves tracking many different contacts and ideas. Job letters will be done in Microsoft Word, but most of us aren't organized enough to track everything in a nice neat Word or Excel document. Again, OneNote is just the place to track all these scattered bits of info.

In the first couple of years after an attorney begins practice as a young associate, the focus is usually on doing legal research in support of partners, writing draft memos, and generally getting rid of the training wheels. Here, associates will find the firm's existing infrastructure a dominant part of their life; they will be writing memos that will be entered in a local storage system. OneNote might be an extremely useful tool for organizing research results especially using the URL pasting features, but, in candor, compatibility with the firm's existing IT environment will be a crucial issue for these young associates. They won't win any points by sharing a OneNote file with a technophobic partner who doesn't have OneNote yet!

Things change as associates mature and they begin taking on independent responsibilities for writing memos, meeting with clients, and appearing in court. Three-to-five year associates have greater control over their interim work product and may be able to adopt OneNote as their standard environment. Associates may be leading interrogatories during the discovery process. Here, associates may be able to use OneNote's audio synchronization to complement or replace an expensive stenographer!

As associates become partners, they lead other associates on projects and they become rainmakers, a setting in which client interaction is paramount. Here, meetings become a much more common aspect of the daily routine, and great concern is expressed over managing a myriad of responsibilities. Partners can usually do what they want as far as software is concerned, so they are free to use OneNote's project folders to organize their disparate activities.

The point I'm making here is that you need to take a careful look at where you are in the life cycle for your profession. If you're a "grunt," you may be somewhat more dependent on your firm's software environment, and you may need to take a careful look at the system requirements discussed in Chapter 2 and the data-sharing issues discussed in Chapter 5. If you're more senior, you're probably freer to be a "lead adopter," and the central issue is whether you feel there's room for improvement in how you track and manage interim work product.

 TIP   If you're working for an enterprise that is considering adoption of OneNote, remember to "segment" target users. People with very similar training and job titles may have very different roles and daily activities that drive different needs in terms of professional note taking and information management.

Interview with Harry Silver, Senior Director, Legal Research System, LexisNexis

Harry Silver is one of the principal architects of the LexisNexis legal research system. He is responsible for providing attorneys with the tools that they need to make legal research as efficient, accurate, and powerful as possible.

Q. Harry, let's begin at a conceptual level. As we know, LexisNexis serves the needs of many types of legal professionals—studen ts, associates, partners, corporate counsel, and professors, to name a few. LexisNexis has known for many years that each of these groups has somewhat varying needs and behaviors with regard to managing information. What is known about how note taking fits into the workflow of these different user segments in the legal profession?

A. Traditional legal research often requires exceptionally "close reading" of primary texts—which include cases, statutes, and regulations. Attorneys frequently take copious notes when reading these documents. When reading directly from books, the notes are often taken on "yellow pads"; but, when the cases are photocopied or printed out from a computer, the tendency is to record marginalia directly onto the document.

Q. Still at a conceptual level, what would you say are the most important needs that various types of legal professionals would express regarding the note-taking task? To what degree are legal professionals willing to contemplate using software to meet those needs?

A. Based on personal experience, at least one distinctive element of legal writing and note taking is the need to record case citations. Uncovering (or tracing) lines of precedent is central to many legal research tasks, and notes frequently contain multiple references in legal citation format.

Q. Now let's move a step closer to the actual day-to-day technology that is used in the practice of law. Although there are certainly exceptions, it's fair to say that various generations of Microsoft Office applications such as Word, PowerPoint, Excel, and Outlook are already deployed in a great many law firms, and that most legal professionals are to some degree familiar with Microsoft Office. Given that background, and given that Microsoft OneNote is a new member of the Office 2003 family, what concerns do you think will be uppermost in legal professionals' minds as they learn about Microsoft OneNote (perhaps via the OneNote Web site at http://www.microsoft.com/onenote), and how would you suggest that they address those concerns?

A. Attorneys are extremely security conscious, and may ask questions about where their notes (or "work product") actually reside. I suspect that clear explanations about the security of data would be well received by the legal community.

[As discussed in Chapter 3, by default OneNote content resides within the My Notebook folder on a local hard drive, where it is as secure as any other content on that hard drive. You may elect to store selected OneNote content within an encrypted folder, in which case it is protected by Windows encryption technology. Finally, OneNote users can elect to store OneNote section files on local area network or wide area network locations (FTP, HTTP). In those cases, the files are protected by the same security as the other data stored at those network locations.—wfz]

Q. LexisNexis and the competitors who followed it into the electronic legal research market originally provided access to their services via specialized Windows programs and now do so primarily via Web browser services. How do you see attorneys wanting to integrate note taking in a specialized program like OneNote with legal research in a Web browser service?

A. In my personal opinion, tools such as Tablet PCs should increase the attractiveness of online note-taking applications. In particular, as attorneys become more comfortable with reading full text documents while on a computer, their interest in annotating these documents "on a computer screen" should also rise.

Q. From what you know about OneNote, what appears 1) most problematic and 2) most promising for legal professionals?

Once again, in my experience, annotating hard-copy versions of numerous documents leads to unwieldy collections of materials when attorneys move to the phase of constructing a memorandum or brief that incorporates these notations. In my opinion, attorneys should appreciate an application that facilitates the process of consolidating marginalia and integrating notes into final work product. *[Note flags might help here.—wfz]* But, as suggested, attorneys will probably need to adopt a form factor that facilitates online reading before the annotation application can enjoy its fullest measure of success.

Mental Health Professionals

The image of the psychoanalyst or psychologist seated in a comfortable leather chair taking notes while a reclining patient speaks is as old as psychiatry. But it must be quite a challenge for a psychologist to actually take good notes while paying close attention to what a patient is saying and appearing (and being) a responsive, concerned listener. I asked Nick Apostoleris, a practicing psychologist, how he deals with this issue.

> *Well, no leather chair for me, and while there is a sofa in my office, it's fabric and folks sit on it rather than lie on it. So, my office may not fit the image too well. The visual you conjure is of classical psychoanalysis—following Freud. I do know an analyst, though they are a rare breed these days; nearly extinct in an era of managed care and evidence-based treatments.*

I do think taking notes is intrusive. I will take notes during some of my initial session, as I get contact and presenting problem info, mental status data, and as I go through my initial semistructured interview. After the initial session, however, I don't take notes. I rely on the neurons to store info until I can dictate. Then I wait for the dictation to return (in .DOC form), proofread it, and put it into session note format. Typing into anything would be disrespectful and therefore unacceptable. The only exception would be for initial info, which can be framed as data gathering rather than assessment or therapy.[2]

It's important to be realistic. As you consider using OneNote in your work as a mental health professional, keep in mind the following points.

- In some situations, even paper note taking isn't the best choice.

- Electronic note taking isn't for everyone.

- Keyboarded note taking is significantly more intrusive and socially problematic than pen-based note taking. If it's time for a new laptop, you might consider the Tablet PC platform.

- Security is an important concern, not just for your OneNote content, but for all the other data on your local and network storage.

OneNote appears to be heading in the right direction to address this set of concerns.

- The entire focus of OneNote is on minimizing intrusion into the PC user's workflow.

- OneNote takes advantage of Tablet PC, Microsoft's best tool for minimizing intrusion into the *social* setting.

- OneNote raises no special security concerns of its own...it's simply dependent on the overall security of your Windows environment.

If these concerns could be overcome, it might be useful to record sessions using OneNote, and indeed it isn't uncommon for trainee therapists to tape-record their work so that they can review their work with supervisors. If the patient gives informed consent, and the therapist can jot down a few "landmark" notes using an unobtrusive Tablet PC, this might be a good use of OneNote.

---

2. Personal communication, 8/5/2003

Truth Is Stranger Than Fiction

The New York Times reported the following on Saturday, September 27, 2003 (page A12):

For years, health insurers have occasionally demanded a look at psychotherapists' notes of their sessions with patients, to ensure that the care they were paying for was appropriate, or that it actually took place.

But now one insurer, Oxford Health Plans, is saying that in many cases, the notes are not enough evidence that the patients received what Oxford paid for. Oxford has audited hundreds of psychiatrists, psychologists, and social workers...deemed their notes inadequate documentation of the sessions, and demanded repayment of thousands of dollars from each provider—in some cases, more than 100,000....

...The rules under Medicare and Medicaid are minimal, requiring a brief description of the session. Dr. Marcia K. Goin, president of the American Psychiatric Association, said that the group has no standards for note taking in therapy, and that in some cases it would be acceptable not to take any notes....

Lawyers in the health care field say insurers generally have the right to review patient records, and they do so from time to time, to combat fraud and rectify lapses in the quality of care.

I'd say that the key takeaway from the examination of this particular profession is that you should take a close look at the social issues around note taking in your profession. If you're taking notes in a situation where the other party is highly aware of your activity, you must be very careful that the tool fits the social requirements of the situation.

Similarly, if you're dealing with sensitive information, you must be sure that OneNote's security (which is basically Windows standard security features) is sufficient for your needs. For example, both legal professionals and mental health professionals are justifiably concerned about security. Bankers, accountants, and tax preparers using OneNote might all want to consider similar issues.

Consultants

Consultants often manage multiple projects, conduct informational interviews, do research, and attend meetings. As such, the consultant profile is a good fit for OneNote's feature set.

Since the whole point of consulting is delivering work product for a fee (although more cynical interpretations are possible), the most obvious opportunity for future enhancement is in the area of increasing OneNote's interoperability with work product tools like PowerPoint and Word by providing more import/export capabilities and OLE support.

Consultant Profile: Ed Kless, Organizational Development Consultant

Q. For what purpose do you use OneNote?

A. As a replacement for note paper. I try to not use paper at all, so the more notes and documents I can get into OneNote the better.

Q. What is your typical usage scenario?

A. Notes from meetings and phone calls, to do list, copy and paste articles for later reading.

Q. Favorite features?

A. The tab-style interface.

Q. Pet peeves?

A. Inability to print anything to a OneNote document. Inability to import "Journal" notes. *[Both issues are discussed in Chapter 5.—wfz]* Pen and select switching is difficult. *[This is improved in the RTM version of OneNote.—wfz]* Paste functionality from HTML is wacky. *[I discuss this issue in Chapter 3.—wfz]* Inability to really link to Outlook. I want to be able to right-click a meeting in Outlook and say "Send to OneNote" and have the attendees, date, time stamps, even an agenda populated in OneNote.

Historians

I wanted to include an example of a highly academic profession in which OneNote might be useful, and I found that academic historians have thought quite a bit about their note-taking needs; in fact, some well-developed software packages already exist in the field. For example, Table 8-2 presents a high-level summary list of the requirements for a popular historical note-taking program called Scribe, matched with a list of the requirements that are met by the first version of OneNote. As you can see, OneNote is already halfway to replacing specialized note-taking tools for historians.

Table 8-2. Comparison of Scribe and OneNote Features

Requirements for Scribe*	OneNote Version 1.0 Features
Create very long **notes** (up to 64,000 characters).	Yes
Store published and archival **sources** (up to 22 types of sources).	Yes
Create, print, and export **bibliographies.**	No
Copy footnote and parenthetical **references** to Clipboard in **Chicago** or **MLA** format.	No
Import sources from **online catalogs** (one at a time only).	No
Index note and source cards using a large number of **keywords.**	Yes
Store contact information and notes on **authors.**	Yes, but not in a contacts database
Add extended **comments** in a separate field.	Yes
Search notes and sources by author, title, keyword, note, comments, and other fields.	Yes—good free text search, although no database search
Perform **word search**: Find and highlight a specific word in the note.	Yes
Link sources to notes.	Yes—URL pasting
Link sources and notes to **images.**	Yes—URL pasting
Create **cross-reference** links.	No
Create an **outline.**	Yes
Create a **timeline.**	No
Create a **glossary** for your project.	No

* http://chnm.gmu.edu/tools/scribe/

As the table suggests, quite a bit of this functionality is already built into OneNote. As is often the case, the introduction of a powerful general-purpose application raises some interesting choices for current and prospective users of specialized applications. People who are already using the specialized application and relying heavily upon its power features, like bibliography exports, won't want to switch just yet. But prospective users who are "on the bubble" and haven't adopted the specialized application may find that the general-purpose application works well enough for their purposes. Future versions of OneNote may make it possible for developers and power users to fill some of the gaps for this specialized audience. And conversely, meeting some of this specialized audience's needs might be very useful for general audiences. How about a timeline that lets users sort notes either by their time stamp *or* by the values of any "smart tag" dates found in a note container?

Writers and Journalists

One of the OneNote team's primary user scenarios was the knowledge worker doing research for a project, so it comes as no surprise that the first version of OneNote offers some extremely useful features for writers and journalists.

- OneNote's navigational structure of folders, sections, page groups, pages, and subpages maps quite well to the busy life of a writer working on a number of projects.

- OneNote's ability to store multimedia content, including text, images, Web content, linked audio, and handwritten ink is a great match for the requirements of today's professional journalist, who often must capture and deliver multimedia graphic, image, and audio as well as plain old text.

- OneNote's synchronization of notes with audio recording is ideal for journalistic note taking, in which it's important to be able to find "landmarks" to help you navigate to the crucial portion of a verbatim quotation.

- The value of automatically saving and backing up should require little elaboration. Even professional journalists still occasionally lose data from time to time.

Journalist Profile: Donna Currie

Q. For what purposes do you use OneNote?

A. Meeting notes for newspaper staff meetings, weekly to do lists, and note taking for newspaper articles and when meeting with computer clients. I have a template set up for monthly newspaper articles/columns, so I can track what's assigned, received, edited, etc.

Q. What is your typical usage scenario?

A. The two things I use most are the to do list, which I check daily, and the notes during the weekly newspaper meetings. The to do's I usually type. The meeting notes I handwrite.

Q. Favorite features?

A. I'm pretty fond of the checkboxes and symbols and other organizational tools that make it easy to see what's done, what's critical, etc.

Q. Pet peeves?

A. The inability to save or import other files into OneNote.

[Remember that you can copy and paste many types of content into OneNote.—wfz]

Q. Wish list?

A. It would be nice to copy some text, move to another tab, and have that tab open so I can paste there.

The ability to set a default new page template for each tab, and/or an easier way to create a new page using templates.

Some way to pin Side Notes to other pages/sections or have them pop up when I open OneNote the first time I use it after creating a Side Note. Or maybe create links from them and paste the links onto other pages.

I've found that it's very helpful to create a standard template for interviews that I conduct using OneNote. The template, shown in Figure 8-2, includes a list of standard questions that I ask everyone.

TIP   Journalists will find that a telephone-to-PC sound adapter is a must have. Charles Hawkins reported, "I recently bought a 'TELEPHONE RECORDER & PLAY ADAPTOR' off of eBay for about $10 including shipping. If you know eBay, you can view the auction at #3047888261. The seller's handle is cardzrmine, so you can search on his handle. He seems to have a bunch of them for sale." Others have reported success with units from Dynametric and Teletool.

While there is no programmatic way to find all your audio notes in OneNote, there is a simple workaround that journalists may consider useful. Create a Custom note flag called Audio and attach it to every audio interview. Then you can create a note flag Summary Page that lists all your audio interviews.

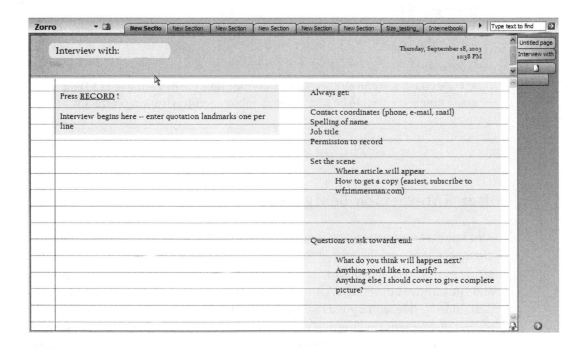

Figure 8-2. Journalist's interview template

The template is available at http://www.OneNoteInfoCenter.com.

Q. For what purpose do you use OneNote?

A. I record interviews for the articles I write.

Q. What is your typical usage scenario?

A. I'll record interviews, which typically last 15–30 minutes while I type notes. Later, when I'm writing the story, I'll review my notes and play back portions I'll use for direct quotes or need to review for accuracy.

Q. Favorite features?

A. The audio icon, which takes me directly to the portion I need to review. No rewinding and fast forwarding, and no accidentally recording over important interviews.

Q. Pet peeves?

A. It doesn't let me modify OneNote files over the network. I have to transfer the entire file instead.

Q. Wish list?

A. I wish there were an audio volume indicator (like the flickering red LED on many tape recorders) to be sure the microphone setup is working correctly.

User Interaction Designers

Also known as human factors engineers, information architects, and usability engineers, these are the people who build user interfaces to software; it's an interesting profession that requires a combination of technical, psychological, cognitive, and substantive knowledge. A group near and dear to my heart, as I spent five years side by side with a great team at LexisNexis. Their work practices are characterized by frequent small-group meetings, 1:1 observations of customers using products, storyboarding, rapid prototyping, and painstaking efforts to document what the software should do in a zillion different situations. OneNote might have been tailor-made for them.

Figure 8-3 shows the page tabs for a multipage OneNote section designed to facilitate rapid storyboarding of a typical user interaction scenario beginning with login, progressing through registration, to submitting a query and evaluating the results. This section is available in the OneNote Stationery Archive at http://www.OneNoteInfoCenter.com.

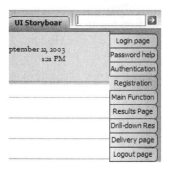

Figure 8-3. Multipage OneNote section for UI storyboarding a scenario beginning with login and progressing through to delivery of results

The nice thing about this set of pages is that it provides semistructured support for walking through a user scenario with a logical flow from beginning to end. A team can put standard information and standard issues on the template, so that certain issues are always asked. If the user interaction designer has a Tablet PC, she can sketch simple wireframes and page layouts. When discussing the storyboarding results, the team can flip rapidly from page to page—almost like having a presentation tool built in. Later notes can be accumulated above the original ones, and the resulting file shared via e-mail or network.

Future needs: better support for drawing tools so that designers can create *wireframes,* or simple outline sketches that illustrate ideas without committing prematurely to particular visual details.

Personal Information Architecture for Note Taking: Interview with Lou Rosenfeld, coauthor of *Information Architecture for the World Wide Web* (2nd ed.)

Lou Rosenfeld is an independent information architecture consultant. He was instrumental in establishing the field of information architecture, and in articulating the role and value of librarianship within the field. With Peter Morville, Lou coauthored the best-selling book, *Information Architecture for the World Wide Web,*[3] Amazon.com's "Best Internet Book of 1998," which has been acclaimed as a classic and is used as a standard text in many graduate-level classes. Here, Lou provides an information architect's perspective on note taking in general and OneNote in particular.

---

3. O'Reilly, 1998; second edition, 2002.

Q. Lou, before we talk about the particulars of the program Microsoft OneNote, let's talk about what the discipline of information architecture has to offer to an individual who wants to become more productive, accurate, and efficient in her note taking for school, work, or personal tasks.

A. Information architecture is usually focused on making large bodies of content more accessible to audiences, such as the users of a Web site. We're actually trying to help people who create information move away from designs that only make sense to themselves and toward more broadly understandable approaches. So our goal is a bit different than that of the individual who is drowning in personal information.

Interestingly, in the foreword to our book's second edition [http://www.useit.com/books/rosenfeldmorvilleforeword2.html], Jakob Nielsen predicts that "personal information architecture may turn out to be even more important than corporate information architecture." And he may be right: The skills and methods that help us organize information for broader audiences should certainly help us organize our own information better. And even if we are the only people who will ever use our own information, we change over time and may forget what we were thinking when we originally labeled that crowded folder "important stuff".

On the other hand, a pessimist might counter that most well-funded corporations who rely on their information systems to support employees and customers don't bother to invest in information architecture. If they don't see the incentive for well-organized information, why would individuals? Well, I'm an optimist, and as I see the demand for "impersonal information architecture" grow, I'm hopeful that individuals will begin to value personal information architecture as well.

Q. Now let's zoom in a bit to the world of actual software. Microsoft OneNote doesn't require Microsoft Office to run, but many people will encounter it for the first time as part of the Office 2003 suite. When most people think of Office, they think of power, integration, and, yes, complexity. Although there are alternatives, for many of us, programs like Word, Excel, PowerPoint, and Outlook are the standard desktop productivity environment. How can a sense of personal information architecture aid the end user in dealing with the complex world of Microsoft Office?

A. Perhaps the designers of those tools might be kind enough to use OneNote to annotate their applications' many and often confusing features? This may sound like yet another slap at Microsoft, but their applications' user documentation is notoriously poor, failing especially when it comes to providing useful contextual help. I'd love to see some sort of alternative to the current help system, and perhaps forcing Office developers to take notes on their own applications might be a step in that direction.

Of course, I'd hope that if Microsoft went this route, they'd have a team of technical communicators edit these notes. Hmm. That sounds more like a group note-taking system, not so much a personal system. Which makes me wonder: Will OneNote's output be shareable, exchangeable, and editable by more than one individual? *[Yes— multiple individuals can edit, one at a time, by file sharing. See Chapter 5.—wfz]* If so, that would be pretty impressive! Almost like overlaying a wiki on top of any form of digital content. *[A wiki is a "piece of server software that allows users to freely create and edit Web page content using any Web browser."[4]—wfz]*

Q. Now add the ten-second explanation of OneNote to the equation: It's a new member of the Office family that is intended to support Office users in note-taking scenarios in meetings, in class, or in personal projects. What information architecture concerns would you suggest should be uppermost in the user's mind as she familiarizes herself with OneNote?

A. My concerns are more related to usability than information architecture. I'd suggest that users give OneNote's tires a good kick, with special attention paid to usage context. For example, if you're planning on using OneNote to take notes during a lecture, make sure that its interface won't slow you down to the point that you can't keep up with the lecturer. Another concern is integration: The existing Office suite applications aren't as well integrated as they could be, and these tools have been around and packaged together for quite some time. Will OneNote be any better integrated? I hope so; the product won't be especially useful if OneNote's designers haven't closed that loop.

Q. Take a look at the official Microsoft OneNote Web site (http://www.microsoft.com/onenote) and let me know what is your experience, as an information architect, from examining the relatively detailed "official" information presented there. What are the most interesting and important things that you learned about OneNote? What do you want to know next?

A. If I understand it correctly, OneNote supports a hierarchy (notebooks, folders, and pages), which I'm quite happy to see; although simple hierarchies aren't the best or only way to organize large amounts of information, they do come in quite handy from time to time. I do hope there are ways of connecting note content across these hierarchical branches as well.

OneNote seems to provide limited support for metadata; even if users keep their choice of metadata fields simple, they'll often trip over which metadata values or terms to apply. Language is so ambiguous, and it's hard to see many people populating their metadata fields with clear and consistently applied terms. And as always with personally applied metadata, most users won't bother anyway. (Be honest: How many of you complete the summary tab in Microsoft Word's Properties?)

The OneNote site itself does a nice job by providing usage scenarios. And the product summary is short and sweet; it does make me want to learn more.

Q. Lou, you're an expert in enterprise information architecture. Let's say that the CEO of a client tells you that his Microsoft account rep recently gave an impressive presentation on Office 2003 and that he (your client) is excited about the idea of making his organization and its employees more productive by using OneNote as a tool to add value to information gathering-note taking— that is today informal and unstructured (scribbles on a yellow pad, as it were). He wants you to take a close look at OneNote for this purpose. What considerations about OneNote, and the enterprise in which it's deployed, are going to be uppermost in your mind as you approach this task?

---

4. http://wiki.org/wiki.cgi?WhatIsWiki

A. While I might suggest that my client continue to investigate OneNote as a means of improving employee productivity, I'd steer him away from OneNote as an enterprise tool. It doesn't seem to be especially strong at making content accessible to a broader audience of users, such as an enterprise's research team. *[Unless you use Windows SharePoint Services.—wfz]* Why? Because personal information management is about making your content accessible to yourself first and foremost; other users' needs are secondary at best. So while tools like OneNote may help users capture or create new content objects, they won't help make these objects accessible, searchable, browsable, and most of all under-standable to a wider audience of users.

Instead I'd be taking a long hard look at k-logs and wikis; they seem to hold much more promise for solving information problems in the enterprise environment.

["All k-logs are Web logs. K-logs are a species of Web logs. K-logs are Web logs used specifically for the purposes of sharing/documenting knowledge and/or sharing the process of knowledge-making."[5]]

Storyteller Profile: Marc Orchant

I am the storyteller at VanDyke Software, a software development company in Albuquerque, New Mexico. The three major areas of activity in which I engage in storytelling and use OneNote are managing content development for our Web site, public relations, and marketing communications.

I have been looking for a tool that offers the section and document approach OneNote uses as its paradigm, and have for some time relied on a shareware tool called Black Hole Organizer. It's been a good tool but uses an Explorer-tree orga-nization system that frankly is kind of dull.

Also, I "live" in Outlook and am really looking forward to the new 2003 version with its improvements. Adopting OneNote seems like a good plan going forward. I realize the integration between OneNote and Outlook is limited in the initial release, but I foresee great potential for tighter integration as the product matures.

One of the things I enjoy most about OneNote that no other tool handles as nicely is the source stamping when pasting information from the Web or another file. I've been using one section in OneNote as a scrapbook of sorts for gathering source material before I start drafting a new Web page or article.

Another feature that has proven indispensable is the note flags. I've customized a flag for each of my major activity areas so that when I'm drafting a project brief that covers these different areas, it's quite easy to see at a glance what kind of

---

5. http://radio.weblogs.com/0106698/2002/10/26.html

ratio there is between marketing, PR, and Web work. The checkbox feature of the flags aids in getting a quick visual assessment of project status.

OneNote is also a great palette for organizing reviewer's comments. I drag and drop commentary from e-mails onto a review page and then consolidate and organize the information after I've finished harvesting. It's really quite a flexible environment for collection, organization, and review of information.

I need the word count tool because I write a lot of press releases, and the cost to distribute them over the wire is predicated on the number of words. A few too many, and the cost of a release goes up by a couple of hundred dollars! I also maintain listings for the evaluation versions of our seven software titles on a large number of download sites, many of which are restrictive in how many words can be used in a short, medium, or long description of the product.

I'm also developing a manuscript about a project discipline I've been developing over the past few years that utilizes mind mapping to generate the project "building blocks"—Outlook for assignment and interactive progress management on specific tasks, and MS Project for more traditional Gantt charting, resource allocation, and baselining. Of course, each section of the manuscript is a separate OneNote section and each chapter (draft) is a OneNote page. This makes moving elements of the manuscript around quite simple and much more creatively liberating than anything I can do in Word once I move past the outline stage.

Software Professionals

Software professionals are usually well represented in beta test populations, and this poses a challenge for both product developers and computer journalists, because software professionals may have substantially different requirements than the mainstream users who will determine the product's commercial success. To judge by early results, one aspect of OneNote that strikes a chord with software professionals is its strength at keeping track of multiple small bits of information. For better or worse, mastery of a large amount of arcana is an important skill for software professionals, and it's great to have a place to stick those paths, mnemonics, and snippets of information. Where OneNote begins to encounter difficulty, as the profile illustrates, is when it's pushed too far. There's a tendency to want it to behave like a code editor instead of a note-taking and outlining tool!

Software Professional Profile: David Salahi

Q. For what purpose do you use OneNote?

A. Collecting many bits of information and ideas on a wide variety of topics.

Q. What is your typical usage scenario?

A. It would be hard to pick a single scenario, as I use it for several purposes both at home and at work. At work I use it to collect bits of information about the software development projects and technologies I work on. At home I use it for various personal projects that I am working on, including my volunteer work as well as ideas and research for a novel.

Q. Favorite features?

A. Its free-form data entry nature; folders, sections, and pages/subpages structure; search capabilities; and ability to paste graphics and Web pages together with text anywhere on a page. There's good keyboard support. I'm also looking forward to using handwriting and voice input when I get a notebook or Tablet PC.

Q. Pet peeves?

A. If you paste text with a lot of tabs or spaces, OneNote reformats your text into columns, which it thinks look nice. This wreaks havoc with code fragments that I try to paste into it. I've also had the problem on occasion with noncode text pasted from other apps.

Also, some keyboard support is missing (e.g., moving to the beginning/end of a note).

Senior Executives

"C-level" executives in corporations—such as chief executive officers, chief information officers, chief technology officers—can expect to hear about Microsoft OneNote, if only because OneNote is an optional add-on to Office 2003. When to migrate to the next version of Office is a major corporate decision that typically must be blessed by the C-level executives, and Microsoft has a large international sales force dedicated to encouraging corporations to upgrade Office as fast as possible. These facts almost guarantee that C-level executives will be presented with a "yea or nay" recommendation about OneNote as part of a presentation about when to upgrade Office 2003. The recommendation will probably take the form "We plan to deploy Office 2003 (when). We're going to deploy (some number) of OneNote licenses and (have some plan for deciding what to do next)." The following sidebar will help you understand how one chief technology officer might approach the formulation of such a recommendation.

....

A Chief Technology Officer's Perspective: Interview with Dan Woods, author of *The Evolved Technologist*

Dan Woods is the founder and editor in chief of Evolved Media Network. Dan was CTO for two Internet companies, TheStreet.com and Capital Thinking, and a director of Editorial Technology at Time Warner New Media. He is writing a book, entitled The Evolved Technologist,[6] *about improving the performance of technology executives. Here, Dan provides an evolved technologist's perspective on meeting OneNote.*

Q. Dan, your situation may be not unlike that of many CTOs and senior technologists as they encounter Microsoft OneNote for the first time. You have heard something about it from friends or colleagues (in this case, me!), but you have not yet had occasion to become familiar with it. The ten-word explanation is that OneNote is a new member of the Office 2003 family focused on note taking and research organization. What questions does that spark in your mind?

A. I have long been a fan and user of free text databases, and I think now that an entire generation has been raised to be proficient types, the time has come for this technology.

The most profound benefit for me of OneNote and similar programs is the flexibility that they offer. *You must be organized. No program will do it for you. [Emphasis mine.—wfz]* OneNote provides a container flexible enough to contain the notes and other fragments of information to match the ad hoc structure of almost any project.

I use free text databases to jot information down on the six or seven projects that I am usually working on. I find that the notes are great ticklers for my memory and I never feel any more like I've lost good ideas.

Q. Take a look at the official Microsoft OneNote Web site (http://www.microsoft.com/onenote) and let me know how you approach the relatively detailed "official" informat ion presented there. What elements of the "official" explanation of OneNote are most striking to you? What are the "unofficial" points of information that you are now most curious about?

A. I think there isn't enough emphasis on the management of small chunks of text, which will be the most useful part of the program.

---

6. Addison-Wesley, forthcoming

Q. Let's say that your friendly local Microsoft account rep has had a chance to give your CEO a song and dance about Office 2003, and he has come away from it enthusing about Microsoft OneNote as a tool for improving productivity of your enterprise and its employees. He's asked you and your team to look into the program and make a recommendation about initial deployment strategy. What approach would you take?

A. I would put it in the hands of people who were collaborating about client service like sales or account managers, or people who were working on a development project. I would see if it could act as a local area wiki with a more portable and powerful format.

Summary

I've shown you a number of different uses and abuses of OneNote in this chapter, and I trust certain patterns are beginning to emerge as you consider using OneNote in your profession.

- There's a good chance that OneNote's first version functionality will meet a substantial fraction of your personal information management needs, because most professions have a project orientation, frequent meetings and interviews, and considerable amounts of interim work product.

- It's also likely that the first version of OneNote won't satisfy the power user requirements of your profession, simply because this is the first version and all effort was concentrated on getting a useful set of features out the door for everyone.

- Audio-synced notes are helpful to almost every profession right now.

- OLE support in OneNote will be important for most professions in the future.

- In the future, an API might enable power users and developers to fill "power user" gaps for particular professions.

- Security is a concern in professions that deal with sensitive information. Although Windows provides significant security features, users in such professions might feel better if OneNote had some application-specific security features built in.

- It's important to consider where you are in the life cycle of your profession and in the pecking order of your organization.

In the next chapter, we'll discuss third-party applications (not from Microsoft) that can make your use of OneNote more effective and enjoyable.

CHAPTER 9

Using OneNote with Other Applications

IN THIS CHAPTER I'll discuss several ways of using OneNote with other applications—both to enhance its strengths and to remedy its weaknesses. I'll emphasize at the outset that this discussion of other applications makes no pretense of being comprehensive. There are simply too many other applications out there! But if I omit a program you find to be a good "partner" with OneNote, by all means tell me about it with an e-mail to wfz@onenoteinfocenter.com.

Using Software to Remedy OneNote's Failings

I'll begin with some programs you can use to deal with known limitations in OneNote. These programs are for situations where you know that you're attached enough to OneNote that you want to make the relationship work, but your primary concern is "fixing" its faults. They're marriage counselors, if you will!

Snag-It Captures Web Pages As Is

OneNote handles pasted Web pages in an innovative and clever way, but a lot of people have expressed frustration at the way OneNote translates pasted Hypertext Markup Language (HTML) into an outline format that it can understand (see Chapter 3, "Taking Your First Notes"). The HTML structure of the copied page doesn't always cooperate—it can be difficult or impossible to select just the portion of a Web page that you want when the layout relies on nested tables, framesets, and image maps. Then much of the remaining HTML is stripped away when it's pasted into OneNote.

In many cases, users just want to capture part (not all) of a Web page in OneNote exactly as it appears on their screen. For that situation, an image capture program such as TechSmith's SnagIt can be just right. The great thing about using SnagIt with OneNote is that you can capture just the portion of the screen you want and paste it into OneNote like a scrapbook, annotated with nearby text containers as you want (see Figure 9-1).

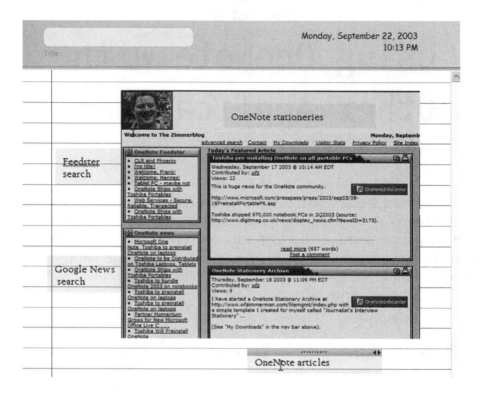

Figure 9-1. Partial Web page (http://www.OneNoteInfoCenter.com) *captured as an image with SnagIt and annotated in OneNote*

TIP   If you want to copy the Uniform Resource Locator (URL) from the original page, highlight a space or a single character and paste it in underneath the SnagIt image.

This works much better than copying an equivalent section of the same Web page and pasting it into OneNote (see Figure 9-2).

(Note that the Paste As Image option wasn't available because the content pasted is a mixture of HTML and images.)

If your use of OneNote will involve frequent "scrapbooking" of Web pages, SnagIt is a great tool for a modest price (http://www.techsmith.com).

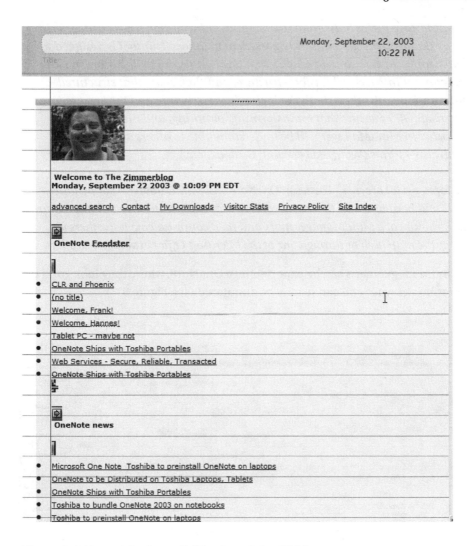

Figure 9-2. Doesn't look much like the original Web page

MindManager Helps You Visualize Projects

MindManager from Mindjet is a well-regarded and popular visual tool for brainstorming and planning. Its highly visual nature complements OneNote well. Hobie Swan, a Mindjet spokesman, says the following:

> *OneNote seems to be designed for individual users—a way for them to build personal repositories of personal information. OneNote is really great for capturing images, sounds, Web site content, etc. and building a kind of scrap book of personal information.*

MindManager helps individual users capture information too—but does so in a way that content can be quickly passed on to others. Our tool is designed to help people capture content quickly and without regard to linear order, place this content into a clearly visible structure, and then share that structured information with others. Both the hierarchical structure and the exports to Microsoft Office ensure that brainstorming, planning, and meeting notes captured in MindManager will be understandable to others and available in multiple forms (Word, PowerPoint, Outlook, etc.).

We foresee a lot of synergy between OneNote and MindManager: For instance, users will be able to take the varied content they capture in OneNote, put it into the structure of a MindManager map, and then communicate it to others via either the map itself or through one of the Microsoft Office exports we support.

MindManager maps can be exported into OneNote, where they look good in the scrapbook layout and can readily be annotated (see Figure 9-3).

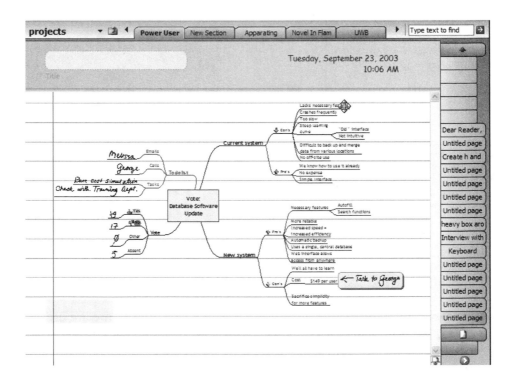

Figure 9-3. You can export a MindManager map into OneNote. (Note that end nodes contain both ink and text.)

Conversely, you can drag content in OneNote containers into MindManager. The easiest way to do this is to have two program windows side by side (see Figure 9-4).

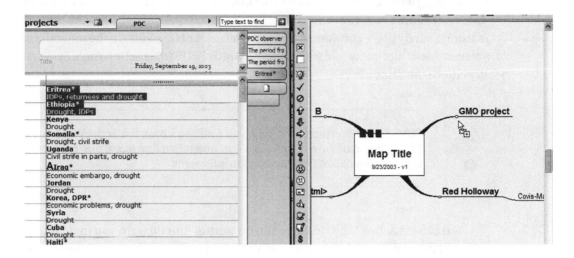

Figure 9-4. OneNote and MindManager side by side

Content dragged from OneNote into MindManager automatically creates new tree branches in MindManager—pretty cool! (see Figure 9-5).

Figure 9-5. These phrases dragged from OneNote containers become attached to MindManager end nodes.

 CAUTION Hold down Ctrl as you drag from OneNote to MindManager so that your OneNote content is copied, not cut. Because OneNote autosaves the current page every *n* seconds, cut content may be difficult to retrieve.

If you're a visual thinker, MindManager will be a great complement to OneNote.

ActiveWords PLUS Accelerates Time Stamping and Text Entry

One missing feature in the first version of OneNote is the ability to insert the current date and/or time anywhere in a note on command. This relatively straightforward feature is surely being considered for future releases of OneNote. In the meantime, you can use a third-party tool such as ActiveWords PLUS from ActiveWords Systems to achieve the same effect.

 TIP   To do date/time stamping, you must purchase the ActiveWords PLUS edition of the software, and you must then download the free InPlace application from ActiveWords Systems.

You can set ActiveWords PLUS to run on startup (but I'll warn you that I found it slowed things down a bit then), or you can configure it at any time via My Programs. The program comes with a few preset keyboard equivalencies, and you can add many other powerful commands via prepared dictionaries or on an ad-hoc basis. The interface to ActiveWords PLUS is a simple drop-down menu that pops up wizards as needed. See, for example, the ActiveWords Add Wizard in Figure 9-6.

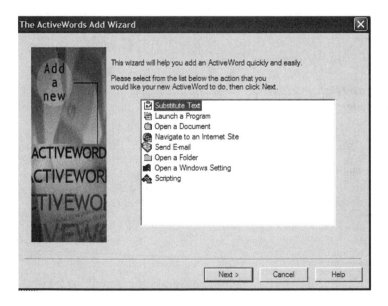

Figure 9-6. Adding an ActiveWord

Note that new ActiveWords can do a variety of functions, including substituting text, launching a program, opening a document, navigating to an Internet site, sending an e-mail, opening a folder, and scripted sequences of ActiveWords commands. ActiveWords PLUS runs throughout your Windows environment, not just in OneNote. Whenever you type a string, it recognizes the ActiveWord, and the program does a predefined action such as substituting a text string, launching a program, or running an ActiveWords script.

The great strength of ActiveWords PLUS for OneNote users is that the two programs reinforce each other. OneNote is all about quick, intuitive entry of information. The guiding metaphor of ActiveWords PLUS, according to Chief Executive Officer Buzz Bruggerman, is enabling users to go smoothly "from an impulse to an utterance to a predictable result." In other words, the ActiveWords user knows that if he has the merest impulse to take an action, all he has to do is to type a quick acronym such as *dt* for date and time, and the computer will translate it into a formal utterance and deliver a predictable result.

The commands available in the InPlace application include several flavors of date and time stamping as well as mathematical calculations. The most useful one for OneNote users is probably the Date & Time Stamp, which I have customized to *dt* in my system (see Figure 9-7).

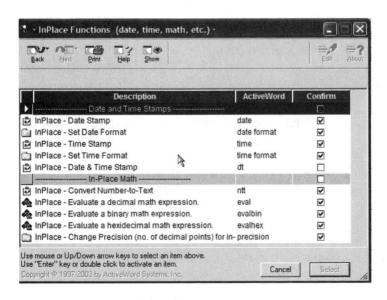

Figure 9-7. I changed the Date & Time Stamp to dt and turned off confirmation.

If you're the sort of person who prefers the command line interface and likes keyboard shortcuts, you'll like ActiveWords PLUS from `http://www.activewords.com`.

> **TIP** The AutoCorrect feature in Office and OneNote is limited to text substitutions inside those applications and doesn't support date/time stamping. ActiveWords PLUS is far more flexible and programmable and can insert date/time stamps in OneNote.

Forced Marriages

A few programs are so ubiquitous that they simply need to play well with OneNote, even if neither the program manufacturer nor Microsoft particularly cares about interoperability between OneNote and the other program. The leading example of this "forced marriage" situation is Adobe Acrobat and the Portable Document Format (PDF) standard. There's little reason for Adobe to care about being compatible with OneNote, and Microsoft has been pushing competing standards to PDF for years. But OneNote users, especially in the educational market, which is one of Microsoft's top priorities, are bound to encounter PDF content, and it's only natural for them to want to be able to use it in OneNote.

Getting PDF into OneNote Is Frustrating

The most straightforward solution would be for OneNote to be able to import PDF files, but that's not available in this first version.

The next most straightforward solution would be to create a "print to OneNote" driver so that users could print PDF files into OneNote format, but that's not available in this first version either.

These barriers have caused frustration among some users. As Michael Costello of Boston University observed in a Usenet posting to news:microsoft.public.onenote:

> *The [OneNote] pitch as an academic note taker is really a nonstarter for many classes. With outside readings as PDF and notes distributed by the professor (usually Word, PDF, or PowerPoint), the inability to incorporate these items into the whole of one's notes is a severe handicap.*

In a later posting, Costello gave some additional detail about why importing PDF into OneNote is so important for some types of academic users:

> *My original remarks were based on my experience in an economics Ph.D. program. In this arena, PDF is the coin of the realm for academic papers. This isn't likely to change. Moreover, these papers are highly technical and include a lot of equations, etc. It is invaluable to be able to make "inline" notes, within the document, as one reads it or goes through it in a class. Journal does a great job of this, but I do miss some of the niceties of OneNote when I use that approach.*

In response to these challenges, OneNote users have evolved a variety of workarounds.

PDF Workarounds

The following are workarounds for using PDF in OneNote:

- Use Acrobat Reader's copy text and copy image capabilities to paste the content into OneNote one chunk at a time. (Admittedly, this isn't a very attractive option because you'll lose all the PDF formatting, which is the whole point of PDF.)

- Create a local relative file link in the following manner: Drag your PDF document to the OneNote toolbar, wait a moment, and then release while the mouse is over the OneNote page. A shortcut of the form *<file: pdf_filename.pdf>* will be created in the current OneNote page. You can click this link from within OneNote, and the PDF document will open in Adobe Acrobat.

TIP   Courtesy of Usenet poster Charles Hawkins: For a blank space in the filename, you have to type the escape of *%20* for each blank space.

- Create a local relative link to a shortcut to the PDF file. "Right-click the file in question in Windows Explorer. Make a new shortcut of the file. Drag this onto your OneNote page. Now OneNote makes a copy of the shortcut file instead of the original. I can live well with multiple copies of the shortcut and, in fact, can send them along with the .ONE file, changing the shortcut pointer in the shortcut file as necessary." —Charles Hawkins[1]

- "ScanSoft makes a product called *PDF Converter* that converts PDFs into Word documents. [They do not yet make a] version for OneNote [but perhaps they will fairly soon]. In the meantime, you could convert the documents to Word format and then cut and paste into OneNote." —Grant Robertson[2]

- If you are a Tablet PC user, print the PDF file to Windows Journal and mark the document up in Journal. Then use OneNote note flags to mark the places in OneNote where you will insert Journal files. —Michael Costello[3]

---

1.   Posting to news:microsoft.public.onenote
2.   Posting to news:microsoft.public.onenote
3.   Posting to news:microsoft.public.onenote

OneNote into PDF Is Easy

Although going from PDF into OneNote is hard, going from OneNote to PDF is easy. You can print from OneNote to the Acrobat print driver, which means you can turn OneNote documents directly into PDFs. Figure 9-8 shows an example. Very cool!

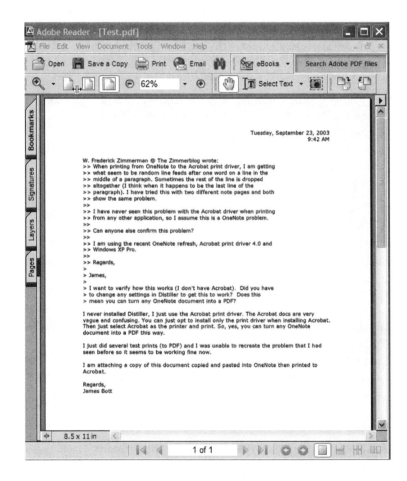

Figure 9-8. A OneNote document printed to Acrobat

 CAUTION Some users have reported difficulty when right margins are set very narrow on the OneNote page. Changing the margin fixed the problem.

Info Select

Micro Logic's Info Select, once known as *Tornado*, is an all-in-one organizing tool with a long history (since 1986) and some devoted users. There's some overlap between the Info Select and OneNote audiences because both groups include "early adopters" of personal organizing tools. I'll spend a moment talking about Info Select and OneNote to illustrate another "forced marriage" scenario, where the challenge is harmonizing your use of OneNote with the use of a different intuitive note-taking tool.

Info Select has a clean user interface that's organized around a living outline (see Figures 9-9 and 9-10).

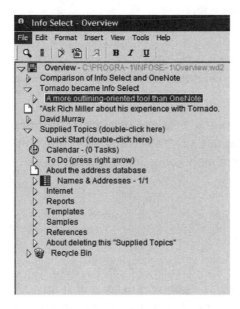

Figure 9-9. Info Select

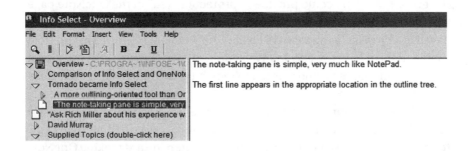

Figure 9-10. The note-taking tool is a simple white screen that appears to the right of the outline tree.

Info Select and OneNote can play together to a limited degree. You can take notes in OneNote, and then paste them into Info Select. You can also go the other direction. In each case, you're going via the Clipboard. This has some interesting effects when you go from OneNote to Info Select because OneNote pages are posted to Info Select as images (see Figure 9-11).

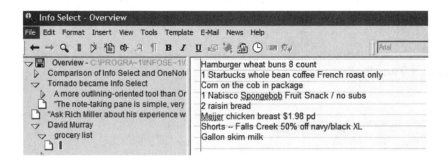

Figure 9-11. This grocery list was pasted from OneNote into Info Select as an image.

The fundamental issue is whether you want to have two separate repositories for notes. Probably not! In situations such as this, the "forced marriage" probably won't work. The bottom line is that you're probably going to wind up having to choose between Info Select and OneNote.

Web and Database Integration

The first version of OneNote doesn't provide very flexible tools for transmitting queries to remote Web and database services. The only way to go "out" from OneNote to data stored elsewhere is either to click a hyperlink in OneNote—which takes you out of OneNote to a browser—or to use Office 2003's Research pane, which unfortunately is rather limited in its first incarnation.

It'd be great if OneNote could provide a "protected area" in the OneNote page so that a user could paste an HTML form into the OneNote page. Even if the results are displayed in a browser (as opposed to inside OneNote), HTML forms in OneNote would enable users to leverage existing Web applications. For example, imagine if you heard an unfamiliar term and wanted to look it up without leaving your note-taking page.

Other Office applications, such as Word and Excel, now allow the user to insert content into the current document via a call to a remote server. Adding such capabilities to a future version of OneNote would be a long step toward making OneNote a more flexible tool for educational publishing—imagine a .ONE file for a physics class filled with latest experiment results from a database server!

Summary

This chapter's discussion of complementary programs just scratches the surface. As the OneNote user base becomes larger, and as new versions of OneNote are released, undoubtedly other useful partnerships will emerge. The chapter covered the following:

- SnagIt is great for image capture and scrapbooking.

- ActiveWords lets you insert time and date stamps.

- The educational market needs a better way to get PDFs into OneNote.

- OneNote is most likely to be complementary with third-party applications that are highly focused on manipulation of specific types of data—text, images, audio, and pasted HTML.

- OneNote is most likely to cause frustration when users have a strong need to bring data from a third-party application or format, such as PDF, that's simply very different.

- OneNote is most likely to conflict with applications that also have ambitions to be "all-in-one" managers.

In the next chapter, you'll look at the future of OneNote.

Looking to the Future of OneNote

IN THIS CHAPTER I'll provide a speculative look at the future of OneNote. I want to leave you with the thought that this first version of OneNote is just that. The dominant maker of personal productivity software has decided that note taking is serious, and good news will keep coming for people who are interested in making themselves more productive.

Of course, it's too early to make any definitive statements about the details. If past experience is any guide, Microsoft will probably not commit to any future release dates or specific features in those releases until a few months before the actual release dates. But I can help you understand what may happen in the future.

First, I'll discuss some of the experiences that trial users had during the OneNote beta. Of course, the Release to Manufacturing (RTM) product was substantially improved over the beta, but it's still possible to make some strongly qualified observations about what seemed to work and what seemed to be problematic.

Second, I'll present a few "wish lists" from lead users. Research in product development and usability testing (of which Microsoft is well aware) has shown that engaging lead users can be a useful way to guide the development of software in certain conditions.

Third, I'll tell you a bit more about the implications of the Office 2003 launch, which includes OneNote.

Finally, I'll close with a few thoughts about why OneNote is revolutionary and important.

Learning Lessons from the OneNote Beta

The OneNote beta was public and involved tens of thousands of end users, so it's fair to discuss some of the themes that emerged during the beta. Again, I stress that the beta software was just that, beta test software, and that the RTM version was considerably improved in many ways. As you read the following sections, bear that in mind.

Using Beta Versions

The latest version of the beta software doesn't expire until January 31, 2004, so it's possible you may purchase this book while still running the beta version of the software. If you're in any doubt as to whether you're running the beta, there's an easy way to tell. Look at the title bar on the OneNote window. If it says *Microsoft Office OneNote 2003 Beta,* you're running the beta.

There were two major versions of the beta software—the first major release in the spring of 2003, commonly referred to as *beta 2,* and a second major release in the summer, commonly referred to as the *beta 2 technical refresh,* or B2R. The B2R fixed a lot of bugs and ran much more smoothly than the first beta. There were minor changes between B2R and the RTM version of OneNote.

Learning from People Who Didn't Like the Beta

A fundamental principle of reasoned discussion is that one of the best ways to understand what's good about something is to see what someone else thinks is *bad* about it! It's for that reason that it's worthwhile to spend a few pages giving you a sample of a few negative reactions to the beta software.

The OneNote beta prompted a number of interesting *cris du coeur* (cries from the heart) from prospective OneNote users who found obstacles they couldn't overcome. I've reproduced a couple of the more thoughtful early negative reactions to OneNote, with permission, to illustrate what OneNote may need to conquer to convert some of its doubters.

David Terron, Disappointed OneNote Beta Tester

David Terron is a 22-year veteran of the British Army and an Information Technology (IT) administrator who is now a teacher of English literature in northern Scotland. He wanted to use OneNote to help him prepare his courses:

> *I've tried—oh, Lord, how I've tried—to use this software to hold all my notes for lectures and seminars on the early poets such as John Donne, Alexander Pope, and so on. Milton would never have written* Paradise Lost *had he used OneNote!*

But if he had written it using OneNote, he wouldn't have lost it, thanks to OneNote's automatic backup feature (a point suggested by beta tester Andrew Watt)! David continues:

I thought having looked at the FAQ, the handouts, the Web site examples, and so on that OneNote would do the job for me. Alas alack! It is…way too complicated for the simple tasks most people need and is really more suitable for the "gadget fiends" with their tablets. Perhaps in a few years OneNote will come of age. Until then…bye-bye, OneNote; you're the weakest link on my laptop and my PC and are hereby exterminated via the waste bin.[1]

David continues:

The other thing I wanted to do with OneNote is keep quotes, both literary and essay ones for future use by myself or students. Again, OneNote doesn't do this perfectly. Admittedly, a database program would be ideal, and thus I've turned to WizQuote from the same people who gave us TexNotes and now have some 54,000 quotes by subject, author, and suitability for inclusion in essays.

I also looked at a program called Writer's Block, which is quite good for planning and then writing essays because it shows Post-it-type blocks in columns that you can review and move around. Another excellent one is Scribe, which I use for my honors history course. It's ideal for keeping quotes and notes and at the same time maintaining a bibliography of what, where, when (and so on) the information has come from. It's ideal for research into my regimental history for a forthcoming book.

So although I felt OneNote had potential, I've found other, more suitable programs that do the job for free or a very low price…and have potential for improved productivity. OneNote I believe is suitable for tablet or small laptops, for use onsite as it were, where information is gathered and needs to be input quickly. Moreover, the chances are that much of the information gathered is actually better manipulated within a spreadsheet or database, and I foresee screams from the beta testers for better export/import facilities so they can gather the info, put it into Access or Excel, get the data or forecast they want, and then bung it back into OneNote. Again, I appreciate that it's a beta and that 90 percent of the bugs and problems will be resolved prior to RTM (November 2003?). But for what I want it to do, OneNote is still not there yet.[2]

To be sure, David is in some ways atypical of the OneNote target user. For example, it's evident he has a higher tolerance for installing and experimenting with new software than many of us do. But many of the points he raises are ones that'll sound a chord for other prospective users. Indeed, OneNote must become

---

1. Posted to Usenet news:Microsoft.public.onenote, May 29, 2003; message ID: 524501c325ea$f595b530$a301280a@phx.gbl

2. Personal communication, David Terron, June 2, 2003

better at importing and exporting other types of information, both from Web pages and from more structured information tools such as spreadsheets and databases. David continues:

> *Okay, it's a replacement for the yellow legal pad. Hmmm. I just opened Notepad on XP, turned on the built-in handwriting recognition in XP, and scribbled away. My scribbles got translated into text in Notepad. And Notepad will append a time and date stamp to the file. I can write anywhere on screen, too. And amazingly it doesn't even cavil about the refresh rate of my USB mouse or my USB pen.*

> *It sounds like the primary market is [Microsoft] employees going to [Microsoft] meetings, and [Microsoft] wants to cut down on the noise of the keystrokes. I suspect "knowledge workers" will need something a lot more fully fleshed than OneNote—something that has timelining, date stamping, and the ability to relate and interconnect things, for example, Scribe or even old Ecco.*

The cry for more power features is a familiar one, and experience suggests two perspectives. First, no development team can focus entirely on power features. Especially with a first release of personal productivity software, it's far more important to develop a set of basic features that meet the needs of a large group of people. Second, time will resolve some of the desire for power features as new versions of OneNote include more power features and as users become accustomed to those existing power features that are unique to OneNote. David continues:

> *Taking notes is not an end in itself; the notes are always part of a process, part of the means to some end. OneNote doesn't facilitate reaching any end.*

David's last point is an important and provocative comment although, in all likelihood, an incorrect one. It's food for thought, though. I suggest that perhaps the most important takeaway is whether you, as a prospective OneNote user, have a clear end in mind.

Microsoft has taken on a challenging problem. Hitherto, note taking was a poorly supported part of knowledge workers' daily workflow, and OneNote is a wonderful step forward. But Microsoft, having "grasped the nettle," must continue, in future releases of OneNote, to improve the process of turning notes into final work product.

David Parody, Fundamental Resistance to Change

David Parody was another beta tester who had a negative response to OneNote:

I've given up trying to find a use for this program. Yes, the cool gimmick value of this product is fine, but finding a real-world application for it is too much. I've already deleted it from my system.

If I need digital ink notes, I'll use Journal (but a scrap piece of paper is better!), which has better handwriting recognition. Otherwise, I'll use Word to write notes using the Tablet PC Input Panel. I can't see desktop users converting to OneNote for any reason.

I think Microsoft has tried to take the pen and paper metaphor too far by even changing the present metaphor beyond what people can understand. With OneNote, Microsoft wants to change the way we work; I'm an old dog, and you can't teach me new tricks.

Sorry, but I'd rather have software work for me rather than the other way around....

What this comment highlights is that OneNote's unique user interface represents change, and decades of experience with personal computing software shows that dramatic user interface changes are always risky and that there are many people who simply resist change.

What Office 2003 Means for OneNote's Future

OneNote was first released as a stand-alone companion to the Office 2003 family of programs. This relationship raises some interesting possibilities for OneNote's future.

Office Shared Services

The individual Office programs already share many services that enable them to offer common functionality. OneNote has already benefited from these services in a number of ways with features such as fonts, bullets, and AutoCorrect. It's likely that future releases will see OneNote take advantage of other Office shared services. Essentially, if the feature is already present in two or more of the Office family of programs, it's likely that the cost of adding it to OneNote is less than the cost of building a new feature of equivalent complexity.

The primary limitations on this process are technical (in many ways, OneNote, with its unique page surface, is quite different from the other applications) and conceptual; the OneNote team will likely focus on adding features that enhance

OneNote's core user scenarios for note taking by students, consultants, researchers, and knowledge workers.

A Comment on Getting Outlook E-Mail into OneNote

It'd certainly be great if there was an automatic way to get OneNote content into Outlook! In a perfect world, this would even work with Outlook Rules, so you could populate you OneNote folder with important e-mail as you go along.

The more fundamental issue this raises is the long-term relationship between OneNote and other Microsoft information repositories. If OneNote is a convenient and pleasing place to put note content, why wouldn't you want to put other content, such as e-mail content or Word documents, into that same interface? Flipping through several OneNote sections looking for a saved e-mail would be considerably more enjoyable than looking through several Outlook saved e-mail folders.

In the long term, it's for Microsoft to resolve these inconsistencies by providing a unified user interface that manages all types of user data (at least, all document-style data) in a page display format that puts all types of Object Linking and Embedding (OLE) objects on equal footing and provides several alternative views of the organizational hierarchy. That's something like the Personal Knowledge Base vision that Richard Miller, Ph.D, articulates in Chapter 1 and maybe something like the Longhorn vision of a "unified database" about which you hear rumors from Microsoft. Time will tell.

Application Programming Interface (API)

Many Microsoft applications, including the main Office tools, have what's called an Application Programming Interface (API). An API is essentially a set of commands that allows third-party developers to build extensions and add-ons to an existing program. The first release of OneNote *doesn't* have an API. There was considerable speculation on the OneNote newsgroup during the beta about why there wasn't an API in version 1.0. An incautious Microsoft employee, not affiliated with the OneNote team, made a speculative comment in a personal blog that suggested the absence of an API was for security reasons. Not so!

Chris Pratley, head of the OneNote technical team, put the matter to rest in the following Usenet posting, which shed considerable light on the API issue:

I manage the OneNote design team. [The person who made that comment] has nothing to do with OneNote. Here are the actual reasons we don't have a programmability model or API in version 1 (2003):

1. *It was a lot of work, and we prioritized the end user experience and value over extensibility for our first release.*

2. *We didn't want to design, build, and support a programmability model while we were still designing the application. That would relegate us to supporting old legacy extensions to OneNote long after the application had changed unrecognizably (a first release means the application changes a lot during development).*

3. *We want to design extensibility once we have real user feedback on what they want to extend OneNote to do, not just take a shot in the dark and enable a bunch of random stuff.*

4. *The VBA style of programmability is getting pretty old, and .NET-managed code is coming to the desktop. It didn't seem right to jump on the old bandwagon when the new one was arriving.*

I could go on, but these are the main reasons. A side effect of not having any programmability is that it's pretty hard to find a security exploit in OneNote, but in any case we've run the automated tools and done the security training and test passes as all development teams do in the trustworthy computing world. I think that [the person who made the comment] may have been jumping to conclusions about our motivations for not having an API.

We fully expect to add extensibility in following releases of OneNote, but we'll do it in a controlled, secure way, using feedback from real customers on what they want from us. Make sense?

So, good news—watch for an API in future releases of OneNote.

Extensible Markup Language (XML)

One of the major themes of Office 2003 is the introduction of deep, explicit support for Extensible Markup Language (XML). It's difficult to overstate the importance of these developments for corporate IT organizations, which are rapidly settling on XML as a standard for data exchange. Yet this first version of OneNote has no support for XML.

This suggests that at some point Microsoft will address the gap. Microsoft's Chris Pratley commented early in OneNote's beta process:

> *The file format isn't XML, but it's a structured binary format that can quickly become XML. We decided not to do XML on this release because it wasn't core to basic note taking. But we architected it for the ability to do XML in our next release very easily.*[3]

XML capabilities in OneNote would enable much richer enterprise uses of OneNote, such as transforming individual notes into more standardized and publishable formats, managing individual data as corporate assets in "electronic lab notebooks," and directly linking note taking to forms and enterprise data repositories.

Partner Endorsements

One of the most important business developments that emerged from the marketing launch of Office 2003 was Toshiba's decision to put OneNote on every laptop it makes. Toshiba sold almost 4 million laptops in 2002 and at one point in 2003 had about 21 percent of the total notebook computer market. So Toshiba's endorsement essentially guarantees that there will be many million OneNote users for the foreseeable future. That's an important point to ponder as you consider becoming a OneNote user. There will be support for you.

Lead User Wish Lists

Lead user wish lists can be an enlightening way to stimulate thought about future product opportunities. This comment from an expert on product development in a letter to the *Wall Street Journal* is informative:

> *Eric von Hippel at MIT has studied the history of seminal inventions (those that create new categories of products or industries). He found that many new categories were not the results of inventions by the manufacturers that commercialized them but were invented by users or leading-edge customers. Our work with Eric and others has shown that the owners of technology are invariably overly optimistic in their forecast because they have too much vested interest in the outcome. Lead users (customers at the leading edge of a change) are much more likely to accurately capture emerging technology requirements and identify the technologies that are most likely to be adapted to this need.*

---

3. http://www.infoworld.com/article/02/12/05/021206hnpratley_1.html

In other words, cutting-edge academic research suggests that you're in a better position than, say, Microsoft, to project the future of OneNote! This is because user needs will determine Microsoft's choices, and as a lead user, you're closer to those needs than the Microsoft team. Microsoft will listen to you! And, as a corollary, this view suggests that lead customers are in a better position than Microsoft is to project the evolution of note-taking solutions in your particular space!

On the other hand, you're probably not in a good position to guess whether OneNote will be a commercial success:

> *But lead users can't foresee how fast new inventions will be adopted by the marketplace either. This is best done by market tests with potential customers.*

The Toshiba endorsement mentioned previously is a great sign:

> *For further reading on lead users in technology forecasting, you might want to read Von Hippel, Sonnack, and Thomke's article in the Sept/Oct 1999 issue of Harvard Business Review "Creating Breakthroughs at 3M," and Chapter 10 of the* PDMA ToolBook for New Product Development *entitled "Lead User Research and Trend Mapping." As author of the chapter, I would strongly encourage [those interested in the future of software to] interview technically sophisticated customers about emerging markets and technologies rather than the companies trying to create them. The vision is much better from the customer's perspective.[4]*

With this perspective in mind, the following sections provide a few representative wish lists posted to Usenet news:Microsoft.public.onenote by a couple of pioneering figures in the online OneNote community.

Ed Garay's Wish List

Ed Garay is a technologist at the University of Illinois Chicago (UIC) who is deeply involved in instructional technology and an early adopter of OneNote. His wish list includes the following:

> *1. A toggle switch to use OneNote in "as is" mode (in other words, telling OneNote not to try to outsmart itself into guessing whether users want bullet lists, numbered lists, special automatic formatting, or some such (all Office system components should have this toggle switch).*

---

4. Wall Street Journal Online, April 18, 2003, Portals Exchange. "Readers Say Predictions of Future Are Crapshoot."

2. *Intuitive support for collapsible/expandable bullet lists such as in the Apple Newton note application.*

3. *A lasso capability that works like in Windows Journal on Tablet PCs (to select text, ink, drag it, and so on).*

4. *OneNote in simple-mode operation. Sometimes all of OneNote's bells and whistles get in the way. Users should be able to operate OneNote with the same simplicity and reduced feature set of Windows Journal. Essentially, it should work like Journal, with better integrated support for typed text (and of course, the tab-based filing metaphor).*

5. *OneNote support for the Eudora e-mail client. It'd be terrific if OneNote had good support for other e-mail clients such as Eudora, not just Outlook.*

6. *Advanced searching.*

7. *Support for Microsoft Word dictionaries, exception dictionaries, and custom dictionaries, such as medical, pharmaceutical, legal, IT, and other custom dictionaries.*

8. *Support for virtual staples, not only when creating sets of documents but after the fact, when you need to go back and attach/affix another document, image, or object to a given document set. Virtual staples should be available from anywhere within Office System 2003 to logically group document (aliases) together regardless of where they're stored.*

 NOTE   This is a great idea on Ed's part!

---

9. *Native automatic handwriting recognition support for mathematics and special symbols. That is, all UIC students could use Tablet PCs in class, using the UIC Digital Backpack and OneNote to annotate their college class materials, which are already online. Whenever they're taking a math, statistics, or chemistry class, for example, they'd toggle a button to instruct OneNote to automatically convert their handwriting using special mathematics/chemistry algorithms.*

10. *Native automatic support for smart shape. This is similar to the previous item but for lines, circles, squares, and so on as in Corel Grafigo. Students should be able to do as much as possible within OneNote. Furthermore, OneNote should become an environment— an environment for learning, for writing, for organizing information, for many things.*

11. *Native and solid support for HTML and Portable Document Format (PDF). HTML publishing is there, but it shouldn't be Microsoft-centric. Being able to publish to Acrobat PDF would be great, too.*

12. *Native speech synthesizer. It'd be nice if users could have the options to have OneNote read the OneNote documents.*

Brian Collins's Wish List

Brian Collins is a OneNote early adopter who took it on himself to write a lengthy and thoughtful wish list:

1. *How about file management? Like being able to view all the audio files related to the page(s) and subpages from within OneNote itself? Also, I think the audio recording toolbar should have more functionality, such as microphone and speaker volume as well as bit rate selection.*

2. *I'd like to see better folder/section arrangement and easy transfer from one folder/section to another, preferably by dragging. This has been improved from the previous beta 2, but there still is room for more improvement. (For example, let's say I'd like the folder Systems 1 to appear to the left of the folder Pathology, instead of where it is now— to the right. How could that be done from within OneNote itself? Office help specifically says it can't be done. With sections, one can only move the selected section to the right, not the other way around, which is therefore unnecessarily complicated. Why can't it be as simple as drag and drop? Pages and subpages can be selected and dragged to wherever someone wants to place them, so I think the same should apply to folders and sections.*

3. *The ability to customize the title page header (for example, the date— maybe it could show the weekday in addition to the day of the month). It should all be customizable. Plus, the ability to adjust the date and time of the page would prove especially useful for students (one of the main target audiences of OneNote) because lectures are in their timetable, and if you could create the note before the lecture actually starts*

while maintaining the original date and time of the lecture, you could be better prepared and organized. Say, for example, there's a lecture on Monday, Sept. 22, at 11 a.m., it'd be cool if you could create a page with a dialog box that pops up asking for all the details of the page, such as title, date and time, lecturer information, lecture type, and so on. These could be fields that the student defines. This could also be helpful in an office/business environment. This point is further explained below.

4. *The ability to add more information about each page in metatags or something similar. This would be especially useful in a school lecture environment, where you could note every lecture in a page and sub-pages of that page and include extra information such as the following:*

   a. *Lecturer name*

   b. *Lecture type—for example, Computer Aided Learning (CAL), Practical, Tutorial, and so on*

   c. *Location of lecture*

   This way you could easily search and display all lectures by a given lecturer or all lectures of a certain type (CAL, Practical, and so on), all lectures that took place in a certain location, and so on. This feature is similar to the Categories function in Outlook's Calendar. You can assign each appointment to multiple categories, and then when you perform a search, you can tick more than one category, such as Practical and Dr. Jones to find all the Practical lectures given by Dr. Jones. This is very useful to help organize and find notes faster.

5. *OneNote really needs a better search function. It needs a search dialog box to perform more advanced search functions, such as the ones I mentioned previously. Also, the ability to search for notes based on date, size, attachments (such as linked files), and other things would be cool. Basically it should contain the same perfect advanced find dialog box Outlook 2003 has.*

6. *The ability to color-code pages; for example, if it belongs to a particular category, it could be colored that category's default color so that it could be easily located when browsing through the pages in a section. Of course, this only complements the search function, which would more effectively locate notes that belong to a certain category, so it's not a solution to the previous point. It also isn't that important.*

7. The ability to drag and drop more than just text and pictures, such as video, Flash content, and so on. Well, Flash isn't that important, but I can really see a need to import PowerPoint files into OneNote, especially because most lectures are in PowerPoint format, so it'd be a better way to organize all the content relating to that lecture/meeting/appointment in the "page" for that lecture/meeting/appointment. This is the other reason why a more advanced file viewer and search dialog box are needed—when you drag and drop a file (such as .DOC, .PDF, and so on), you'd be able to remember where you put it if you forget and have a lot of pages. Plus, if you delete the link to the file from OneNote, how come the file isn't deleted from the folder? Even if you delete the whole page, the file won't get deleted. Does it all have to be done manually?

8. Better integration with Outlook's calendar, such as the ability to automatically create a page in a certain section of OneNote upon entering appointment details in the calendar. Also, if OneNote had better view options, you could see all the notes entered in a specific day, week, or month, sort of like looking at appointments in Outlook.

9. Better file organization in My Notebook—instead of all files and audio recordings for all sections in a folder being placed in the same folder, it could be arranged to be placed in subfolders, preferably with the same names as the section the file belongs to; for example, if a file is called Presentation.ppt and belongs in the Meetings section in the Work folder, then there should be another folder in the Work folder called Meetings Files, which would contain all the included files of the section. Similarly, audio recordings should have a folder, such as Meetings Audio within the Work folder. In this way, the files would be arranged better.

10. I'm writing this point to commend the programmers who have written OneNote. It's a marvelous piece of work, which has been improving rapidly from beta to beta, and I hope the final product will include some of the suggestions I mentioned. Thank you.

I hope this comment conveys some of the enthusiasm that early adopters feel about OneNote and its future.

Why Is OneNote Revolutionary?

In closing, I'll provide a couple of points to stimulate thought about OneNote and its future.

In Stanford usability guru Terry Winograd's classic collection, *Bringing Design to Software* (Addison-Wesley, 1996),[5] Peter Denning and Pamela Dargan looked at four award-winning and highly innovative software packages, including Quicken and the original Macintosh interface. They "asked the designers of these software packages what they had chosen to achieve a good design. There was a surprising level of unanimity in their answers:"

> "Pick a domain in which many people are involved and that is a constant source of breakdowns for them. (For example, the designer of Quicken chose personal finance.)"

> "Study the nature of the actions that people take in that domain, especially of repetitive actions. What do they complain about most? What new actions would they like to perform next?"

> "Deploy prototypes early in selected customer domains. Observe how people react and what kinds of breakdowns they experience."

> "[B]reakdowns…are interruptions of standard practices and progress caused by tools breaking, people failing to complete agreements, external circumstances, and so on (in personal finance, these breakdowns include errors in writing or coding checks, missing payments, discrepancies between ledger and bank statement, lost deposits…)."

> "Define software routines that imitate familiar patterns of action. Include functions that permit actions that most users have wished they could do, but could not do manually. (In personal finance, these functions include presenting screen images of template checks, allowing electronic payments, and providing a database that records transactions by income-tax type.)

When the breakdowns observed are mission critical to a significant body of end users, and the new software solutions are efficient and intuitive, "action-centered design" is a recipe for revolutionary innovation. It appears that this is the process that Microsoft has applied to the domain of individual note taking with OneNote. Note taking is a domain in which almost everyone is involved at some time or another and is a frequent source of breakdowns. OneNote will continue to be revolutionary as long as Microsoft continues to identify the places where the process of note taking "breaks down" and as long as the OneNote team innovates new solutions to those problems.

---

5. http://hci.stanford.edu/bds/

Why Is OneNote Important?

The great science fiction writer Robert A. Heinlein once wrote the following:

> *A human being should be able to change a diaper, plan an invasion, butcher a hog, con a ship, design a building, write a sonnet, balance accounts, build a wall, set a bone, comfort the dying, take orders, give orders, cooperate, act alone, solve equations, analyze a new problem, pitch manure, program a computer, cook a tasty meal, fight efficiently, die gallantly. Specialization is for insects.*[6]

Note taking is an important part of at least 14 of the 21 tasks Heinlein mentions (the exceptions being, perhaps, changing diapers, butchering hogs, setting bones, comforting the dying, pitching manure, fighting efficiently, and dying gallantly). For better or worse, note taking is an important and ubiquitous part of life, and OneNote helps you do it better.

---

6. *Time Enough for Love* (Reissue edition: Ace Books, 1994)

Not Your Father's Keyboard Shortcuts

Keyboard shortcuts are important. A substantial slice of the population likes to memorize quick key combinations that help them do things faster. And observation of posts to the Usenet newsgroup Microsoft.public.onenote confirms that OneNote users like to tell each other about keyboard shortcuts.

Table 1 presents a quick (and subjective) list of the most useful keyboard shortcuts in OneNote.

Table 1. Top 10 OneNote Keyboard Shortcuts (and Why)

Number	Keyboard Shortcut	What It Does	Why You Should Care
10	Alt+Ctrl+"+" (plus sign on numeric keypad)	Zooms in to the current page.	Did you know you could do this?
9	Alt+Ctrl+- (minus sign on numeric keypad)	Zooms out.	Get the "big picture" on your notes.
8	Ctrl+1 through Ctrl+5	Applies the To Do and other predefined note flags to selected text.	The Note Flags Summary feature is only useful if you explicitly add this metadata to your notes.
7	Ctrl+6	Applies custom note flag to selected text. I recommend that you define this note flag as "Audio."	This makes your audio files findable in the Note Flags Summary pane.
6	Ctrl+Shift+E	Sends selected pages as e-mail.	Joy shared is joy doubled.

Table 1. Top 10 OneNote Keyboard Shortcuts (and Why) (Continued)

Number	Keyboard Shortcut	What It Does	Why You Should Care
5	Ctrl+-	Applies strikethrough formatting.	Great for checking items off your to do list.
4	Ctrl+Shift+K	Creates task in Outlook 2003.	Brings your notes into Outlook where you can track them.
3	Ctrl+Shift+M	Opens a small SideNote window.	Very useful for jotting super-quick notes and reminders.
2	Ctrl+N and Ctrl+Shift+N.	Creates new OneNote page and subpage.	Lets you add pages rapidly.
1	Ctrl+A	Selects all items (repeat to broaden the scope of the selection).	Helps you understand and manipulate containers, the fundamental building blocks of OneNote.

TIP A full list of keyboard shortcuts is available in OneNote Help (search on "keyboard shortcuts"). It's organized by function and by where you are in the program (Help, toolbars, edit boxes, and so on).

The following series of tables shows the proximity relationships among OneNote's keyboard shortcuts. If you are a touch typist, this may strike a chord!

Remember that not all keyboards are laid out exactly the same. This series of tables is merely representative of a typical keyboard layout (that used on my Microsoft Bluetooth keyboard).

Tables 2 through 7 present all the possible meanings of each keystroke combination. A particular keystroke combination (for example, Alt+Ctrl+right arrow) can have more than one meaning, depending on the part of the screen where the cursor is located—the Help screen, a OneNote menu, or the OneNote page display surface. Usually, the meanings for the same keystroke combination in different modes are fairly similar, but not always. So these tables may also be of benefit to those who remember a particular combination but don't remember exactly what it does in each situation.

Table 2. Keyboard Shortcuts for OneNote—Function Keys Row

Key	Unshifted	Shift	Ctrl
F1	Display the Help task pane.		Close and reopen the current task pane.
F2	Not applicable ()— no special function in OneNote.		
F3			
F4			Close the current session.
F5			
F6	Move from the Help task pane to the Find box to the current page.		
F7	Open the Spelling task pane.		
F8			
F9			
F10	Select the menu bar, or close an open menu and submenu at the same time.	Display the shortcut menu.	
F11			
F12			

Table 3. Keyboard Shortcuts for OneNote—Number Row

Key	Unshifted	Shift	Alt	Ctrl	Alt+Shift	Ctrl+Shift	Alt+Ctrl+ Shift
`							
1				Apply the To Do note flag to the selected text.	Show selected outline through level 1.		
2				Apply the Important note flag to the selected text.	Show selected outline through level 2.		
3				Apply the Question note flag to the selected text.	Show selected outline through level 3.		
4				Apply the Remember for Later note flag to the selected text.	Show selected outline through level 4.		
5				Apply highlighting note flag to selected text.	Show selected outline through level 5.		
6				Apply a custom flag (defined by you in the Customize My Note Flags task pane) to the selected text.	Show selected outline through level 6.		
7				Ditto	Show selected outline through level 7.		
8				Ditto	Show selected outline through level 8.		

Table 3. Keyboard Shortcuts for OneNote—Number Row (Continued)

Key	Unshifted	Shift	Alt	Ctrl	Alt+Shift	Ctrl+Shift	Alt+Ctrl+Shift
9				Ditto	Show selected outline through level 9.		
0				Ditto	Show all levels of the selected outline.	Make selected text body text.	
-				Apply strikethrough formatting.	Show body text for visible headings of the selected outline.	Select the current paragraph and its subordinate paragraphs.	Zoom out.
=		+		Apply subscript formatting to selected text or following insertion point.	Hide body text of the selected outline.	Apply superscript formatting to selected text or following insertion point.	Zoom in.
Backspace	Backspace	Delete selected text.	Delete selected text.	Delete selected text.	Redo the selected action.		

Table 4. Keyboard Shortcuts for OneNote—QWERTY Row

Key	Unshifted	Shift	Alt	Ctrl	Ctrl+Shift
Tab	In the Help window, select the next hidden text or hyperlink. In a dialog box, move to next option or option group. In OneNote, increase indent by one level.	Move to previous hidden text or hyperlink, or the Browser View button at the top of a Microsoft Office Web site article. In a dialog box, move to previous option or option group. In OneNote, decrease indent by one level.		Switch to next tab in a dialog box. Go to next section.	Switch to previous tab in a dialog box. Go to previous section.
Q					
W					
E				Center between margins.	Compose an e-mail message.
R				Justify on the right margin.	
T				Move the insertion page to or away from the page header.	
Y				Redo the last action.	
U			Connect or disconnect the Help window from OneNote.	Apply underline to selected text or subsequent insertions.	

Table 4. Keyboard Shortcuts for OneNote—QWERTY Row (Continued)

Key	Unshifted	Shift	Alt	Ctrl	Ctrl+Shift
I			When followed by Alt+N, adds or removes space on the page. Use the up/down left/right arrows to select direction.	Apply italics to selected text or subsequent insertions.	
O					Formats selected text as a numbered list.
P				Print the current help topic.	
[					
]					
\					

Table 5. Keyboard Shortcuts for OneNote— ASDF Row

Key	Ctrl	Ctrl+Shift
A	Select all items. (Repeat to broaden the scope of the selection.)	
S		Open the Page List task pane.
D		
F	Move the insertion point to the Find box.	
G		Open a vertical view of the OneNote folder/section hierarchy.
H		
J		
K		Create a task in Microsoft Outlook 2003.
L	Justify on the left margin.	Create a bulleted list.
;		
,		
Enter		
]		
\		

Table 6. Keyboard Shortcuts for OneNote—the Z Row

Key	Ctrl	Ctrl+Shift	Alt+Ctrl
Z			
X	Cut the selection to the Clipboard.		Increase or reduce the size of the page header.
C	Copy the selection to the Clipboard.		
V	Paste the selection from the Clipboard.		
B	Apply bold to selected text or following insertion point.		
N	Add new page at the end of the section.	Add a new subpage to the current group of pages.	
M	Open a new OneNote window.	Open a small Side Note window.	
,		Reduce size of page header.	
.	Create bulleted list.	Increase size of page header.	
/			

Table 7. Keyboard Shortcuts for OneNote—Navigational Keys

Key	Unshifted	Shift	Alt	Ctrl	Alt+Shift	Ctrl+Shift	Alt+Ctrl
Escape	Close an open menu or submenu.						
Insert	Turn overtyping on or off.						
Delete							
Home	Move to the beginning.	Select backward from the insertion point to the beginning.	Go to first page in section.	Scroll to top of current page.			
End	Move to the end.	Select forwards from the insertion point to the end.	Go to last page in section.	Scroll to end of current page.			
Page Up	Move up one page.		Go to first page of currently visible set of pages.	Go to the previous page in the section.			
Page Down	Move down one page.		Go to last page of currently visible set of pages.	Go to the next page in the section.			

Table 7. Keyboard Shortcuts for OneNote—Navigational Keys (Continued)

Key	Unshifted	Shift	Alt	Ctrl	Alt+Shift	Ctrl+Shift	Alt+ Ctrl
Up arrow	In Help table of contents, select previous item. In OneNote menu, select previous command.			Go to previous paragraph.	Move selected page tab up.	Move selected page tab up.	Move insertion point up in current page, or expand the page up.
Down arrow	In Help TOC, select next item. In OneNote menu, select next command.	Open the selected menu.	Open a selected drop-down list. On OneNote display surface, go to next note container.	When a shortened menu is open, display the full set of commands (the ones missing below the double arrow). Go to next paragraph in note container.	Move selected page tab down.		Move insertion point down in current page, or expand the page down.

Table 7. Keyboard Shortcuts for OneNote—Navigational Keys (Continued)

Key	Unshifted	Shift	Alt	Ctrl	Alt+Shift	Ctrl+Shift	Alt+ Ctrl
Left arrow	Move one character.	In edit boxes, select or unselect one character to the left.	In Help, move back to previous task pane. In HelpToc, move back to previous item. In task panes, reverse the sequence of task panes you opened. Go back to last page visited.	In edit boxes, move one word to left.	Decrease indent by one level. If you have right-to-left languages installed, set writing direction left-to-right.	Select or unselect one word to the left.	Move insertion point left in the current page, or expand the page left.
Right arrow	Move right one character.	In edit boxes, select or unselect one character to right.	In Help, move to next task pane. In Help, move to next item. In task panes, repeat the sequences of task panes you opened. Go forward to next page visited.	In edit boxes, move one word to right.	Increase indent by one level. If you have right-to-left languages installed, set writing direction right to left.	Select or unselect one word to the right.	Move insertion point right in the current page, or expand the page right.

Table 7. Keyboard Shortcuts for OneNote—Navigational Keys (Continued)

Key	Unshifted	Shift	Alt	Ctrl	Alt+Shift	Ctrl+Shift	Alt+ Ctrl
Space bar	Open the selected menu, or perform the action assigned to the selected button.		Display title bar shortcut menu.	Open the menu of task panes. In the toolbar, display the Toolbar Options menu.			
+sign on numeric keypad							Zoom in.
- sign on numeric keypad							Zoom out.

The Lighter Side of Keyboard Shortcuts

If you're interested in an amusing take on keyboard shortcuts, the online humor magazine *The Onion* published the definitive piece on keyboard shortcuts in the summer of 2003.

Area Man Knows All the Shortcut Keys

NEW BRITAIN, CT—Catalog copywriter Roger Turlock knows all the keyboard combinations that execute a computer's common commands, the Comfort Uniforms employee said yet again Tuesday...[1]

For the full text, go to *The Onion* and search on "shortcut."

---

1. http://www.theonion.com/onion3929/area_man_knows_all.html

Index

Symbol

A

M

X

See the Appendix for a comprehensive list of shortcuts.